Political Loneliness

Philosophical Projections

Series Editor: Andrew Benjamin, Distinguished Professor of Philosophy and the Humanities, Kingston University, UK, and Professor of Philosophy and Jewish Thought, Monash University, Australia

Philosophical Projections represents the future of modern European philosophy. The series seeks to innovate by grounding the future in the work of the present, opening up the philosophical and allowing it to renew itself, while interrogating the continuity of the philosophical after the critique of metaphysics.

Titles in the Series
Foundations of the Everyday: Shock, Deferral, Repetition, Eran Dorfman
The Thought of Matter: Materialism, Conceptuality and the Transcendence of Immanence, Richard A. Lee
Nancy, Blanchot: A Serious Controversy, Leslie Hill
The Work of Forgetting: Or, How Can We Make the Future Possible?, Stephane Symons
On the Brink: Language, Time, History, and Politics, Werner Hamacher, edited by Jan Plug
Political Loneliness: Modern Liberal Subjects in Hiding, Jennifer Gaffney
Refugees: Towards a Politics of Responsibility (forthcoming), Nathan Bell

Political Loneliness

Modern Liberal Subjects in Hiding

Jennifer Gaffney

ROWMAN & LITTLEFIELD
Lanham • Boulder • New York • London

Published by Rowman & Littlefield
An imprint of The Rowman & Littlefield Publishing Group, Inc.
4501 Forbes Boulevard, Suite 200, Lanham, Maryland 20706
www.rowman.com

6 Tinworth Street, London SE11 5AL, United Kingdom

Copyright © 2020 by Jennifer Gaffney

All rights reserved. No part of this book may be reproduced in any form or by any electronic or mechanical means, including information storage and retrieval systems, without written permission from the publisher, except by a reviewer who may quote passages in a review.

British Library Cataloguing in Publication Information Available

Library of Congress Cataloging-in-Publication Data
Names: Gaffney, Jennifer, 1987- author.
Title: Political loneliness : modern liberal subjects in hiding / Jennifer Gaffney.
Description: Lanham : Rowman & Littlefield, 2020. | Series: Philosophical projections | Includes bibliographical references and index.
Identifiers: LCCN 2020008579 (print) | LCCN 2020008580 (ebook) | ISBN 9781786606945 (hardcover) | ISBN 9781786606952 (epub) ISBN 9781538148310 (pbk)
Subjects: LCSH: Alienation (Philosophy) | Communities. | Political science—Philosophy. | Arendt, Hannah, 1906-1975.
Classification: LCC B808.2 .G34 2020 (print) | LCC B808.2 (ebook) | DDC 320.01—dc23
LC record available at https://lccn.loc.gov/2020008579
LC ebook record available at https://lccn.loc.gov/2020008580

Contents

Introduction   1

1   The Peculiar Loneliness of the Current Age:
Heidegger on Being-With   21
     Modern Subjectivity and the Forgetfulness of Being   23
     Phenomenology and the Modern Subject   26
     Being Together with Things and Others   31
     The Peculiar Loneliness of Being-With   37
     Authenticity   41

2   Reclaiming Community: Alterity, Exteriority,
and Plurality   51
     The Legacy of Our Peculiar Loneliness   53
     Nancy on the Limits of Heidegger's *Mitsein*   60
     Nancy's Ontology of the "We"   65
     Relationality and the Plural Event   71
     Thinking the Common Politically   76

3   The Politics of Being-With: Hannah Arendt on the
Space of Appearance   81
     Arendt's Critical Appropriation of Heidegger   85
     The Politics of Techno-Scientific Rationality   90
     Natality, Plurality, and the Space of Appearance   94
     The Politics of Modern Subjectivity   98

4   Loneliness and Liberty: Arendt's Critique of Liberal
Subjectivity   107
     From Political Freedom to Private Liberty   110
     Liberty and the Political Emancipation
of the Bourgeoisie   116

	Fatal Consequences: Liberty and Statelessness	120
	The Loneliness of Liberal Subjectivity	122
5	The Politics of Loneliness: Another Origin of Totalitarianism	129
	From Statelessness to Loneliness	131
	Solitude, Isolation, and Loneliness	136
	Loneliness and Totalitarianism	144
	Loneliness and Liberal Citizenship	148
	Beyond the Loneliness of Liberal Subjectivity	149
6	Political Loneliness Today: America's Hidden Trump Supporter	157
	America's Hidden Trump Supporter	161
	Loneliness and Neoliberal Subjectivity Today	171
	Political Loneliness and the Hidden Trump Supporter	176

Conclusion	187
Bibliography	201
Index	209

Introduction

Never before have we been so interconnected, so accessible to one another. The global networks of technology and commerce that order our daily lives have made even the furthest corners of the earth reachable in a single Skype call. They have made possible the exchange of commodities across every part of the world, and they have granted to anyone with a smartphone and a social media account access to the most important political and cultural movements taking place across the globe. Never before have we been able so vigilantly to keep track of one another, to communicate so quickly our ideas and opinions, and to share so publically the details of our private lives. And yet, while these things no doubt mark our age as one of heightened togetherness, it is the provocation of this work that we have never before been so lonely. This paradox—that we are more extremely together and more extremely apart than ever before—makes the loneliness of the current age especially peculiar. The task of the present inquiry is to develop a framework for interpreting this peculiar loneliness—or the fact that in an era of hyperbolic interconnectedness, there is nevertheless a widespread sense that we belong nowhere, that we have lost our nearness to others, and that we are neither supported by nor responsible for the communities in which we find ourselves.

Philosophical inquiry into the peculiar loneliness of the current age is by no means new. Martin Heidegger, for instance, draws attention to it in his 1951 essay "The Thing" when he says:

> *All distances in time and space are shrinking.* Man now reaches overnight, by plane, places which formerly took weeks and months of travel. He now receives instant information by radio, of events which he formerly learned about only years later, if at all . . . the peak of this abolition of every possibility of remoteness is reached by television, which will soon pervade and dominate the whole machinery of communication. . . . Yet, the frantic abolition of all distances brings no nearness . . . despite all conquest of distances the nearness of things remains absent.[1]

Heidegger's critique of the ordering that modern techno-scientific rationality produces—an ordering that might conquer all distances but that brings us no closer to a genuine sense of belonging—forms a central problematic of much of twentieth- and twenty-first-century continental philosophy. At stake in this problematic is the question of whether and how we might recover a sense of authentic community from out of the peculiar loneliness that characterizes modern life. We see this concern in Karl Jaspers's critique of the technocracy of European society, no less than in Hans-Georg Gadamer's efforts to develop Jaspers's claim that this technocracy has produced an age of "anonymous responsibility" in which human beings approach one another as numbers to be calculatively managed.[2] Gadamer, for his part, suggests that in this "thoroughly rationalized society," we find ourselves at once pressed together while at the same time plagued by isolation or loneliness (*Vereinsamung*), the price of which "is our nearness to others . . . to stand in a communal sphere and to be supported by something communal—this is what we decry when something is lost or disappears in the sadness of loneliness."[3] Whereas Gadamer is led from this to attempt to rehabilitate the concepts of friendship and solidarity, others, such as Jean-Luc Nancy, develop relational ontologies in order to displace once and for all the modern presumption that human beings are isolated, self-conscious subjects who stand at a distant and indifferent relation to the world. For Nancy, the stakes of the techno-scientific ordering of the modern world, and the epistemological subject on which this ordering is based, consist not in the destruction of community per se, but rather in the destruction of authentic forms of communal life that embrace alterity, otherness, and plurality. Whereas this instrumental ordering is always vulnerable to totalizing and reductive ways of being together—ways that are fundamentally lonely—Nancy develops an ontology of the with-structure of existence whereby the possibility of being-with is always already conditioned by the alterity of the other.[4]

We see, then, that the peculiar loneliness of the current age and the problematic it creates regarding the possibilities for authentic communal life is well-trodden territory in twentieth- and twenty-first-century continental thought. Yet, as central as this problematic has been, its political stakes remain underdeveloped. Taking my point of departure from these critiques of the instrumental rationality of the modern age, it is the goal of the present inquiry to develop the peculiar loneliness of the current age in a political register. Central to this work is the claim that neoliberal subjectivity has rendered us lonely in ways that have yet to be fully appreciated but that are nevertheless decisive for thinking the possibilities for authentic communal life today. In this, my aim is to frame the problem of loneliness in terms of the political alienation of modern life, a form of alienation that I will suggest owes its existence to the political structures that we have inherited from the liberal tradition and the forms of subjectivity that these structures produce.

Whereas much has been said about the existential, psychoanalytic, and social dimensions of loneliness, scholarly inquiry into the political significance of this problem has only recently begun to take shape. Jill Stauffer has carved out a space for thinking the problem of loneliness politically in her recent work *Ethical Loneliness: The Injustice of Not Being Heard*. Stauffer conceives of loneliness as a symptom of the unwillingness, often on the part of just-minded people, to listen to those who have suffered injustice. She thus defines loneliness as

> the isolation one feels when one, as a violated person or as a member of a persecuted group, has been abandoned by humanity, or by those who have power over one's life possibilities. It is a condition undergone by persons who have been unjustly treated and dehumanized by human beings and political structures, who emerge from that injustice only to find that the surrounding world will not listen to or cannot properly hear their testimony— their claims about what they suffered and about what is now owed to them—on their own terms.[5]

Stauffer emphasizes those who find themselves cast out from the dominant discourse and for whom the inability to be heard produces a profound and abiding loneliness. Turning especially to the work of Emmanuel Levinas, she puts into relief the loneliness that arises among those who have suffered historical forms of oppression and exclusion, and who find themselves unable to give testimony even upon being fully enfranchised within their political communities. In this, Stauffer has taken an important first step in developing the problem of loneliness in a political register, using it as a lens to think beyond the juridical framework that is often employed in discourses concerned with political reconciliation and transitional justice.

My aim is to take the next step in advancing this discourse. Whereas Stauffer frames the problem of loneliness in terms of the ethical responsibility we have to listen to those who have historically been excluded from liberal democratic spheres of political discourse, I emphasize the peculiar loneliness that is already at stake in the forms of subjectivity that these spheres produce. In this, my goal is not to deny the importance of the loneliness that Stauffer identifies, but rather to approach this problem from a different vantage point, considering the ways in which the peculiar loneliness of the current age is affirmed and reproduced by the very structures that organize liberal and allegedly open societies. The central argument of this work is that the political structures that we have inherited from the liberal tradition—such as the emphasis on representation rather than deliberation, the anonymity of the vote, and the priority placed on securing and expanding the right to pursue private self-interest—have eroded the space of politics, leaving even those endowed with the full rights of liberal citizenship hidden from one another, unable to see themselves as belonging to a common world. Turning to the work of Hannah Arendt, I wish to suggest that it is precisely this loss of a world—a loss that arises from the destruction of the political sphere—that renders human beings lonely. Drawing on Arendt's characterization of totalitarianism as "organized loneliness," I argue that the consequences of this experience are as dire as they are urgent.[6] Whereas we might take for granted the liberal political structures that organize modern life and even call for their expansion in the service of ending political alienation and exclusion, I wish to suggest that these structures do not promise such an end; quite to the contrary, they reproduce the very loneliness that makes modern individuals vulnerable to totalitarian domination.

By developing the problem of loneliness in its political significance, this work makes two distinct contributions. First, it deepens and challenges discourses in current continental philosophy that seek to address the peculiar loneliness of the current age by establishing the conditions for authentic communal life. By offering an account of the loneliness of liberal subjectivity, my aim is to bring to light a further, underappreciated dimension of modern subjectivity that keeps this possibility from being realized. Turning especially to Heidegger's notion of "being-with," Nancy's conception of the "we," and Andrew Benjamin's more recent discourse on what he calls the "plural event," I consider the central role that the problem of loneliness has played in recent continental thought.[7] In an effort to contravene this loneliness, these figures introduce decidedly important ontologies that displace the modern epistemological subject by establishing the relationship between the meaningfulness of the world and the way in which this meaning is only able to emerge in and through our relations with others. As important as these discourses have been, however, I maintain that they nevertheless leave unanswered the question of how the political structures of modern life reinforce isolated and instrumental forms of subjectivity that perpetuate the problem of loneliness. By considering the role that the political plays in holding open a space for the appearance of such meaning, and by clarifying the dangers involved in losing such a space, I aim to address this lacuna and open new paths to envisioning the possibilities for authentic communal life.

Second, the present inquiry contributes to debate in contemporary political theory by introducing a new voice to critical discourses concerning the assumptions of the liberal political tradition. There are, of course, myriad ways to engage critically the global expansion of liberal and neoliberal politics. One might, for instance, draw on neo-Marxist perspectives in critical theory to consider the way in which liberalism exploits the machinery of capitalism and, in so doing, reinforces the alienation of modern mass society. One could also turn to figures who critically appropriate the structures of Enlightened liberalism, rehabilitating them in the service of expanding the opportunities for democratic discourse and fostering a more inclusive and progressive political sphere.[8] Yet, whereas much work has already been done to develop these critical perspectives, I turn to Arendt to consider how her phenomenological approach to the political offers new ways of thinking the dangers and limits of the legacy of the liberal tradition. It is from out of this phenomenological framework that Arendt is able to develop these dangers and limits in terms of the problem of loneliness, which I will suggest offers a novel but underappreciated point of departure for interpreting the relationship between neoliberalism and totalitarianism in the context of political life today.

Undoubtedly influenced by the tradition of existential phenomenology, Arendt nevertheless distinguishes herself from her contemporaries in the significance she attributes to the political sphere of human existence. In contrast to the spheres of labor and work, Arendt argues that the political constitutes a "space of appearance," or that space in which we become visible to one another in our irreducible singularity and irrevocable interdependence. The political is where we speak and act with others in order to introduce new meaning to the world, saving it from "its normal 'natural' ruin," or the necessity that governs ordinary life.[9] In other words, it is the space for the appearance of human freedom and, thus, she says, "the *raison d'être* of the political is freedom and its field of experience is action."[10] Only in this space are we able to appear, not as interchangeable entities, but as radically unique and capable of acting against the overwhelming odds of statistical laws and probability.[11] Only here, Arendt argues, do the reductive metrics of utility lose their relevance, disclosing a more authentic possibility for human action, one that enables a common world constituted by the irreducible singularity and plurality of its actors, to appear.

And yet, Arendt is clear that it is precisely this space that has been lost in the modern era. She attributes this loss to the emphasis in the liberal political tradition on the expansion of rights and liberties in the private sphere and the elevation of the security of these rights and liberties to the paramount aim of politics. Though Arendt takes it to be a pillar of all civilized government to protect the private rights and liberties of individual citizens, she argues that the liberal political tradition has transformed this into the *sole* concern of politics, enabling the necessity that drives "the pursuit of 'enlightened' self-interest" and national investment in the expansion of these interests, to rule supreme.[12] In Arendt's view, the liberal credo that freedom begins where politics ends has thus had a devastating effect; it has destroyed the space of appearance, leaving behind lonely, atomized individuals, who, though pressed together into a great mass, nevertheless remain hidden, unable to appear to one another in the fullness of their humanity.

It will be a central concern of this work to clarify the relation of Arendt's critique of the liberal tradition to her concern for the vulnerability of lonely individuals to totalitarianism. As Arendt says, "What prepares men for totalitarian domination in the non-totalitarian world is the fact that loneliness, once a borderline experience usually suffered in certain marginal social conditions like old age, has become the everyday experience of the evergrowing masses of our century."[13] Loneliness, Arendt argues, arises when human beings discover that they no longer belong to a world with others who can bring the fullness of their humanity into relief. A symptom of what she calls "worldlessness" or "world-alienation," loneliness sets in when human beings have been deprived of their political existence and severed from the meaningful nexus of relations that constitute the common world. It is in view of this that Arendt says, "world-alienation, and not self-alienation as Marx suggested, is the hallmark of the modern age."[14]

In contrast to solitude and even isolation, Arendt describes loneliness as the anxiety one has over the loss of self that occurs upon being severed from a common world that can confirm the truth of one's experience.[15] This anxiety causes individuals to lose trust in who they are and "the elementary confidence in the world which is necessary to make experiences at all. Self and world, the capacity for thought and experience are lost at the same time."[16] Upon falling into despair over this loss of self and the surrounding world, human beings become disoriented; loneliness overwhelms us with doubt and uncertainty regarding the truth of our experience, leaving us without a tangible reality in which to ground ourselves. For this reason, she explains, the feeling of loneliness is "among the most radical and desperate experiences of man."[17] It is precisely in this desperation—a desperation, Arendt argues, that stems from the feeling of being superfluous—that human beings become willing to surrender their humanity to the delusional fellowship promised by totalitarianism.

In Arendt's view, it is only possible to appease the despair of loneliness by remaining consistent in one's reasoning, which provides "the only reliable 'truth' human beings can fall back upon once they have lost the mutual guarantee, the common sense, men need in order to experience and live and know their way in a common world."[18] Totalitarian ideology is driven not by an idea, such as dialectical materialism or racism, but by the coercive force of the logical process itself.[19] Whereas totalitarian movements like National Socialism are often thought to arise because of the sense of community they promise, Arendt maintains that this notion of community is delusional; what appeals is not a real possibility for belonging, but rather the stringent logicality that drives totalitarian ideology. In addition to emancipating thought from experience by subordinating all perceptible reality to an ideological truth, totalitarianism rescues men from their loneliness, preying on the fear lonely individuals have of contradicting themselves.[20] Upon accepting the first premise of the movement's ideology, lonely individuals must follow through with the deduction it prescribes, or else risk rendering their lives meaningless.[21] In view of this, Arendt suggests that totalitarianism can only rule over lonely individuals who have become desperate enough to surrender their inner freedom of thought to the sheer force of logic that drives totalitarianism.

For Arendt, then, loneliness is a symptom of the loss of a common world, a loss that she attributes to the increasing decay of the political sphere of our lives in the modern age. By developing this problem in a political register, Arendt thus offers a unique vantage point from which to interpret the peculiar loneliness that continues to saturate even the most densely populated spaces. With this, she provides a framework to interpret several of the perplexities and presumptions of modern political life. First among these is the way that totalitarian movements like National Socialism, which ordinarily appeal to the outer edges of the political spectrum, become mainstream. Though we may be inclined to attribute this appeal to the sense of community such movements promise, this is not enough to account for the vast demographics across which they are able to cut. To be sure, such movements do promise a heightened sense of togetherness. Yet, Arendt's analysis offers an important critical perspective on this heightened togetherness, clarifying that in order for totalitarianism to have such wide and undifferentiated appeal, the masses must have already been atomized and isolated to the point of loneliness. Rather than promising genuine belonging through a collective cause or consciousness, totalitarian politics represents the most refined form of the peculiar loneliness of the current age, pressing individuals into an indistinguishable mass whose sole purpose is to accelerate the necessary movements of nature and history. Her analysis thus issues an urgent call, not to dismiss these movements as aberrations, but to confront the breeding ground that loneliness creates for them to become mainstream.

Second, Arendt's political interpretation of the problem of loneliness provides a platform to critique our received ideas and assumptions about the liberal political tradition, highlighting the loneliness that these structures produce and the vulnerability of this loneliness to totalizing and dangerous forms of communal life. Whereas mainstream discourses in liberal political theory call for the expansion of the structures that organize Western liberal democracies to address the exclusion and alienation of modern life, Arendt's analysis puts into relief the way in which this can affirm and reproduce the very loneliness that makes modern individuals susceptible to totalitarianism. Figures like Stauffer have already done important work to clarify the dangers of the problem of loneliness for those who have been cast out of their political communities. Equally important has been the work that scholars since Heidegger have done to make philosophically significant the peculiar character of the loneliness of modern mass society. Yet, Arendt provides a novel point of departure for interpreting the relation of this peculiar loneliness to the liberal political structures that organize Western democracies and the ways in which we implicate ourselves in the reproduction of this loneliness by uncritically calling for their expansion.

Third, and perhaps most importantly, Arendt provides a framework for interpreting the loneliness that remains at work in political life today. The notion of political loneliness opens new paths to understanding our own "post-truth" era, a time in which "fake news" and "alternative facts" are referred to regularly to express suspicion over the reliability, not just of the words and deeds of others, but also of the reality of the world itself. It provides a basis to interpret the use of terms like the "hidden Trump supporter" to describe vast swaths of the American electorate, no less than the tendency to turn to the echo chambers of Twitter and Facebook to advance one's political views. That the language of hiddenness could become so ubiquitous and our predominant modes of political discourse so self-referential warrants our attention. By considering the ways in which neoliberal subjectivity has rendered modern individuals lonely, it is the goal of this work to provide a platform for interpreting these phenomena and, moreover, their relation to the recent ascendance of right-wing populism in what purport to be the most enlightened, liberal, and democratic nations on earth. This ascendance, I will argue, is perhaps best interpreted not as a deviation from the liberal political structures that organize modern life, but as symptomatic of the lonely forms of subjectivity that these structures produce.

On the basis of this, it is the goal of this work to suggest that we are called upon by the problem of political loneliness to develop a politics of appearance—or a politics that draws neoliberal subjects out of their hiding and into the full illumination of the public realm—in order to reclaim those spaces in which the possibilities for authentic communal life might be fulfilled. To be sure, figures like Jacques Derrida and Judith Butler have raised important objections to the notion of appearance for perpetuating a metaphysics of presence that reinforces reductive forms of subjectivity. Yet, I nevertheless wish to suggest that a politics of appearance—one keyed to the shared responsibility to make one another visible in the public realm—does not fall prey to such an objection, but rather offers an important antidote to the distinctive form of loneliness that remains at work in political life today.

This work will unfold in three parts. I will begin by developing the centrality of the problem of the peculiar loneliness of the current age in recent continental thought. I will then consider Arendt's contribution to these discourses through her distinctive critical perspective on the liberal political tradition, one that exposes the possible risks for totalitarianism in the loneliness of liberal subjectivity. Finally, I will draw on the framework Arendt offers to interpret the loneliness that may remain at work in Western liberal democracies today and the increasing vulnerability of these societies to far-right populist politics.

Chapter 1, "The Peculiar Loneliness of the Current Age: Heidegger on Being-With," gives contour to the philosophical significance of the problem of loneliness, locating the starting point for inquiry into this problematic in the work of Martin Heidegger. Though Heidegger's critique of modern techno-scientific rationality is perhaps most pronounced in his later writings on technology and language, I turn in this chapter to his 1927 masterwork *Being and Time*. A work best known for its radical intervention in the tradition of Western metaphysics, equally important is the way in which this intervention makes visible as a philosophical problematic the peculiar loneliness of the current age. The goal of this chapter is to suggest that in displacing the modern subject with the relational structure of being-in-the-world, Heidegger at the same time discovers a distinctive form of alienation, one to which Dasein, in its excessive possibility and irrevocable interdependence, is always already vulnerable. This, I will suggest, comes into view in Heidegger's assertion that "being-in is *being-with* [*Mitsein*]."[22] While we might expect Heidegger to be led from this to insist that Dasein finds itself originally at home in the world, it is a crucial if underappreciated insight of *Being and Time* that he does not. Instead, Heidegger maintains that Dasein initially and for the most part finds itself in its relations with others in a leveled down, inauthentic way. That is, Heidegger discovers in Dasein's native relationality a compulsion toward the "they-self," or a way of being together with others that is shrouded in anonymity, leaving Dasein hidden and alone even as it finds itself crowded in by others.[23]

In turning to the "they-self," I will suggest that Heidegger discovers at the ground of Dasein's existence the possibility for a peculiar kind of loneliness, one that is felt most profoundly with others and that is only intensified by the movement of care (*Sorge*). It is precisely because Dasein does not enter into relation with the world through the intentional structure of consciousness, but instead indwells these relations though care, that it finds itself always already reaching out in order to make more proximate and familiar the world into which it has been thrown. Yet, it is also in this native reaching out, this longing to bring closer that which seems far away, that Dasein's care harbors the possibility for the reduction of one's communal relations and responsibilities to the metrics of utility, metrics that may promise proximity and familiarity, but that also totalize and render invisible the excessive possibility and singularity of those with whom it shares the world.

Many have criticized Heidegger's discourse on the "they-self" for depicting too pessimistically the dynamics of social life.[24] Yet, in our own era of hyperbolic interconnectedness, we are by no means strangers to this longing for accessibility and proximity, nor are we immune to the reductive metrics and algorithms that organize our ways of being together with others. I therefore wish to take a different angle of approach to this aspect of *Being and Time*, conceiving of it as the starting point for philosophical inquiry into the peculiar loneliness of the current age. In this, I will argue that Heidegger's insight creates an enduring problematic in twentieth- and twenty-first-century continental philosophy. In discovering that this loneliness is at once an inevitable and intolerable dimension of being-in-the-world, Heidegger raises the question of how we might recover from out of this peculiar loneliness authentic forms of communal life. Though Heidegger's own answers to this question have, for both philosophical and political reasons, proven largely unsatisfying, the legacy of the question itself nevertheless remains central. Therefore, while *Being and Time* may offer no solution, it nevertheless makes visible as a philosophical problematic the peculiar loneliness of the current age, a problem that I will suggest has only become increasingly urgent today.

In chapter 2, "Reclaiming Community: Alterity, Exteriority, and Plurality," I develop the legacy of this problem in the main currents of continental thought. The question of how we might recover authentic forms of communal life from out of this paradox is central to figures from Karl Jaspers to Judith Butler. These thinkers, to be sure, recognize the urgency of the problem of the peculiar loneliness of the current age—or the fact that while we may be able to conquer all distances through technological and scientific advancement, we nevertheless remain no nearer to ourselves, others, or the world. They also remain guided by Heidegger's radical intervention in modern notions of subjectivity, following him in advancing ontologies of relation that displace the modern subject. Yet, they recognize, too, that while Heidegger himself endeavors to answer the question of authentic communal life from out of this problem, he is unable to think these possibilities in ways that are as responsive to Dasein's irreducible singularity as they are to its irrevocable interdependence.

Turning especially to the work of Jean-Luc Nancy, I consider this perceived limitation in Heidegger's early formulation of the project of fundamental ontology as it takes shape, on the one hand, in Heidegger's discourse on Dasein's singularity in the mode of authenticity and, on the other, in his emphasis on the collective destiny of a people in his discourse on Dasein's historicity. Nancy, for his part, argues that as groundbreaking as Heidegger's insights into the with-structure of existence might be, Heidegger himself fails to think being-with ontologically. Nancy recognizes not only in Heidegger's project, but in the Western philosophical tradition more generally, an inability to conceive of being-with in a way that neither sets singular Dasein apart from its relationality nor absorbs this singularity into a totalizing collective.[25] The question of authentic communal life thus turns on finding a way between these alternatives. In view of this, we find that figures like Nancy, and more recently, Andrew Benjamin, endeavor to develop relational ontologies that emphasize how the singularity of one's own existence cannot be thought apart from an original exposure to alterity and difference—which is to say, an original relation.[26] Both thus emphasize that thinking the "we" depends on thinking the plural, such that neither the singular nor the communal are lost.

Chapter 2 will therefore consider the importance of the problematic that Heidegger introduces and the difficulty that his own inability to resolve this problem poses for the thinkers who build on his project. These discourses suggest that addressing the problem of our peculiar loneliness depends on discovering authentic forms of communal life that are neither alienating of our relations nor reductive of our difference. Whereas the former only intensifies the peculiar loneliness of modern life, the latter contains within it dangerously totalizing possibilities. In consequence of this, each of the figures considered in this chapter turn to a notion of communal life that emphasizes an original exposure to the alterity and exteriority of the other, an exposure in virtue of which Dasein's singularity becomes possible. By asserting that being-with can only be thought ontologically if it is keyed to this exteriority, these discourses take important steps in advancing the original problem that Heidegger discovers in his own efforts to upend modern notions of subjectivity. Yet, as important as these discourses are, more may nevertheless be said about the political significance of the peculiar loneliness of the current age and the importance of the political sphere for conceiving of the singularity of existence in and through our relations with others.

In view of this, I turn to Arendt in chapters 3, 4, and 5 to consider how her efforts to develop the problem of loneliness in a political register open new paths to thinking the possibilities for authentic communal life. In chapter 3, "The Politics of Being-With: Hannah Arendt on the Space of Appearance," I consider how, in turning to the political, Arendt attempts to think the "we" in ways that are at once responsive to the peculiar loneliness that Heidegger identifies and at the same time keyed to a conception of communal life that is grounded in plurality, alterity, and difference. To this end, I trace Arendt's critical appropriation of Heidegger's fundamental ontology through the development of her own political ontology, one that treats the political as the site of both self- and world-disclosure, or that space in which human beings are able to appear to one another in their singularity as members of a common world. By turning first to her critical engagement with Heidegger in her writings from the 1930s and 1940s and then to her transformation of this into a positive political project in such works as *The Human Condition*, we find that she, in much the same way as the thinkers considered in chapter 2, is working to answer the question of how we might recover authentic forms of communal life from out of the peculiar loneliness of the current age. Yet, by developing this question in a political register, we find that she also discovers a further danger of modern subjectivity, one that is born out of the liberal political structures that organize modern life and that offers a distinctive vantage point from which to view the modern subject's vulnerability to this distinctive and peculiar form of loneliness.

In chapter 4, "Loneliness and Liberty: Arendt's Critique of Liberal Subjectivity," I develop Arendt's novel critical perspective on the liberal tradition, one that exposes the possible risks for totalitarianism in the loneliness of liberal subjectivity. At stake in Arendt's concern is the way in which the political sphere of human existence has been forgotten in the modern era, a forgetfulness that cannot be thought apart from the emphasis within the liberal tradition on the security and expansion of the right to pursue one's private self-interest as far as possible. Rather than undertaking a destruction of the history of Western metaphysics, as Heidegger does, Arendt undertakes a destruction of the history of Western politics, emphasizing the way in which this loss of the political can be traced through the transformation of the idea of freedom from a communal, political activity to a property of thought or the will. While freedom was originally thought to be most proper to the political sphere of human existence, Arendt argues that it was ultimately relocated to the inner dwelling of thought or the will in late-antiquity, a consequence, she thinks of the fall of the Roman Empire and the decay of the political sphere. An apolitical and worldless notion of freedom, Arendt argues that it was nevertheless this conception of freedom that was inscribed into the foundations of the liberal political tradition. This, she argues, is exemplified by the elevation of the security of rights and liberties in the private sphere to the highest aim of politics. While we may take for granted the liberal credo that "freedom begins where politics ends," Arendt argues that it is precisely this sentiment that has led to the loss of the political sphere in the modern era. Arendt develops the relation of this credo to the destruction of the political sphere through her analysis of historical events such as the political emancipation of the bourgeoisie, the birth of the nation-state and the Rights of Man, and the apparent meaninglessness of these rights in her discourse on the rise of stateless people in the period between the world wars. At stake in all of this is a concern for the ways in which the liberal political structures of modern life have destroyed the space of politics, leaving behind lonely and rootless individuals who have lost the ability to appear to one another in their singularity as belonging to a common world. While we may find ourselves increasingly pressed together into a great mass, Arendt argues that modern individuals have never before been so lonely, the consequences of which, she thinks, were no more apparent than in the rise of European totalitarianism.

In chapter 5, "The Politics of Loneliness: Another Origin of Totalitarianism," I turn to Arendt's analysis of totalitarianism to elucidate the consequences of the loneliness of liberal subjectivity. Totalitarianism, Arendt argues, distinguishes itself from tyrannical government insofar as it does not destroy its subjects' external freedom movement, but rather colonizes its subjects from within, reducing human beings to nothing more than laboring animals and closing off any possibility for the spontaneity of human action. Arendt is clear that this inner colonization is only possible after individuals have already become lonely. Loneliness leaves human beings overwhelmed by a sense of worldlessness and superfluity. It makes them desperate to belong and prepares them, in turn, to surrender their humanity to the delusional fellowship promised by totalitarianism. It is in view of this fact that Arendt describes totalitarianism as "organized loneliness," a form of political organization that draws its energy from the peculiar loneliness of modern mass society.

On the basis of this, we find that Arendt's analysis of the political loneliness of modern life helps to bring into focus the dangers and limits of the liberal political structures that we tend to take for granted. As I will suggest in this chapter, Arendt's political philosophy has received renewed attention in recent years for the contribution it makes to current debate concerning the global possibilities for liberal democratic practice. Yet, the emphasis scholars have placed on Arendt's notion of "the right to have rights" in order to advance these debates threatens to overshadow the scope and depth of her critical relation to the liberal tradition. By turning to Arendt's analysis of the problem of loneliness, I aim to show that this aspect of Arendt's work guides a prescient critique of the forms of subjectivity that underlie notions of citizenship within the liberal political tradition. On her view, these forms of citizenship do not secure liberty but instead reproduce the very loneliness that makes modern subjects susceptible to totalitarian domination. In view of this, I maintain that indwelling our communal relations and responsibilities authentically will depend above all on contravening this loneliness by rehabilitating the political existence of the lonely liberal subject.

Chapter 6, "Political Loneliness Today: America's Hidden Trump Supporter," examines the prescient framework that Arendt's discourse on the loneliness of liberal subjectivity provides for interpreting political life today. There are many phenomena that are worthy of attention in this regard, including the widespread appeal to "fake news" and "alternative facts," nationalistic responses in both Europe and the United States to global mass migration, and the impact of social media on democratic discourse. I will suggest in this chapter that one exemplary but underappreciated phenomenon can be found in the "hidden" Trump supporter, a term that became popular in the wake of the 2016 U.S. presidential election. This term was used by major media outlets to account for the failure of polling data to predict Donald Trump's victory, indicating that those who had intended to vote for Trump hid this preference from pollsters for fear of being ostracized, reporting instead that they were undecided or that they planned to vote for a different candidate. There has been much debate among political scientists about whether hidden Trump supporters contributed to the surprising outcome of this historic election.[27] Yet, whereas these debates have focused on the statistical significance of this phenomenon, we have yet to examine the broader implications of the use of the language of hiddenness to describe a vast swath of a democratic electorate.

A phenomenon that is easily overlooked, I wish to suggest that this language of hiddenness is itself emblematic of the political loneliness to which Arendt draws our attention. In addition to highlighting the political loneliness that may remain at work in Western liberal democracies today, this phenomenon helps to show how this loneliness might render Western liberal societies vulnerable to right-wing populist politics. It is, of course, crucial to recognize the complex nature of the circumstances that have led to the rise of right-wing populism today, no less than the specific conditions under which Arendt was developing her account of European totalitarianism in the early twentieth century. It would not only be overly simplistic to neglect these complexities, but also inconsistent with recent scholarship in Arendt studies that cautions against reductive approaches to these complex political environments.[28] Yet, while it is crucial to acknowledge these complexities, Arendt's analysis nevertheless provides a useful framework for interpreting the loneliness that may remain at work in our own society today, and the vulnerability that this creates to totalizing forms of communal life. Whereas much work has been done to discuss other factors—for instance, growing economic inequality, globalization and technological change, the failure to hold banks accountable for the financial crisis, the distinctive rhetorical style of today's populist political leaders—this chapter emphasizes an element not typically explored, namely, the vulnerability of the liberal subject per se to right-wing populism in order to provide a broad framework for critically engaging more specific contexts like the contemporary political situation in the United States. Hence while we must acknowledge the contingent factors of the 2016 context, no less than the distinctive ways in which right-wing populism is taking shape in other regions, I nevertheless wish to suggest that we may turn to the loneliness of liberal subjectivity to consider how such contingent factors achieve their determining power.

By way of conclusion, I argue that in taking seriously Arendt's analysis, we are called upon by the problem of political loneliness to develop a politics of appearance or a notion of politics that draws lonely liberal subjects out of their hiding and into the full illumination of the public realm. I will argue that it is only by reclaiming our political existence that we can appear to one another in our singularity for the sake of renewing the meaningfulness of the world. This, I maintain, will depend on thinking beyond liberal subjectivity to establish political spaces that produce forms of political agency that remind us of our humanity and our responsibility to the world that makes possible its appearance. A politics of appearance, understood as an antidote to the problem of political loneliness, thus opens new paths to thinking the possibilities for authentic forms of being-with, possibilities that are crucial for overcoming the loneliness and atomization that dominates communal life in the present age.

NOTES

1. Martin Heidegger, "The Thing," in *Poetry, Language, Thought*, trans. Albert Hofstadter (New York: Harper Collins Books, 1971): 163–180, 163–164, emphasis in original.

2. Hans-Georg Gadamer, "Friendship and Solidarity," *Research in Phenomenology*, 39 (2009): 3–12, 3.

3. Hans-Georg Gadamer, "Isolation as a Symptom of Self-Alienation," in *Praise of Theory: Speeches and Essays* (New Haven: Yale University Press, 1988): 101–113, 101–102. This is based on a modified translation by Adrian Costache in "On Solitude and Loneliness in Hermeneutical Philosophy," *Meta: Research in Hermeneutics, Phenomenology and Practical Philosophy*, 5.1 (2013): 130–149, 133.

4. Jean-Luc Nancy, *Being Singular Plural* (Stanford: Stanford University Press, 2000), 6.

5. Jill Stauffer, *Ethical Loneliness: The Injustice of Not Being Heard* (New York: Columbia University Press, 2015), 1.

6. Hannah Arendt, *The Origins of Totalitarianism* (New York: Harcourt Inc., 1974), 477.

7. This project is in conversation with a myriad of recent works on this topic, including *The Common Growl: Towards a Poetics of Precarious Community*, ed. Thomas Claviez (New York: Fordham University Press, 2016), a collected volume that focuses on the approaches of figures such as Jean-Luc Nancy, Jacques Rancière, and Homi Bhabha to the possibilities for authentic community in the modern world. This theme appears in Greg Bird's recent work, *Containing Community: From Political Economy to Ontology in Agamben, Esposito, and Nancy* (Albany: SUNY Press, 2016). Whereas Bird draws on Agamben, Esposito,

and Nancy to rethink community in ways that overcome notions of propriety in communal life, my aim is to bring the underappreciated contribution of Arendt to bear on this discourse. Similarly, Anya Topolski's recent work *Arendt, Levinas, and a Politics of Relationality* (New York: Rowman and Littlefield, 2015) offers an account of relationality and community, doing so in direct reference to Arendt's work. Yet, Topolski does not consider this with reference to the theme of loneliness. As the present inquiry suggests, it is precisely Arendt's concern for the problem of loneliness that brings into focus a dimension of the alienation of modern political life that must be addressed if we are to begin developing a framework for politics that supports alterity and plurality.

8. In turning to Arendt to undertake a critique of the neoliberal tradition, this work complements several recent related texts. For instance, Dotan Leshem's The Origins of Neoliberalism: Modeling the Economy from Jesus to Foucault (New York: Columbia University Press, 2017) draws on Arendt's analysis of the destruction of the political sphere in late-antiquity to recast traditional interpretations of the history of liberalism and neoliberalism in terms of its Christian origins. The present inquiry also engages themes similar to those that are addressed in David Chandler and Julian Reid's recent work *The Neoliberal Subject: Resilience, Adaptation, and Vulnerability* (New York: Rowman and Littlefield, 2016). Yet, whereas Chandler and Reid orient their debate within mainstream discourses in liberal political and economic theory, my work brings these debates to bear on recent discourses in current continental philosophy concerning the possibilities for authentic communal life. Bonnie Honig's recent work *Public Things: Democracy in Disrepair* (New York: Fordham University Press, 2017), as well as Wendy Brown's *Undoing the Demos: Neoliberalism's Stealth Revolution* (New York: Zone Books, 2015), will be important resources later on in this work for thinking about neoliberalism today.

9. Hannah Arendt, *The Human Condition* (Chicago: University of Chicago Press, 1998), 247.

10. Hannah Arendt, "What Is Freedom?" in *Between Past and Future*, ed. Jerome Kohn (New York: Penguin Books, 2006): 142–169, 145.

11. Arendt, *The Human Condition*, 178.

12. Hannah Arendt, *The Origins of Totalitarianism* (New York: Harcourt Inc., 1974), 145.

13. Ibid., 478.

14. Arendt, *The Human Condition*, 254.

15. Hannah Arendt, "On the Nature of Totalitarianism: An Essay in Understanding," in *Essays in Understanding 1930–1954: Formation, Exile, and Totalitarianism*, ed. Jerome Kohn (New York: Schocken Books, 1994): 328–360, 336.

16. Arendt, *The Origins of Totalitarianism*, 477.

17. Ibid., 475.

18. Ibid., 477.

19. Arendt, "On the Nature of Totalitarianism," 355.

20. Arendt, *The Origins of Totalitarianism*, 478.

21. Ibid., 473.

22. Martin Heidegger, *Being and Time*, trans. Joan Stambaugh, rev. Dennis J. Schmidt (Albany: SUNY Press, 2010), 116.

23. Heidegger, *Being and Time*, 123.

24. See Richard Wolin, *The Politics of Being: The Political Thought of Martin Heidegger* (New York: Columbia University Press, 1990), 49 and Fred Dallmayr, *Twilight of Subjectivity: Contributions to a Post-Individualist Theory of Politics* (Amherst: University of Massachusetts Press, 1981), 56–71.

25. Jean-Luc Nancy, "The Being-with of Being-there," *Continental Philosophy Review* 41 (2008): 1–15, 5.

26. See Jean-Luc Nancy, *Being Singular Plural*, 6, and Andrew Benjamin, *Towards a Relational Ontology: Philosophy's Other Possibility* (Albany: SUNY Press, 2015), 2.

27. See for instance Peter Enns, "Understanding the 2016 US Presidential Election Polls: The Importance of Hidden Trump Supporters," *Statistics, Politics and Policy*, 8.1 (2017): 41–63 and Alexander Coppock, "Did Shy Trump Supporters Bias the 2016 Polls? Evidence from a Nationally Representative List Experiment," *Statistics, Politics, and Policy*, 8.1 (2017): 29–40. See also Samara Klar, Christopher R. Weber, and Yanna Krupnikov, "Social Desirability Bias in the 2016 Presidential Election," *The Forum* 14.4 (December 2016): 433–443 and Andy Brownback and Aaron Novotny, "Social Desirability Bias and Polling Errors in the 2016 Presidential Election," *Journal of Behavioral and Experimental Economics*, 74 (June 2018): 38–56.

28. See, for instance, Ian Storey, "The Politics of Defining Today: Towards a Critical Historicism of Judgment," *Arendt Studies*, 1 (2017): 61–86, DOI: 10.5840/arendtstudies2017957.

1

The Peculiar Loneliness of the Current Age: Heidegger on Being-With

This chapter considers Martin Heidegger's insights into the peculiar loneliness of the current age and the stage this sets for philosophical inquiry into the possibilities for authentic communal life. As we have seen, the peculiarity of this loneliness consists in the fact that while we may be able to conquer all distances through scientific and technological advancement, we are nevertheless no nearer to ourselves, to one another, or to the things around us. Though Heidegger's critique of modern instrumental rationality is perhaps most pronounced in his later writings on language and technology, I turn in this chapter to his 1927 masterwork *Being and Time*. A work best known for its radical intervention in the tradition of Western metaphysics, replacing its metaphysics of presence with an ontology of existence, equally important is the way in which this intervention makes visible the problem of our peculiar loneliness.

Heidegger's radical intervention in *Being and Time* consists in his displacement of the isolated modern subject in favor of the relational structure of "being-in-the-world." Heidegger conceives of this relationality not in terms of the epistemological structure of consciousness but rather in terms of care (*Sorge*) or our pre-cognitive tendency "toward nearness" from out of which Dasein makes more proximate and familiar its world. Coming to understand these ontological structures, he argues, depends not on the metaphysical presumption that beings are constituted by fixed, pre-given essences but rather on recognizing that we are constituted by the excessive and irresolute possibility of existence, an excess from which all philosophical questioning begins.[1] As groundbreaking as each of these insights are, it is the goal of this chapter to consider how, in discovering this ontology of existence, Heidegger at the same time discovers a distinctive form of alienation, one to which Dasein, in its irreducible possibility and irrevocable relationality, is always already vulnerable. I begin by considering the central problematic of *Being and Time* and its importance for elucidating what Heidegger describes as the vacuity of modern notions of subjectivity. I then turn to Heidegger's claim that insofar as Dasein is always already in a world, Dasein is at the same time "always already being-with," together, not just with things, but also with others in an originary and pre-thematic way. While we might expect Heidegger to be led from this to insist that Dasein finds itself originally at home in these relations, it is crucial for our purposes that he does not. Instead, turning to his analysis of the "they-self," we find that Heidegger discovers in this native relationality the possibility for being together with others in a way that is reductive, instrumental, and totalizing, shrouding Dasein in anonymity even as it finds itself crowded in by others. In view of this, I will suggest that the "they-self" points to a peculiar kind of loneliness, whereby Dasein finds itself at once pressed into an indistinguishable mass and at the same time hidden from those with whom it shares the world.[2]

That being-with does not promise immediate belonging for Dasein but instead begins in inauthenticity is a decisive if underappreciated insight of *Being and Time*. It indicates that the very movement of care—its drive to make accessible and familiar the world into which it has been thrown—is the very same movement that makes possible the loneliness and anonymity of the they-self. Many have criticized Heidegger's discourse on the "they-self" for depicting too pessimistically the dynamics of social life.[3] Yet, in our own era of hyperbolic interconnectedness we are by no means strangers to this longing for accessibility and proximity, nor are we immune to the reductive metrics and algorithms that organize our ways of being together with others. Rather than treating this aspect of *Being and Time* as overly pessimistic, I therefore wish to take a different angle of approach, conceiving of it as the starting point for philosophical inquiry into the problem of our peculiar loneliness. As I will suggest in subsequent chapters, Heidegger's insight creates an enduring problematic in twentieth- and twenty-first-century continental philosophy. In discovering that this loneliness is at once an inevitable and intolerable dimension of being-in-the-world, Heidegger raises the question of how we might recover from out of this peculiar loneliness authentic forms of communal life. Though Heidegger's own answers to this question have, for both philosophical and political reasons, proven largely unsatisfying, the legacy of the question itself nevertheless remains central. Therefore, while *Being and Time* may offer no solution, it nevertheless makes visible as a philosophical problematic the peculiar loneliness of the current age, a problem that I will suggest is only becoming increasingly urgent today.

MODERN SUBJECTIVITY AND THE FORGETFULNESS OF BEING

In order to clarify how Heidegger's discovery of his ontology of existence makes visible the problem of our peculiar loneliness, it is necessary to begin by considering the central problematic of *Being and Time*. This problematic comes into view in Heidegger's effort to reawaken our native capacity to be perplexed by the question of the meaning of being. Fundamental to the ancient ontologies of Plato and Aristotle, Heidegger argues, "This question today has been forgotten—although our time considers itself progressive in again affirming 'metaphysics.'"[4] As Aristotle first discovered, the field of inquiry that is directed toward "being as such," or first philosophy, raises the most fundamental questions—questions that must be interrogated if we are to understand particular regions of being such as the being of living things or the being of the material world.[5] Yet, while the question of the meaning of being is the most fundamental, being itself is also the most obscure and indefinable of all concepts. It is at once perfectly universal, while at the same time that which makes possible the manifold of categories within which particular beings belong. Moreover, Heidegger explains, in its *highest* universality, there is nothing higher or more universal to which we can refer in our efforts to define it.[6] And yet, the concept permeates our everyday experience; it is used in all predicating and knowing, raising the question of why the meaning of being is not as comprehensible as the phrase "the sky *is* blue" or "I *am* happy."[7]

These perplexities, to be sure, are the deepest and most difficult to interrogate. Yet, rather than turning toward them, Heidegger maintains that the tendency in the history of Western metaphysics has been to turn away, giving rise to a dogma within this tradition that not only trivializes the question of the meaning of being but "even sanctions its neglect."[8] In consequence of this, Heidegger says, this question has ceased to be *"a thematic question of actual investigation."*[9] Taken to be empty of meaning and impossible to define, inquiry into the meaning of being has come to be understood either as a fool's errand or as something so self-evident that it is unworthy of philosophical inquiry.

It is within this horizon of concerns that Heidegger lays out his early formulation of the project of fundamental ontology. While it has become a habit of Western philosophical thinking to explain away the perplexities of being, Heidegger insists that it is precisely in these perplexities that the fundamental necessity of the question becomes apparent. Since the ancient ontologies of Plato and Aristotle, he argues that the methods that have been employed throughout the tradition of Western metaphysics to answer the question of the meaning of being have led us astray.[10] Whereas these methods have tended to ask this question by observing being as if it were one being among others, Heidegger maintains that being itself requires a fundamentally different method of demonstration. "Not only is the *answer* to the question of being lacking," Heidegger says, "but even the question itself is obscure and without direction. Thus to retrieve the question of being means first of all to work out adequately the *formulation* of the question."[11] In a radical gesture against the tradition of Western metaphysics, Heidegger thus argues that in order to reformulate this question, we must no longer treat as indifferent or passive those who are natively compelled to interrogate the perplexities of being. Instead, adequately formulating the question will depend first on making transparent in its ontological priority that being who is able to ask it in the first place.

Whereas other creatures and things may be indifferent to the question of the meaning of being, Heidegger argues that it is fundamental to the being of human being to be able to ask why there is something rather than nothing. We are the kinds of beings who have being as a concern; we regard being, question it, and seek it out in order to understand it. Hence, the task of *Being and Time* is not only to answer the question of the meaning of being, but to suggest that such an investigation depends above all on elucidating the conditions under which it is possible to have this question in the first place.[12] After all, the question of the meaning of being is *my* question; I am the being for whom being is a concern. It is mine and mine alone, and, therefore, Heidegger argues, formulating the question will depend first on gaining clarity about the kind of being that I am.

What, then, does it mean that the question of the meaning of being is *my* question? How do I begin to understand myself from out of this native capacity to be perplexed by the most obscure questions? Whereas the tendency in Western metaphysics has been to conceive of the human being as one being among others, constituted by a fixed essence or pre-given set of properties, Heidegger argues that we discover in our very capacity to question being that no such material essence can be attributed to us. If this were the case, we would have no need to ask ourselves whether we should be one way or another, as the answer to these questions would already be settled. Therefore, Heidegger argues, understanding being will depend first on offering an analysis of the excessive and irresolute possibility of existence as this is disclosed in our own capacity to be perplexed.

Heidegger insists that we are the kinds of beings who are *there*, who exist, and who are able to ask this question because we must decide for ourselves who to be and how to live. In renaming the human being Dasein or being-there, Heidegger thus wishes to indicate that we exist in this or that way prior to any metaphysical category, property, or essence that is assigned to us. He says:

> Dasein always understands itself in terms of its existence, in terms of its possibility to be itself or not be itself. Dasein has either chosen these possibilities itself, stumbled upon them, or in each instance already grown up in them. Existence is decided only by each Dasein itself in the manner of seizing upon or neglecting such possibilities.[13]

In this, Heidegger argues, Dasein does not understand itself in terms of an essence that can be actualized over the course of a life, nor does it understand itself in terms of fixed properties that it is endowed with from birth. Rather, Dasein understands itself above all in terms of its existence, or its possibilities to be one way or another, possibilities that it must either seize upon or neglect. In other words,

Heidegger says, "*The 'essence'* [*'Wesen'*] *of Dasein lies in its existence* [*Existenz*]. The characteristics to be found in this being are thus not pre-given 'attributes' of an objectively present being which has such and such an 'outward appearance,' but rather possible ways for it to be and only this."[14] Ontologically prior to any metaphysics of presence, the excessive and irresolute possibility of existence is precisely what makes possible the question of the meaning of being in the first place. Fundamental ontology will thus depend, Heidegger argues, on first offering an existential analytic of the being who is able to ask this question.

At stake in Heidegger's concern for this existential constitution is the presumption that Dasein is most fundamentally structured, not by its calculable position in space, but rather by its distinctive experience of time. In view of this, Heidegger says, reformulating the question of the meaning of being depends on "an original explication of time as the horizon of the understanding of being, in terms of temporality as the being of Dasein which understands being."[15] By time, Heidegger does not mean "clock time" or the artificial measurement of successive moments. Ontologically prior to this, he argues, is time as we experience it, whether in our reminiscence of times passed, in the way time lingers when we are completing ordinary, everyday tasks, or in the experience of time pressing in on us when we become anxious about things to come. Rushing headlong into the future from out of a past that it neither chooses nor controls, Dasein is always already structured in its ways of being and relating by this temporality. More specifically, Dasein's finitude—or the fact that its time will one day come to an end, that it will cease to exist—both constitutes its experience of time and creates the horizon within which every understanding and questioning take shape. In placing Dasein's temporality at the center of his existential analytic of Dasein, Heidegger thus wishes to show that Dasein can understand neither itself nor the world in abstraction from this temporality, and, as such, time, understood in terms of the histories and traditions that we inherit and the projects we undertake for the future, sets the limit within which any inquiry takes shape, including our inquiry into the question of being.

PHENOMENOLOGY AND THE MODERN SUBJECT

In order to reformulate this question, Heidegger thus insists that we must offer an existential analytic of Dasein in terms of its temporality. Such an analysis cannot impose categories and properties onto Dasein, but must instead proceed in a manner by which "this being can show itself to itself on its own terms."[16] In other words, such an investigation must be phenomenological, beginning with a description of Dasein as Dasein appears, not in abstraction from the world, but in its "everydayness."[17] In this, Heidegger explains, phenomenology must be understood as a descriptive rather than explanatory method, allowing things to appear as they are in their fullness of being.

In turning to phenomenology, Heidegger wishes to challenge the deeply entrenched assumption in the history of Western metaphysics since Plato that appearances are fundamentally different from the reality of the things we observe. When we encounter phenomena, Heidegger argues, we are not experiencing something superficial and illusory behind which the reality of the thing itself lies; quite to the contrary, in making such observations we are trying to notice the things themselves as they show themselves to us.[18] Hence, for Heidegger, being and appearing are not opposed to one another, but are instead bound together.

In turning to phenomenology, Heidegger thus follows his predecessor, Edmond Husserl, in affirming the dictum "To the things themselves!"[19] Heidegger, like Husserl, believes that the method of phenomenology offers a crucial alternative to the distorted and reductive ways that the modern sciences have come to treat the objects it observes. Heidegger agrees with Husserl that the time has come to challenge the presumption of expertise in the sciences. He also finds compelling Husserl's suggestion that phenomenology, or that method by which we hold ourselves open to things as they appear, enables us to interrogate the pretense of certainty within the modern sciences, no less than the closed-mindedness of the technical and reductive methods that have become the primary tools for understanding modern life. Heidegger thus follows Husserl in his suggestion that the method of phenomenology advances beyond these calculative methods, resisting the tendency to force properties onto the objects we observe and calling instead for a turn inward that enables us to examine the fundamental structures under which these phenomena become possible objects of experience.[20]

Yet, Husserl places the transcendental ego at the center of his inquiry, emphasizing the conditions under which appearances become possible objects of experience for an intending subject.

Heidegger, by contrast, endeavors to deepen and challenge this approach in order to twist free of the epistemological notion of subjectivity that has oriented the modern tradition since Descartes. In Heidegger's view, the forgetfulness of being is expressed perhaps no more profoundly than in the modern emphasis, not on questions of ontology, but on the epistemological concern for discerning what we can know with certainty. Heidegger argues that by insisting on the separation between *"res cogitans"* and *"res corporea,"* between mind and body, spirit and nature, Descartes was led by his radical skepticism to posit a vast and seemingly unbridgeable gap between the human being and the world.[21] In consequence of this, the question of how the subject is granted access to the world became the definitive problem of modern philosophical inquiry, a problem that Heidegger argues has caused the fundamental question of the meaning of being to fall into obscurity.

The birth of modern notions of subjectivity thus mark a decisive shift from ontological questions to epistemological ones. In conceiving of knowledge as the method by which we come to understand the world, Heidegger maintains that Descartes creates a platform for the modern assertion that the human being is a knowing subject who stands in a disinterested and distant relation to the world and who only comes into relation with it by consciously intending an object. In positing this distance between subject and object, Heidegger insists that the modern epistemological tradition precludes any inquiry into the meaningfulness of the things with which we are always already involved.

Heidegger, to be sure, is indebted to Husserl in myriad ways. Yet, Husserl, in the manner of Descartes, suggests that phenomenology will enable us to discover a more indubitable foundation for the sciences. In so doing, Heidegger thinks, Husserl implicates himself in the very presumptions of the modern epistemological tradition that he wishes to overcome. In Heidegger's view, Husserl is led by his own presumption of a transcendental ego to treat objects as "indifferent theoretical ways of intending."[22] As such, the distinctive and situated ways in which appearances are disclosed become inconsequential for understanding the fundamental structures that make possible our experience of them. Heidegger thus maintains that Husserl thematizes "objective being," abstracting objects from their embeddedness in the world and our experience of them through his use of the *epoché*, which brackets off the world in order to undertake a phenomenological reduction that is not obscured by error and prejudice.[23] In treating the object as "objective presence," Heidegger believes that Husserl's phenomenological reduction precludes an analysis of the relation between the being doing the intending and the world within which it is already immersed. That is to say, Heidegger believes that this method presumes a self-conscious subject whose historically informed biases, moods, and prejudices are irrelevant to the analysis of the fundamental structures of experience.[24]

In view of this, Heidegger insists that the task of phenomenology must be reformulated so that it no longer investigates the universal structures of intentionality in order to discern the conditions for the possibility of the experience of the conscious subject. Instead, Heidegger argues, phenomenology can only get at the things themselves if it offers a description of the universal structures under which it becomes possible for the human being to question the meaning of being in the first place. He thus attempts to move beyond Husserl's project, insisting that the method of phenomenology is most proper, not to epistemology, but rather to ontology.

That phenomenology is the method most proper to ontology, Heidegger thinks, has two important implications. First, a phenomenological description of existence in its ontological significance requires an analysis that is not bracketed off from the world and the relations that constitute it. Insofar as we are born into a world that we neither choose nor control, we are always already pre-figured by the world and our relations to the things and others that constitute it. Therefore, turning inward in the ways that Husserl recommends in order to gain access to Dasein depends on offering a phenomenological description, not of the conscious subject, but rather of Dasein in its "everydayness." That is, it requires an understanding of Dasein as a being that has already discovered the world in a certain way insofar as it is constituted by and dependent upon the nexus of meaningful relations in which it finds itself. Heidegger therefore argues that in order for phenomenology to be the method of ontology it must offer a description not of the transcendental ego but rather of Dasein as being-in-the-world (*in-der-Welt-sein*).[25]

Second, rather than searching for a more indubitable epistemic ground for the sciences that is free of error and prejudice, Heidegger suggests that it is precisely because the finite temporality of Dasein structures the horizon within which every understanding and inquiry takes shape that we cannot be liberated from error and prejudice. Heidegger takes Husserl to presume that in performing the *epoché*, it becomes possible to ascertain the universal structures of intentionality, offering complete and unfettered access to the phenomenon.[26] Heidegger, by contrast, maintains that while phenomenology allows things to show themselves as they are, it is integral to phenomena that they also conceal themselves. Heidegger is clear that while nothing lies behind the phenomenon, the phenomenon can nevertheless retreat, remain hidden, and fall into obscurity, showing itself only in disguise.[27] Phenomenology, then, is the method by which beings are wrested from their concealedness, discovered or uncovered through our "talking about them," but that always and again fall back into hiding. Whereas Husserl follows Descartes, Heidegger reaches back even further to liberate phenomenology from the quest for epistemological certainty. Turning to the Greek conception of *aletheia*, Heidegger argues that truth is not a fixed property of objects, but rather something that comes to appear upon being uncovered or discovered through our engagement in the world, an engagement that is always set within a horizon and never indifferent to the relations that constitute it.[28] Rather than conceiving of the truth in terms of the correspondence between an object and a knowing subject, Heidegger argues that truth appears as meaningful only insofar as it is "a determination of the being of Dasein itself."[29] That is to say, it comes to appear upon being uncovered or discovered in our effort to interpret the meaningfulness of the world so that we might find a home in it.[30] Hence, Heidegger argues that it is only insofar as Dasein is concerned or worried about the world it has inherited—a concern or worry he ultimately calls care (*Sorge*)—that allows truth to appear.

In undertaking a destruction of the tradition of Western metaphysics, Heidegger thus discovers that Dasein is most fundamentally "being-in-the-world," constituted in and through the nexus of meaningful relations in which it finds itself. He discovers, too, that in this native relationality, Dasein is always already reaching out, indwelling the world through its care or concern for the things and others with which it is involved. It is in these two discoveries—first, that Dasein is not a self-contained, isolated subject, but rather being-in-the-world, and second, that truth is disclosed not by intending the properties of an object, but through our care and concern for the things with which we are involved—that Heidegger radically intervenes in the tradition of Western metaphysics.

Yet, as I will suggest in what follows, it is also from out of these discoveries that Heidegger makes visible a distinctive form of alienation, one to which Dasein in its irreducible possibility and irrevocable relationality is always already vulnerable. To demonstrate this, I will elucidate Heidegger's analysis of being-in-the-world alongside his claim that "Dasein is always already being-with."[31] While we might expect Heidegger to be led from this to insist that Dasein is promised immediate belonging, it is important for our purposes that he does not. Instead, Heidegger argues that Dasein is initially and for the most part together with others in a leveled-down, inauthentic way, having forgotten itself in its irreducible possibility. As I will suggest, Heidegger's very effort to replace the modern epistemological subject with the relational structure of being-in-the-world makes visible a peculiar kind of loneliness, one that is epitomized by Dasein's absorption in what he calls the "they-self." The loneliness of the they-self is at once an inevitable part of being-in-the-world and at the same time an intolerable feature of Dasein's existence. While Dasein finds itself initially and for the most part with others in a leveled-down, inauthentic way, it is precisely this experience that serves as the irritant by which Dasein, in the mood of anxiety, is dislodged from the they-self, finding that it is tasked with deciding for itself who to be and how to live. In view of this, we find that Heidegger's radical intervention in the history of Western metaphysics is important not only for replacing its metaphysics of presence with an ontology of existence, but also for putting into relief a peculiar loneliness to which Dasein, as being-in-the-world, is always already vulnerable.

BEING TOGETHER WITH THINGS AND OTHERS

Finding itself always already thrown into a world or nexus of meaningful relations that are not its own, Dasein is in-the-world to the extent that it is constituted by its temporality. That is to say, Dasein projects from out of this thrownness into the future, seizing upon possibilities that either enable it to be itself or that set it adrift. As such, its relation to the world is not established after a knowing subject has consciously intended an object. Instead, Dasein is pre-cognitively beholden to and constituted by a world that is larger than itself and from out of which it must project its future possibilities.[32] In view of this, Heidegger argues, Dasein has always already discovered the world in its existential constitution as a thrown project.

Though Heidegger wishes to clarify the constitutive structural factors of Dasein as being-in-the-world, this does not mean that we should interpret Dasein as a discrete, objectively present entity that is contained within a larger, objectively present world. Distinctive of traditional ontologies, this latter approach treats "being in" as a categorial characteristic, whereby objects stand in a certain spatial relation to one another—for instance, "the dress is in the closet" or "the water is in the glass." The relation between these objects is indifferent and accidental. The water and dress are "being in" in a way that is unaffected and independent in "being-objectively-present-together."[33] Such an interpretation of the phenomenon of being-in presupposes that "knowing the world" consists in knowing in a formal, scientific way, measuring and calculating the corporeal qualities of "external" things.[34] Yet, Heidegger maintains that "we cannot understand by [the being-in of Dasein] the objective presence of a corporeal thing [*Körperding*] (the human body [*Mendschenleib*]) 'in' a being objectively present."[35] Whereas the relation between stones, tables, pens, desks, and the like may be indifferent and accidental, Dasein is "in" the world in a fundamentally different way. Dasein does not merely stand next to the things that surround it, nor does it understand them as a conscious subject who asks how the representations stored "inside" its conscious mind "correspond" to reality.[36] Instead, Heidegger explains, Dasein is in the world to the extent that it dwells (*wohnen*) in it, inhabiting the world with native familiarity and concern for the things with which it is involved.[37]

Before knowing the world scientifically, Dasein is already taken up in it, absorbed in its everyday dealings with things and others. While knowing in a formal, scientific manner may be one way that Dasein gains new perspectives on the world, this does not establish or verify a relation between the "inner" life of the subject and the "outer" world of the object. As Heidegger explains, "The interpretation of knowledge, still prevalent today, as a 'relation between subject and object' . . . contains about as much 'truth' as it does vacuity. But subject and object are not the same as Dasein and world."[38] Dasein finds itself always already grasping for and reaching toward something beyond itself. He says, "In directing itself toward . . . in grasping something, Dasein does not first go outside of the inner sphere in which it is initially encapsulated."[39] Instead, he explains, in dwelling, caring, perceiving, grasping, "Dasein is always already 'outside,' together with some being encountered in the world already discovered."[40] Moreover, in dwelling together with the beings it encounters, Dasein does not abandon some "inner" sphere. Instead, in being together with its object, Dasein is at the same time always already "inside," aware of itself as being-in-the-world. In its concern for the things with which it is involved, Dasein understands itself first and for the most part through what is not its own. Therefore, prior to "knowing" the world in a scientific and thematic way, the world is already discovered, disclosed in its meaningfulness through Dasein's native involvement with it.[41]

In view of this, Heidegger insists that it is not consciousness but rather care (*Sorge*) that constitutes the fundamental ontological structure by which Dasein becomes visible as being-in-the-world.[42] Insofar as being-in means dwelling, being amid, and being together with the things in the world, Dasein is primordially concerned about the world with which it is already involved.[43] As Heidegger's reference to the story of care teaches us, "[The human being] has the 'origin' of its being in care . . . this being is not released from its origin, but is held fast and dominated by it as long as this being 'is in the world.'"[44] For Heidegger, Dasein's relation to the world is never indifferent or passive. Rather, as a thrown project, Dasein intuitively plans ahead, proposes, and expects in order to cope with the conditions of its existence, which are manifest above all in the anticipation of its own death.[45] It is therefore in virtue of the temporality of Dasein that care is intrinsic to us. As Charles Scott explains, "Whereas care is the origin and meaning of human life in the world, time constitutes the origin and meaning of the unified structure where care takes place."[46] Insofar as we are finite, we are also always already ahead of ourselves, prompted in our care to project into the future. Hence, in being thrown into the world, Dasein is primordially concerned in and about its being, and it is this concern that gives meaning and orientation to the "for sake of which" that directs all of Dasein's activity.[47]

As care, Dasein understands itself initially and for the most part in terms of its everyday dealings with things. In its everydayness, Dasein already sees and has already discovered the world in a certain way. This kind of seeing is not mere perceptual cognition, but arises through "handling, using, and taking care, which has its own kind of 'knowledge.'"[48] Things never originally show themselves as objectively present, discrete entities with certain corporeal properties. Instead, in its everyday dealings, Dasein appropriates the things with which it is involved in the most adequate way possible in order to complete the tasks it sets forth for itself. "This dealing," Heidegger says, "which makes use of things, is not blind, but instead gives them their specific [certainty]."[49] Things are thus initially discovered not through theoretical observation, but rather in their usefulness, or, as Heidegger puts it, their "handiness" (*Zuhandenheit*). Using the example of the hammer, Heidegger explains, "The less we just stare at the thing called hammer, the more we take hold of it and use it, the more original our relation to it becomes and the more undisguisedly it is encountered as what it is, as a useful thing."[50] The hammer is thus disclosed in its handiness through an everyday, circumspect dealing with it, and it is through our work, our projects, and our dealings that the world becomes visible.[51] Therefore, Heidegger argues, this practical, circumspect way of seeing is not subordinate to theoretical observation, but rather fundamental to an understanding of Dasein in its ontological priority as being-in-the-world.

In view of this, we find, too, that care points to Dasein's native tendency to reach out, to bring nearer, and to make familiar the things that it encounters. This can be seen by turning to Heidegger's analysis of Dasein's spatiality, which, he says, "shows the character of *de-distancing* and *directionality*."[52] An aspect of *Being and Time* that is thought by many commentators to be derivative of Heidegger's analysis of the temporality of Dasein, his destruction of vulgar notions of spatiality inherited from modern physics and the tradition of Western metaphysics is nevertheless crucial for understanding his existential analytic of being-in.[53] Moreover, the spatiality of being-in, as Heidegger conceives of it, is equally important for how we might understand Dasein's existential constitution as always already being-with no less than the peculiar loneliness that I will suggest he discovers in light of this.

Insofar as Dasein is not objectively present but is rather always already being-in, it deals with the things it encounters in the world in a familiar and heedful way.[54] "De-distancing," Heidegger says, "means making distance disappear, making the being at a distance of something disappear, bringing it near."[55] While there has been a tendency to take the mathematical measurement of the space in which Dasein exists to be most fundamental, Heidegger maintains that it is Dasein's tendency "toward nearness" that is originating, structuring the horizon of every encounter we have, including those that prompt us to calculate mathematically the distance between two points. As Heidegger explains, "When Dasein in taking care brings something near, this does not mean that it fixes upon something at a position in space which has the least measurable distant from a point of its body. Bringing near is . . . rather toward headful being-in-the-world, that is, what that being-in-the-world initially encounters."[56] Insofar as Dasein essentially dwells in this de-distancing, it never overcomes remoteness in the sense of crossing over the space between point A and point B, but is always de-distancing, reaching out, and bringing nearer. In this de-distancing, Dasein also continually seeks out signs and directions that orient it toward its world. As such, de-distancing also has the character of directionality, promising familiarity and proximity that orients Dasein within its world.

For Dasein, then, spatiality discloses itself not in terms of mathematical principles, but rather as the meaningful context within which Dasein decides to be one way or another, a decision that is structured by its temporality.[57] This nexus of meaningful relations is always already discovered before any individual thing comes to appear, and its meaningfulness depends on the way in which Dasein indwells it.[58] In this, Dasein is never "in" the world in the sense of being in another objectively present thing.[59] Rather, Dasein dwells insofar as it has this native familiarity and concern for the things with which it is involved and is thus existentially and pre-thematically constituted by care. Dasein's own possibilities to be one way or another are constituted by its facticity or the fact that Dasein is bound up with what is outside of it. As Heidegger explains, "Dasein understands itself as bound up in its 'destiny' with the being of those beings which it encounters within its own world."[60] Facticity thus points to the fact that Dasein finds itself always already in a world that is larger than its own making, a world that it neither chooses nor controls.[61] While we may not be in the mood to acknowledge our relation to the world, we are never outside of or free from being-in it. Rather, we are always already reaching out and bringing nearer in order to make more proximate and familiar the world in which we find ourselves.

Though Heidegger's initial inquiry into being-in-the-world unfolds with respect to the things and tools that we use in our every day lives, he clarifies that this cannot be thought apart from our relation to the others who are there with us. Whereas Dasein is always already "in" the world to the extent that it cares for the things with which it is involved, Dasein is also already "with" the world to the extent that it finds itself in relation to others. While Heidegger elucidates the way in which useful things are initially discovered in their "handiness" through our work with them, he insists that it is only insofar as we also encounter these things in relation to others that their meaningfulness is disclosed. Rather than constituting a mere addition to useful things, Heidegger maintains that even when one is alone in a workshop, using a hammer to build a chair or a table, both the task and the tools discovered through that task carry possible references to other Daseins. The chair is being built for someone to use in their own everyday dealings, and, in this way, others are always there when we discover the hammer and nails in their usefulness. Likewise, once the chair or table is finished, sold, and incorporated into the life of another Dasein, the chair always contains a reference to its maker. Discovering the chair in its usefulness is thus always already bound up with the other who made it. While this reference may only be tacit and understood in an indeterminate way, it is nevertheless always together with the useful things that we encounter in our everyday dealings.

Though the things we use are only ever encountered in relation to those others who are involved with them, Dasein pre-thematically understands that there is a difference between useful things and the others it encounters. Whereas useful things and tools are initially discovered in their handiness, other Daseins are encountered as being-there-with in a way that tools and things are not. These others dwell in the world, appearing not in their usefulness or objective presence, but instead in their care and concern for the world with which they are involved. Dasein thus encounters the world initially in terms of the "being-there-too" of the others who are there with it. Never simply an "I," Dasein thus originally finds that "the world is always already one that I share with others."[62] Though Dasein certainly can identify itself as "I here," this "I" is never originally isolated in the sense of being a self-contained subject. Not only is this "I" spoken in relation to what is "over there," but even before Dasein distinguishes itself, it is already being-with-others.

Because of this, Heidegger says, "Dasein understands itself initially and for the most part in terms of the world, and the Dasein-with of others."[63] This originary being-with is not negated by the feeling of being alone, nor is it undermined in those moments when we reduce others to their objective presence, merely passing them by or treating them only in their utility. This, to be sure, is one mode of relating, but even here, Dasein is still "with" others in an originary way. As such, Heidegger says, "Being-in-the-world is being-with."[64] Being-with, he argues, belongs to the being of Dasein, and thus, in just the same way that being-in sets the horizon within which Dasein understands itself and the world, so too does its being-with-others.[65] Moreover, in just the same way as Dasein's spatiality takes shape in its effort to bring nearer the world of things in which it finds itself, so too does its attempt to bring nearer and make more proximate those with whom it shares the world. Yet, as we shall see, this proximity and familiarity do not promise immediate belonging with others. While this tendency toward nearness is fundamental to the being of Dasein, it is this very same impulse that I will suggest conditions Dasein's entanglement in the they-self, or a way of being-with others that is fundamentally lonely insofar as it is reductive of Dasein's own most possibilities to be.

THE PECULIAR LONELINESS OF BEING-WITH

In asserting this native relationality, we might expect Heidegger to insist that Dasein finds itself initially and for the most part at home in the world with others, promised genuine belonging from the outset. Yet, Heidegger makes a different gesture, one that is especially important for the purposes of this discussion. In its native tendency "toward nearness," seeking out signs and directions that make proximate and familiar what it encounters, Dasein first indwells these relations in terms of its facticity or the fact that it is always already bound up with what is external to it and not its own. That is, in having its being in care, Dasein initially and for the most part seeks out signs and guideposts that promise proximity and familiarity, not just with the things it encounters, but also with the others who are always already together with those things. Yet, in seeking out these signs and directions from what is external to it, Dasein loses itself, letting others decide on its behalf who it should be and how it should live.

As such, Heidegger says, "Being-in-the-world, to which being together with things at hand belongs just as primordially as being-with others, is always for the sake of itself. But the self is initially and for the most part inauthentic, the they-self. Being-in-the-world is always already entangled."[66] While Dasein is always already being-with, Heidegger is clear that its concern for others initially takes shape in a deficient and leveled-down way. He explains, "Being for-, against-, and without-one-another, passing-one-another-by, not-mattering-to-one-another are possible ways of concern. And precisely the last named modes of deficiency and indifference characterize the everyday and average being-with-one-another."[67] These deficient modes of concern for others tend to lead us astray such that we find ourselves treating one another as objective presence. Hence, while being-with-others belongs to the being of Dasein, the consequence of this is not that we immediately and originally find ourselves at home in being-with. Quite to the contrary, it is precisely because "Dasein is essentially for the sake of others" that Dasein finds itself first and for the most part in these relations in a leveled-down and inauthentic way.[68]

Dasein's everyday self is constituted by what it takes care of in the surrounding world in a way that is for or against others. All of Dasein's doings and undertakings are considered in relation to those with whom it shares the world. Others thus set the measure by which everyday Dasein sees itself. Initially, Heidegger says, "Dasein stands in subservience to others. It itself *is* not; the others have taken its being away from it. The everyday possibilities of the being of Dasein are at the disposal of the whims of others."[69] These others do not have the appearance of singular individuals. In one's effort to distinguish oneself from these others, one at the same time belongs to them and is unable to see them in their own existential possibilities. As Heidegger explains, others are thus encountered in this mode of being-with not in terms of a who, but instead as an indistinguishable mass that he calls "the they."[70]

When Dasein is absorbed in the they, it enjoys the things that "they" enjoy, judges the world in the way "they" judge it, and withdraws from things that "they" find horrific and shocking.[71] Significantly, Heidegger argues, while Dasein may be together with the "they" in a heightened way, the others with whom Dasein is involved at the same time disappear in their distinctiveness. In this, we might characterize the they-self in terms of a peculiar loneliness, whereby Dasein finds itself pressed together with others and yet nevertheless left hidden and isolated from those with whom it shares the world.

The great mass that appears in place of those with whom Dasein is involved levels down and makes average all who are absorbed by it. Averageness prescribes the ways that Dasein acts, diminishing all uniqueness and obscuring Dasein's own most possibilities to be. Heidegger says:

> This being-with-one-another dissolves one's own Dasein completely into the kind of being of "the others" in such a way that the others, as distinguishable and explicit, disappear more and more. In this inconspicuousness and unascertainability, the they unfolds its true dictatorship.[72]

The "dictatorship" of the they is expressed in its tendency toward averageness. The they is factically constituted by this averageness in "what it does and does not consider validness, and what it grants or denies success. This averageness, which prescribes what may be ventured, watches over every exception which thrusts itself to the fore." [73] In consequence of this, Heidegger says, "Every priority is noiselessly squashed. Overnight, everything that is original is flattened down as something long since known. Everything won through struggle becomes something manageable. Every mystery loses its power."[74] Absorbed by the "they-self," Dasein is thus initially and for the most part in relation to others in an inauthentic way. At stake in this inauthenticity is the loss of one's singularity, rendering those with whom Dasein shares the world anonymous and hidden. Hence, we might describe this mode of being-with as especially lonely, whereby Dasein finds itself at once crowded in by others and at the same time left entirely hidden from them.

Perhaps most striking about this insight is the fact that it is precisely from out of Dasein's existential constitution as being-in-the-world that it finds itself taken in by the they. Heidegger says, "The care of averageness, reveals . . . an essential tendency of Dasein, which we call the *leveling down* of all possibilities of being."[75] Dasein is always already drawn in by this they, finding itself initially and for the most part constituted by it. That is to say, Dasein is originally a "they-self," tending in its everydayness to level down its own most possibilities to be. This averageness and leveling-down, Heidegger argues, may be understood in terms of what he calls "publicness" (*Öffentlichkiet*), which initially controls the way that Dasein and the world are interpreted. For inauthentic Dasein, such interpretations only appear to be correct because they absorb every difference and genuineness. Heidegger explains, "Publicness obscures everything, and then claims that what has been covered over is what is familiar and accessible to everyone."[76] The they disburdens Dasein of its responsibility to be a self, a responsibility that consists in deciding for itself who it has to be. Insofar as "they" are responsible, no one is responsible and thus, he says, "The *they*, which supplies the *who* of everyday Dasein, is the *nobody* to whom every Dasein has surrendered itself, in its being-among-one-another."[77] Dasein, therefore, is not initially an "I" in the sense of having a "self." Instead, Dasein originally understands itself as a "they-self," which is to say, as a nobody. This is not an accidental property of Dasein, Heidegger explains, but integral to Dasein's being insofar as it is constituted by being-with. He says:

> The self of everyday Dasein is the *they-self*, which we distinguish from the *authentic-self*, that is the self that has authentically grasped itself. The they-self is *dispersed* in the they and must find itself.... *Initially*, "I am" not in the sense of my own self, but I am the others in the mode of the they.[78]

Hence, insofar as Dasein is constituted by being-with, Dasein has initially and for the most part fallen prey to the they-self, appearing not in its radical singularity, but rather as everyone and no one, entirely invisible in its own most possibilities to be.

Many have taken issue with this aspect of Heidegger's project, suggesting that Heidegger's interpretation of being-with in *Being and Time* is "disproportionality negative," radically de-valuing the very relationality that he initially seems to affirm.[79] As Richard Wolin has suggested, this makes it difficult to see how Heidegger avoids succumbing to his own critique of Husserl, impoverishing our worldly relations and celebrating a non-relational Dasein who seemingly has no way to enter into these relations authentically. As important as these criticisms are, however, I wish to take a different angle of approach to interpreting this aspect of *Being and Time*. Heidegger's discovery of the relational structure of Dasein involves, at the same time, the discovery of a peculiar kind of loneliness that is epitomized by the they-self and built into Dasein's very existential constitution as being-in-the-world. Dasein's native tendency to bring nearer and make more accessible the world into which it has been thrown is the very same tendency that makes possible its absorption in inauthentic forms of being-with.

In our own age of hyperbolic interconnectedness, this claim is not far from our own experience, nor is Heidegger's insight that such ways of relating leave us lonely and hidden from one another. What is especially significant about this dimension of *Being and Time*, then, is that the loss of self that arises from our entanglement in the they-self at the same time produces an intolerable loneliness, one that is experienced most profoundly when we are with others. This is a crucial if underappreciated insight of *Being and Time*, prompting reflection on the peculiar loneliness that may remain at work in our own era of heightened togetherness. As inevitable as this longing for proximity and familiarity might be, the peculiar loneliness that it produces is equally intolerable, supplying the irritant that displaces Dasein in the mood of anxiety from its entanglement in the world so that it can decide for itself who it has to be.

Heidegger's insights into the loss of self that arises when we are with others in the mode of inauthenticity thus sets up a crucial problematic, raising the question of how we might recover authentic forms of being-with from out of the peculiar loneliness of the they-self. Moreover, in highlighting its intolerability, Heidegger sets the stage for further inquiry into the perils of this loneliness for social and political life. In what follows, I will briefly consider three answers that Heidegger offers to the question of what authentic Dasein, in being constituted by both its radical possibility and irrevocable interdependence, might look like. Though these answers have, for both philosophical and political reasons, proven largely unsatisfying, we nevertheless find that *Being and Time* sets in motion an enduring problematic, making visible the urgency of this problem of loneliness and the need to recover authentic forms of communal life from out of it.

AUTHENTICITY

Heidegger first gestures toward a solution to the problem of this peculiar loneliness by highlighting two positive modes of concern that Dasein can have in relation to others. He calls the first leaping in, which arises when Dasein is with others in the mode of inauthenticity and the second, leaping ahead, which arises when Dasein indwells these relations authentically. The first he says, "can take the other's care away from him and put itself in his place in taking care, it can *leap in* for him."[80] This mode of concern, whereby Dasein treats the other in terms of what needs to be taken care of, robs the other of her own care, displacing her from herself and her own most possibilities to be. This kind of concern makes the other dependent, Heidegger explains, and can even dominate her. While this way of taking care is perhaps most common, Heidegger explains that it is reductive, arising when we take care "of things at hand" and treat others as objects to be dealt with and tasks to be completed.

The other positive mode of concern, Heidegger says, "does not so much leap in for the other as *leap ahead* of him in his existentiell potentiality-of-being."[81] Heidegger argues that this mode of concern gets out in front of the other's own most possibilities to be, not to take her care away, but to create a platform for her to decide for herself who to be and how to live. Leaping ahead, Heidegger explains, thus constitutes an authentic mode of care to the extent that it consists in being-with-another in a way that enables the other to become transparent to herself in her freedom of possibility. No longer thought to be a "what" that needs to be taken care of, Heidegger suggests that leaping ahead enables the "who" to appear. In view of this, he says that the possibility for leaping ahead cannot arise when we are with others who are simply doing and thinking the same things as us. Rather than promoting genuine closeness or belonging, this way of being-with "not only keeps for the most part within outer limits, but also enters distance and reserve."[82] On the other hand, Heidegger explains, when, in taking up something common, each devotes themselves in a way that ensures that the other is able to appear on her own, "authentic alliance" becomes possible. Such an alliance is authentic, Heidegger explains, because it "frees the other for himself in his freedom."[83] From Heidegger's distinction between leaping in and leaping ahead, we thus get a first glimpse into the possibilities for authentic being-with.

This aspect of his discussion, however, is woefully brief. Far more robust is Heidegger's discourse on authentic Dasein in Division II of *Being and Time*. Yet, the question of how authentic Dasein might have an "authentic alliance" with another does not come into view as clearly as one might hope in his analysis of authenticity. Though there is much to be said about Heidegger's discourse on authentic Dasein, I will consider only briefly the way in which care comes to appear in the mode of authenticity. While we might expect Heidegger to conceive of care here in terms of Dasein's relations to others, we find instead that authenticity reaches its summit through the achievement of a certain kind of self-relation that is displaced from the world-relations to which it has fallen prey. As Hans

Blumenberg has suggested, Heidegger's discourse on authenticity is thus characterized by what he describes as the "narcissism" of care, emphasizing that what is most proper to Dasein is a certain kind of care of the self. [84]

As being-in-the-world, Dasein is not an isolated subject surrounded by objectively present things; quite to the contrary, Dasein is always already involved and engrossed in a world or nexus of meaningful relations. We have already seen how, in the mode of inauthenticity, our involvement in the world unfolds in accordance with what is normal, acceptable, and predictable. This way of caring arises in the context of our everyday dealings with people and things, leading us, in this everydayness, to do as we are expected to do and to see ourselves how others see us.[85] Dasein in the mode of inauthenticity is thus shrouded in anonymity, unable to disclose the "who" or individual singular authorship that is constitutive of Dasein's existence. The they disburdens Dasein of the weight of its being as this unfolds in its freedom for its own most possibilities to be. Consequently, Heidegger explains, "Everyone is the other, and no one is himself."[86] We thus find ourselves dispersed in the mode of inauthenticity, lost in the average everydayness of the they and unable to care in a way that allows for self and world disclosure.

In the mode of authenticity, by contrast, Dasein finds itself overtaken in the mood of anxiety, summoned back to itself through a confrontation with its finitude. Upon coming face-to-face, not with its native relationality, but rather with the possibility of its most radical separation from the world and others, Dasein, in being-toward-death, is disclosed as radically individuated and free for its own most possibilities to be. As Heidegger says, death is "Dasein's ownmost nonrelational possibility," a possibility that cannot be bypassed and that *"lays claim* on it as something *individual."*[87] Indeed, while death is Dasein's certain, insuperable possibility, it cannot be calculated as if it were merely objectively present. As the possibility of such radical separation, death is in each instance only one's own and thus "exhibits a different kind of certainty," one that is indefinite, given to us as the anticipation of something that cannot be anticipated, quantified, reduced, or generalized.[88] This anticipation thus takes shape as a call that momentarily displaces Dasein from its normal course of existence as being-in-the-world, uprooting it from the pre-given meanings that structure our ordinary relations to things and others. This call—the call of conscience—reminds us of ourselves and the possibilities that are given to us by the singularity of our existence as this is disclosed in the anticipation of our own death.[89] Characterized by silent and inward resolve, authentic Dasein thus heeds this call in the moment of anticipatory resoluteness, deciding from out of itself who to be and how to live. For Heidegger, then, care takes shape in a way that is most proper to the being of Dasein when it returns us to ourselves, calling upon us to decide to be who to be in light of those possibilities that are most our own. Authenticity thus reaches its summit through a retreat from Dasein's native engrossment in the world, enabling Dasein, in turn, to care for the singularity and unrepeatability of its existence. Finding itself beholden only to the call of conscience, Dasein is thus disclosed as care in the mode of authenticity through a return to itself, taking shape most properly as a certain kind of care of the self.

While care may point to the fact that we are always already exposed to more than we can grasp and, in this, reaching out toward that which is foreign and unfamiliar, Heidegger seems to suggest here that authenticity takes shape through a movement inward and away from this native relationality.[90] In setting authentic Dasein apart from its involvement in the world in the mode of authenticity, we may therefore wonder whether Heidegger leaves crucial possibilities for authentic being-with unfulfilled in the context of our communal relations and responsibilities. That is to say, the question of what it means to "leap ahead" in order to achieve an "authentic alliance" seems to remain unresolved in Heidegger's account of authenticity.

Heidegger is thus led from his account of singular Dasein in the mode of authenticity to develop a notion of authentic being-with that comes into view in his discourse on the historicity (*Geschichtlichkeit*) of Dasein in §74 of *Being and Time*. While this section of the text can perhaps be read as answering the question of what leaping ahead means, we find that Dasein's radical individuation seems to go missing in Heidegger's effort to think authentic historicity in terms of the collective destiny of people. Heidegger explains that upon returning resolutely to its thrownness, Dasein appropriates the traditional possibilities that it has inherited, "although not necessarily as traditional ones."[91] Heidegger explains that it is only upon becoming authentic, "free *for* death," that the possibility for Dasein's authentic historicity emerges. Yet, what is disclosed in this authentic historicity is not an endless multiplicity of its most accessible and least authentic possibilities, "those of comfort, shirking and taking things easy."⁹² Instead, authenticity makes Dasein free for death and thus "brings Dasein to the simplicity of its *fate* [*Schicksals*]."⁹³ It is precisely in this notion of fate—of having been sent—that Heidegger grounds Dasein's authentic possibility as being-with. He says:

> If fateful Dasein essentially exists as being-in-the-world in being with others, then its occurrence is an occurrence-with and is determined as *destiny* [*Geschick*]. With this term, we designate the occurrence of the community, of a people [*Volk*]. Destiny is not composed of individual fates, nor can being-with-one-another be conceived of as the mutual occurrence of several subjects. These fates are already guided beforehand in being-with-one-another in the same world and in the resoluteness for definite possibilities. In communication and in struggle the power of destiny first becomes free. The fateful destiny of Dasein in and with its "generation" constitutes the complete, authentic occurrence of Dasein.⁹⁴

Understood in terms of the historical destiny of a people, Heidegger's formulation of authentic being-with in his discourse on historicity purports to answer the question of the "who" of Dasein, while, at the same time, affirming Dasein's interconnectedness in a way that does not succumb to the inauthenticity of the they-self. Yet, this question of the "who" is answered by its inheritance, not as an individual, but as a part of a collective. A puzzle thus arises regarding how the historicity of Dasein, in being prompted by the anticipation of death and grounded in the categories of history and fate, can at once free Dasein for its radical individuation and, at the same time, form the basis for authentic being-with-others.⁹⁵ There has been much debate about the extent to which Heidegger's concern for fate and destiny can be brought together with his account of authenticity in his analysis of being-toward-death. Equally important has been the question of whether these passages, in emphasizing the historical destiny of a people, contain the undertones of Heidegger's own National Socialist sympathies. Both are important paths of inquiry. For the purposes of this discussion, however, what is most important is that while Heidegger makes visible Dasein's peculiar loneliness in his analysis of the they-self in Division I of *Being and Time*, it is not clear that his own efforts to think more authentic possibilities for being-with resolve this problem.

Woefully brief in his discourse on leaping in and leaping ahead, seemingly at odds with himself in his account of authentic Dasein, and left in the end with the fused, collective destiny of Dasein in its historicity, Heidegger has been interpreted by many to leave unresolved his own answers to the question of what authentic being-with might look like. Even so, he nevertheless makes visible in *Being and Time* a distinctive form of alienation, a peculiar loneliness, to which Dasein, in its irreducible possibility and irrevocable relationality, is always already vulnerable. It is precisely in discovering his ontology of existence that Heidegger also discovers how it is that we can at once be more extremely together and more extremely apart than ever before. Hence, as important as Heidegger's intervention into the tradition of Western metaphysics is, equally important is his discovery of this peculiar loneliness as this takes shape in his analysis of the inauthenticity of the they-self. While *Being and Time* may offer no solution, Heidegger thus makes philosophically significant the urgency of the peculiar loneliness of the current age. It will be the goal of the next chapter to elucidate the long afterglow of this problem in twentieth- and twenty-first-century continental philosophy. In particular, I will consider how thinkers since Heidegger have confronted this inevitable and intolerable loneliness while attempting to recover authentic forms of communal life that do not yield to dangerous and totalizing political possibilities.

NOTES

1. Heidegger uses the language of excess in his 1928 essay "Transcendence." As he explains, "Dasein is itself excess," becoming visible as possibility only insofar as it always exceeds its own grasp. See Martin Heidegger, "Transcendence," in *The Heidegger Reader*, trans. Jerome Veith (Bloomington: Indiana University Press, 2009): 68–78, 75.

2. Martin Heidegger, *Being and Time*, trans. Joan Stambaugh (Albany: SUNY Press, 2010), 123.

3. See Richard Wollin, *The Politics of Being: The Political Thought of Martin Heidegger* (New York: Columbia University Press, 1990), 49 and Fred Dallmayr, *Twilight of Subjectivity: Contributions to a Post-Individualist Theory of Politics* (Amherst: University of Massachusetts Press, 1981), 56–71.

4. Martin Heidegger, *Being and Time*, 1.
5. Ibid., 2.
6. Ibid.
7. Heidegger, 3.
8. Ibid., 1.

9. Ibid.

10. Heidegger begins this critique of the history of Western metaphysics in the initial pages of *Being and Time*, starting with Aristotle's discovery of the problem that the universality of being creates or the fact that this universality must at once transcend even the most generic concepts and at the same time unify particular beings in *Metaphysics* III.4. Heidegger argues that rather than tarrying on this perplexity, the tradition has been led astray either by asserting the primacy of being's universality or by insisting on the primacy of its imminence. See *Being and Time*, Int. I.1–4.

11. Heidegger, *Being and Time*, 3.

12. Richard Polt, *Heidegger: An Introduction* (New York: Routledge, 1999), 2.

13. Heidegger, *Being and Time*, 11.

14. Ibid., 42.

15. Ibid., 17.

16. Ibid., 16.

17. Ibid., 43.

18. Polt, 42.

19. Heidegger, *Being and Time*, 32. See also Friedrich-Wilhelm von Hermann, *Hermeneutics and Reflection: Heidegger and Husserl on the Concept of Phenomenology*, trans. Kenneth Maly (Toronto: University of Toronto Press, 2013), 3.

20. Hermann, 3.

21. Heidegger, *Being and Time*, 91.

22. Soren Overgaard, "Heidegger's Early Critique of Husserl," *International Journal of Philosophical Studies*, 11.2 (2003): 157–175, 160.

23. Much has been said about the limits of Heidegger's critique of Husserl given Husserl's own efforts to develop his phenomenological method within the context of the lifeworld, but it is beyond the scope of this work to consider these debates. For more on the limits of Heidegger's critical appropriation of Husserl, see Overgaard, 157–175.

24. See Overgaard, 160.

25. Heidegger, *Being and Time*, 62.

26. Overgaard, 161.

27. Heidegger, *Being and Time*, 33.

28. Ibid., 31.

29. Martin Heidegger, *Plato's Sophist*, trans. Richard Rojcewicz and Andre Schuwer (Bloomington: Indiana University Press, 1997), 23.

30. Ibid., 11.

31. Heidegger, 117.

32. Heidegger, "Transcendence," 75.

33. Ibid., 55.

34. Ibid., 88–89.

35. Ibid., 54.

36. Ibid., 62.

37. Ibid., 54–55.

38. Ibid., 60.

39. Ibid., 62.

40. Ibid.

41. Ibid.
42. Ibid., 57.
43. Polt, 79.
44. Heidegger, *Being and Time*, 191.
45. Charles Scott, "Care and Authenticity," in *Martin Heidegger: Key Concepts*, ed. Bret Davis (Durham: Acumen Publishing, 2010): 57–68, 59.
46. Ibid., 58.
47. See Jennifer Gaffney, "At Home with the Foreign: Arendt on Heidegger and the Politics of Care," *Epoché, A Journal for the History of Philosophy*, 23.1 (2018): 146–163.
48. Heidegger, *Being and Time*, 67.
49. Ibid., 69.
50. Ibid.
51. Ibid., 70.
52. Ibid., 102.
53. See Peter Sloterdijk, "Nearness and Dasein: The Spatiality of Being and Time," *Theory, Culture, and Society*," 29.4/5 (2012): 36–42. There has been much debate about whether Heidegger succeeds in thinking the exteriority of space ontologically in *Being and Time*. An increasingly important debate in contemporary discourse, it is nevertheless tangential to the argument here. For more on this, see Gunter Figal, *Objectivity: The Hermeneutical and Philosophy*, trans. Theodore George (Albany: SUNY Press, 2011); and John Sallis, *The Logic of Imagination: The Expanse of the Elemental* (Bloomington: Indiana University Press, 2012).
54. Heidegger, *Being and Time*, 102.
55. Ibid., 102.
56. Ibid., 104–105.
57. Ibid., 103.
58. Ibid., 68.
59. Ibid., 54–55.
60. Ibid., 56.
61. Ibid.
62. Ibid., 119.
63. Ibid., 117.
64. Ibid., 115.
65. Ibid.
66. Ibid., 175.
67. Ibid., 118.
68. Ibid., 120.
69. Ibid., 122–123.
70. Ibid., 123.
71. Ibid.
72. Ibid.
73. Ibid.
74. Ibid.
75. Ibid.

76. Ibid., 124.
77. Ibid.
78. Ibid.
79. Richard Wolin, *The Politics of Being*, 50.
80. Heidegger, *Being and Time*, 118.
81. Ibid., 119.
82. Ibid.
83. Ibid.
84. Hans Blumenberg, *Care Crosses the River*, trans. Paul Fleming (Stanford: Stanford University Press, 2010), 139–157.
85. Polt, 86.
86. Ibid., 124.
87. Heidegger, *Being and Time*, 252.
88. Ibid., 254.
89. Ibid., 264–269.
90. The consequences of this come into view in Heidegger's call for a hermeneutics of facticity in his 1923 lecture course, *Ontology—The Hermeneutics of Facticity*, as well as in *Being and Time*. Indeed, this question of the hermeneutical displacement that arises in our encounter with the foreign and unfamiliar has become a central concern of contemporary discourse in philosophical hermeneutics. See, for instance, Dennis Schmidt, "Black Milk and Blue: Celan and Heidegger on the Pain of Language," in *Readings of Paul Celan*, ed. Aris Fioretos (Baltimore: Johns Hopkins University Press, 1994): 110–129; Günter Figal, *Objectivity: The Hermeneutical and Philosophy*, trans. Theodore D. George (Albany: SUNY Press, 2010); James Risser, *The Life of Understanding: A Contemporary Hermeneutics* (Bloomington: Indiana University Press, 2012); Donatella Di Cesare, *Utopia of Understanding: Between Babel and Auschwitz*, trans. Niall Keane (Albany: SUNY Press, 2012); and Theodore D. George, "The Responsibility to Understand," in *Phenomenological Perspectives on Plurality*, ed. Gert-Jan van der Heiden (Leiden: Brill Publishing, 2014): 103–120.
91. Heidegger, *Being and Time*, 365.
92. Ibid.
93. Ibid.
94. Ibid., 366.
95. Wolin, *The Politics of Being*, 61.

2
Reclaiming Community: Alterity, Exteriority, and Plurality

The purpose of this chapter is to develop the legacy of the problem of Dasein's peculiar loneliness in the main currents of continental thought. As we have seen, Heidegger makes visible this loneliness as a philosophical problematic through his analysis of the inauthenticity of the they-self. That Dasein is at once constituted in and through its relations to others and at the same time always already vulnerable to indwelling these relations in ways that are reductive of the excessive possibilities of existence is a decisive if underappreciated insight of *Being and Time*. It indicates that the possibility for a peculiar form of loneliness lies at the ground of Dasein's being, creating the conditions under which Dasein can find itself desperately lonely even as it is crowded in by others. As peculiar as this loneliness is, however, it is a form of alienation that is by no means marginal; on the contrary, it has only become increasingly pervasive with the advance of the techno-scientific ordering of modern life, an ordering that at once promises to conquer all distances while at the same time yielding no genuine sense of belonging.

The question of how we might recover authentic forms of communal life from out of this peculiar loneliness is central to figures from Karl Jaspers to Judith Butler. These thinkers, to be sure, recognize the urgency of the problem of the peculiar loneliness of the current age—or the fact that even as we find ourselves increasingly interconnected, we nevertheless remain no nearer to ourselves, others, or the world. They also remain guided by Heidegger's radical intervention in modern notions of subjectivity, following him in advancing ontologies of relation that displace the modern subject. Yet, these figures recognize, too, that while Heidegger himself endeavors to answer the question of authentic communal life from out of this problem, he is unable to think these possibilities in ways that are neither alienating of Dasein's relationality nor reductive of the radical singularity that emerges from its excess of possibility.

Turning especially to the work of Jean-Luc Nancy, I consider in this chapter these perceived limitations in Heidegger's early formulation of the project of fundamental ontology. For Nancy, these limitations take shape, on the one hand, in Heidegger's discourse on the "mineness" of Dasein's singular existence as this is disclosed in its being-toward-death, and on the other, in Heidegger's emphasis on the collective destiny of a people in his discourse on Dasein's historicity. Nancy, for his part, argues that as groundbreaking as Heidegger's insights into the with-structure of existence might be, Heidegger himself does not adequately think the ontological significance of being-with. Nancy recognizes not only in Heidegger's project, but in the Western philosophical tradition more generally, an inability to conceive of being-with in a way that neither sets singular Dasein apart from its relationality nor absorbs this singularity into a totalizing collective.[1] The question of authentic communal life thus turns on finding a way between these alternatives. In view of this, figures like Nancy, and more recently, Andrew Benjamin, endeavor to develop relational ontologies that emphasize how the singularity of one's own existence cannot be thought apart from an original exposure to alterity and difference—which is to say, an original relationality.[2] This relationality, however, is irreducible to any unity. Rather, both emphasize that thinking the "we" depends on thinking the plural, such that neither the singular nor the communal are lost.

Chapter 2 will therefore consider the importance of the problematic that Heidegger introduces and the difficulty that the perceived limitation of his own resolution to this problem poses for the thinkers who build on his project. These discourses suggest that addressing the problem of our peculiar loneliness depends on recovering authentic forms of communal life that neither obscure our relationality nor absorb our irreducible difference and singularity. Whereas the former only intensifies the peculiar loneliness of modern life, the latter yields totalitarian political possibilities that undermine the potential for authentic communal life. In consequence of this, each turns to a notion of communal life that emphasizes an original exposure to the alterity and exteriority of the other, an exposure in virtue of which Dasein's singularity becomes possible. By asserting that being-with can only be thought ontologically if it is keyed to this exteriority, these discourses take important steps in advancing the original problem that Heidegger discovers in his own efforts to upend modern notions of subjectivity. Yet, as important as these discourses are, more may nevertheless be said about the political significance of the peculiar loneliness of the current age and the importance of the political sphere for conceiving of the singularity of existence in and through our relations with others. Hence, upon considering the legacy of Heidegger's insights into Dasein's peculiar loneliness in the main currents of continental thought, I will turn in subsequent chapters to the work of Hannah Arendt whose concern for the political significance of the problem of loneliness opens new paths to thinking the possibilities for authentic communal life.

THE LEGACY OF OUR PECULIAR LONELINESS

The problem that I have described as the peculiar loneliness of the current age is by no means Heidegger's alone, nor is he the only thinker to identify a promise and risk in this loneliness. This loneliness constitutes a promise insofar as it is the condition under which Dasein might be displaced from the inauthenticity of the they-self and freed for its own most possibilities to be. It constitutes a risk insofar as it is intolerable, creating the conditions under which Dasein, in the desperation of this loneliness, might rush headlong into any hope of fellowship, no matter how delusional, totalizing, or reductive. In addition to Heidegger, we see this promise and risk brought into focus by figures such as Karl Jaspers, who offers a similar analysis of the ways in which the techno-scientific ordering of modern life has generated this peculiar loneliness.[3]

In *Man in the Modern Age*, a work written in 1930 just after the publication of *Being and Time* and just before the ascendance of National Socialism in Germany, Jaspers explains that the advance of Western civilization has been guided by three principles: first, by an unflinching rationalism, or the weighing and measuring of the data of experience and the achievement of technical mastery; second, by the subjectivity of selfhood, an idea that has come to be understood in terms of individuality and that was correlated from the outset with rationalism; and third, by the idea that the world is a tangible reality in time whose assurance is guaranteed through the principles of rationalism and subjective selfhood, both of which cognize reality and seek to master it.[4] Jaspers explains that these principles, though distinctive of the advance of Western civilization since antiquity, have only been fully developed over the last two centuries. As a result, he says:

> The surface of the world became universally accessible; space capitulated. For the first time, man was able to dwell wherever he would on our planet. All things are interrelated. The technical mastery of space, time, and matter advances irresistibly . . . in the course of which discovery itself has been systematized and subjected to purposive endeavor.[5]

Guided by these three principles, modern advances in science and technology have led to unprecedented population growth, the lengthening of life expectancies, and far greater access to basic necessities. These advances have brought about improvements in the speed of transportation and communication and have enabled extraordinary innovation in enterprise and production.

Yet, Jaspers is clear that these advances have not promised a genuine sense of homecoming or belonging, but have instead produced mass societies of atomized individuals. The processes that drive this technical ordering have become so highly systematized and refined, he argues, that individuals appear as nothing more than a part of their machinery. "Today," Jaspers explains, "it is taken as a matter of course that human life is the supply of mass needs by rationalized production with the aid of technical advances."[6] In the quest to simplify everything, this technical and systematic ordering seeks a universal language, not just for production and commerce, but for all modes of social and political life, establishing rules and norms that promote uniformity, order, and ease in all relationships.

While such rules might promise great accessibility, they also level any hope of having what Jaspers describes as a remarkable experience. He says, "Thanks to the technical conquest of time and space by the daily press, modern travel, the cinema, wireless, etc. a universalization of contact has become possible. No longer is anything remote, mysterious, wonderful. All can participate as witness of events accounted great or important."[7] While this technical and systematic world-order might have at first ensured the self-preservation of the masses, Jaspers argues that by the beginning of the twentieth century, "Man was bereft of his world. Cast adrift in this way, lacking all sense of historical continuity with past or future, man cannot remain man. The universalizing of the life-order threatens to reduce the real man in a real world to mere function."[8] He thus describes the modern masses as feeling "adrift and forsaken," not just because they find themselves alienated from their work, but because the character of life in general has lost its specifically human quality.[9] He says, "When the average functional capacity has become the standard of achievement, the individual is regarded with indifference. No one is indispensable. . . . It is as if man thus deracinated and reduced to the level of a thing, had lost the essence of humanity."[10] No longer connected with oneself or one's fellow human beings, Jaspers suggests that modern individuals find themselves swallowed up by the apparatus that drives modern life, an apparatus that renders human beings invisible, anonymous, and expendable.

This apparatus is itself guided and sustained by what Jaspers describes as the "bureaucracy" of the state. Bureaucracy, he explains, reduces those who work within it to a functional apparatus, preferring blind obedience to any real leadership. "In mass-organization," he says, "dominion or leadership assumes wraith-like invisibility."[11] What has authority and what bears responsibility is no longer the individual leader, but the apparatus itself, giving rise to a kind of anonymous responsibility in which "each individual is a tiny wheel with a fractional share in the decision, but no one effectively decides."[12]

In view of this, we find that Jaspers, much like Heidegger, identifies a danger in the techno-bureaucratic apparatuses of modern life, apparatuses that render human beings anonymous, hidden, and devoid of any shared sense of belonging or responsibility. Though Heidegger develops this in *Being and Time* in the context of his project of fundamental ontology, their respective concerns for the vulnerability of human existence to leveled down and inauthentic forms of communal life are resonant. Jaspers, like Heidegger, recognizes that as pervasive as this apparatus has become, and as accessible and familiar as we might be to each other, the peculiar loneliness that this produces is intolerable. Jaspers, for his part, argues that the collapse of such a world-order is imminent, though the consequences of this collapse are unknown.[13] In the desperate search for meaning and fellowship, the possibility for a world in which life once again becomes meaningful is no doubt in the offing. So, too, however, is the possibility for unprecedented rebellion, bloodshed, and idolatry of an individual who might rescue the masses from their loneliness. The question thus arises as to how we might envision authentic forms of communal life from out of this loneliness—or the fact that while science and technology might grant us greater proximity and familiarity than ever before, there is nevertheless a widespread sense that we belong nowhere and are neither supported by nor responsible for the communities in which we find ourselves.

We thus see in Jaspers a similar concern for the predicament of this peculiar loneliness, the echoes of which resonate in the work of major figures in twentieth- and twenty-first-century continental thought no less than in their contemporary commentators. At stake in these discourses is the question of how we might recover authentic forms of being-with without thinking our communal relations and responsibilities in ways that are reductive and totalizing of the excessive possibilities of existence. In the field of philosophical hermeneutics, for instance, we see this in the work of Hans-Georg Gadamer. Gadamer, following both Heidegger and Jaspers, suggests that in this "thoroughly rationalized society," we find ourselves at once crowded in by others while at the same time plagued by isolation or loneliness (*Vereinsamung*).[14] The price of this experience, Gadamer explains, "is our nearness to others . . . to stand in a communal sphere and to be supported by something communal—this is what we decry when something is lost or disappears in the sadness of loneliness."[15] In response to this peculiar loneliness, Gadamer suggests that it is necessary to think more fully than Heidegger the possibilities for being-with. For Heidegger, Gadamer argues, being-with "was a concession that he had to make, but one that he never got behind."[16] Gadamer maintains that while Heidegger's insights into the with-structure of existence mark a radical intervention in notions of modern subjectivity, Heidegger nevertheless fails to realize fully the other as conditioning of Dasein's existence, focusing instead on the historicality of Dasein's thrownness and treating being-with as "more a 'letting the other be' than an authentic 'being-interested-in-him.'"[17] As James Risser has argued, Gadamer thus emphasizes in his writings after *Truth and Method* that being-with-one-another is essential to a hermeneutics of facticity.[18] He develops this concern in his efforts to rehabilitate notions of friendship and solidarity in response to Jaspers's diagnosis of the problem of the "anonymous responsibility" of modern life, keying these ways of being together to an originary experience of hermeneutical displacement in one's encounter with another.[19]

We find this concern not only in the work of major figures in hermeneutics, but also in deconstruction, especially in Jacques Derrida's discourse on justice, law, and politics. As Nicholas Dungey has argued, Derrida repeatedly remarks on his indebtedness to Heidegger, while also insisting that deconstruction is political. While these threads of Derrida's thought are often treated separately, Dungey argues that they must be thought together in terms of Derrida's effort to engage critically Heidegger's notion of being-with in *Being and Time*.[20] Derrida, like Heidegger, rejects the notion of a worldless subject whose substance is defined apart from the lived world and the relations that constitute it.[21] It is neither the case for Heidegger nor for Derrida that Dasein understands itself apart from its relations with others. An understanding of others always lies within Dasein's mode of being, along with an understanding of its excessive possibility and singularity of existence. In view of this, we see Derrida attempting to deepen this claim in Heidegger's discourse in such works as *Politics and Friendship*, where he locates our understanding of our relations in the economy of call and response. Dungey says:

> Like Heidegger, Derrida suggests that subjectivity is opened in and through a disclosive webbing of relationships. Unlike Heidegger, though, Derrida conceives of our being-with-others as more transitive; it comes from the other, upon us, demanding a response. For Derrida, responding to the call of the other is evidence of our situated, worldly being.[22]

Significantly, Derrida, like Heidegger, recognizes that in positing a notion of the self that is constituted in and through these relations, the possibility for a distorted form of being-together-with-others arises. For Heidegger, Dasein's fall into publicness is as distorting of Dasein's authentic relationality as it is an inevitable feature of Dasein's existence. Derrida, for his part, takes up this vulnerability of Dasein's native relationality in his analysis of logocentrism—the phenomenon that binds thought and speech to self-presencing. He argues that this is a similarly "natural" way of interpreting experience. As Dungey says, "Just as Dasein does not 'choose' to fall into the anonymity of the 'public,' the self that interprets its being logocentrically does not 'choose' self-presence and autonomy; it simply finds itself *there*, 'objectively' present amongst others."[23] Derrida, perhaps more so than Heidegger, is therefore clear that it is precisely this native impulse toward logocentrism that makes possible the impulse toward nationalism, racism, and other totalizing forms of being together with others. It is in view of this, Dungey argues, that Derrida is led to develop a notion of justice that is separate from the reductive universality of the law, thinking it in terms of "disassociation, heterogeneity, and a recognition of otherness in ourselves."[24] In this, we see that Derrida, like Gadamer, recognizes the importance of Heidegger's insights into the vulnerability of being-with to inauthentic and totalizing forms of relationality. We see, too, that Derrida's political writings might be interpreted as an effort to conceive of being-with in ways that are neither alienating of Dasein's relationality nor reductive of its irreducible singularity.

There are myriad figures within the tradition of continental thought who are concerned to think the possibilities for authentic communal life from out of the problematic that Heidegger makes visible. A dimension of this seems to be at stake in the work of Maurice Merleau-Ponty in his phenomenology of the body, and in particular in his notion of touch. As Beata Stawarska has argued, it is precisely this notion of touch that allows Merleau-Ponty to develop the inexhaustibility of the subject in a way that is also intersubjective.[25] Equally important is Emmanuel Levinas's critique of Heidegger's ontology of being and his concern for emphasizing an ethics of the face of the other. Chantal Bax has argued that if we consider carefully Levinas's critique of Heidegger, we discover that what is most significant about his concern for the nationalistic impulse he sees in Heidegger's fundamental ontology is that it demonstrates that a "radical break with situatedness does not automatically fare better than a firmly enrooted account of (co-)existence. . . . This in fact offers a valuable lesson, not just for present day reception of Heidegger, but also for thinking about community and communities today."[26]

As much as these themes are apparent in the work of classical figures in the continental tradition, so too are they present in more recent discourses in continental thought that are oriented by questions in social and political philosophy. We see this, for instance, in Judith Butler's recent work on the ethics of cohabitation, which raises the question of how we might come to understand ourselves as responsible for others who are radically different from us, but with whom in a globalized world we find ourselves increasingly interconnected.[27] Even more recently, a similar concern comes to the fore in the work of Latina feminist phenomenologist Mariana Ortega, who puts Heidegger in dialogue with figures such as Gloria Anzaldúa in order to deepen and challenge Heidegger's discourse on being-with in light of the simultaneous and conflicting identities of those belonging to different worlds, such as immigrants, exiles, and inhabitants of borderlands.[28]

It would be a bridge too far to suggest that all of these discourses directly engage the problem of our peculiar loneliness as I have defined it. Yet, we might nevertheless trace the echoes of Heidegger's discovery of this problem through the work of these and other scholars. This concern for thinking communal life anew in terms of an original exposure to difference and otherness may be seen as a response to the question that Heidegger raises through his discovery of Dasein's peculiar loneliness. That our native relationality does not promise immediate belonging but, quite to the contrary, runs the risk of producing forms of being together in ways that are reductive, violent, and totalizing has proven to be a perennial problem, one that is only becoming increasingly pressing in our own era of hyperbolic interconnectedness. Yet, while the question itself remains urgent, Heidegger's own solutions to this problem have been perceived by many to fail to capture fully the nature of being-with and the role that an originary exposure to alterity and otherness plays in opening up a possibility for authentic communal life. I turn now to Jean-Luc Nancy who brings into focus this concern, no less than an attunement to the problem that Heidegger's discovery of our native relationality poses. In view of this, Nancy and, more recently, Andrew Benjamin are led to develop relational ontologies that conceive of the "we" not in terms of a collective historical destiny but rather in terms of an original exposure to exteriority, alterity, and difference. In this, both offer what may be interpreted as responses to the peculiar loneliness that Heidegger makes visible in his analysis of the inauthenticity of the they-self.

NANCY ON THE LIMITS OF HEIDEGGER'S *MITSEIN*

The platform for Nancy's project is squarely and undeniably rooted in Heidegger's fundamental ontology. Nancy, like Heidegger, insists that meaning is not a property of being, but is instead what being always already is. Nancy argues, too, that the site for the disclosure of this meaning is existence and, specifically, the existence of that being who is able to ask the question of the meaning of being—namely, the human being. Finally, Nancy remains close to Heidegger in his efforts to displace the epistemological Cartesian subject, affirming Heidegger's existential characterization of Dasein as being-in-the-world and our fundamental relation to the things and others with which we are involved.

Yet, while Nancy takes his point of departure from Heidegger, he also identifies a limitation of Heidegger's understanding of being-with.[29] As we have seen, Heidegger insists that Dasein, understood as being-there, is at the same time "being-with"—*mitsein*, always already together with others. Being-with is not a mere matter of things being next to each other, but is instead essential to the existential constitution of Dasein. Yet, Nancy argues that while Heidegger locates being-with at the heart of Dasein's existential constitution, the concept itself nevertheless remains obscure throughout *Being and Time*, receiving far less systematic attention than concepts like care, world, anxiety, or being-toward-death. Though Heidegger identifies inauthentic being-with in the indifference and anonymity of the they-self, Nancy maintains that he rushes from this, first to an isolated notion of authenticity in his discourse on being-toward-death and then to a notion of authentic being-with that is characterized no longer by the "they" but instead by a notion of *volk* or an authentic community bound together by a common historical destiny [*Geschick*]. In this, the essential "with" comes to be understood as a people whose singular possibilities are superseded by the communal or collective possibility of Dasein's historicity.[30]

Nancy notes that this emphasis on the destiny of a people has unsurprisingly led many to criticize Heidegger for being nationalistic and communitarian, offering further evidence of how his formulation of the project of fundamental ontology goes seamlessly together with his involvement in the Nazi party in the early 1930s. Yet, Nancy argues that it would be imprudent to dismiss Heidegger's project for these reasons alone. Heidegger makes explicit that we are essentially being-with, and it is precisely because of this that we are essentially vulnerable to totalizing forms of communal life. In this, Nancy recognizes the importance of Heidegger's insight into the with-structure of existence, both for displacing reductive notions of modern subjectivity and for putting into relief Dasein's native vulnerability to inauthentic forms of being together with others. Yet, Nancy argues that while a critique of such totalizing forms of community is in the offing in Heidegger's project, Heidegger himself fails to thematize fully the structure of the "we" in light of Dasein's existential constitution, leading him toward a notion of collective destiny that is not only politically problematic but inadequate to the structure of the "with" itself. What is especially significant about Heidegger's project, then, is that while he takes this with-structure to be constitutive of Dasein's existence, he nevertheless fails to think being-with ontologically. This, however, is not the fault of Heidegger alone. It is Nancy's view that Heidegger stands at the end of a long-standing failure of Western thought to investigate the nature of the "we" ontologically. The decline of political life in the current age and the ascendance of nationalistic sympathies across the Western world, Nancy argues, are sufficient testimony to our failure to think being-with in an adequate way.[31] Hence, in response to this long-standing failure, Nancy argues that there is today an urgent need to think the "we" ontologically, though this is something that Western thinking has not yet done.

Though Heidegger does not answer as fully as we might hope the question of what "being-there-together" looks like, Nancy suggests that in characterizing being-with as an existential condition of human existence, Heidegger nevertheless raises the question of how we are to understand ourselves as co-habitants or co-existents of the world to which we belong. As Nancy says, "From *Being and Time* onward, it becomes noticeable how co-existence constitutes an *experimentum crucis* for our thinking."[32] What, then, does "being-there-together" or being in common look like? Nancy insists that there are three possible modes by which we might envision ourselves as being in common. First, one can be together in a banal way, simply standing alongside in anonymity and indifference. This mode of being-together, of simply standing in a crowd, is a form of extreme exteriority whereby the other confronts us as someone from whom we are alienated. Second, one can be together in such a way that one is able at once to appear in one's singularity while at the same time as a being that is together with and shaped by the others with whom one shares the world. Nancy explains that this modality of being together consists in a mixing and sharing of properties, such that the individual appears in her singularity as co-constituted by the others with whom she is involved. The third mode of being-together consists in understanding the common as a collective or community in which the singular individual is absorbed. Here, the individual has no weight beyond her ability to transcend her singular possibilities for the sake of a communal destiny.

Nancy explains that only the first and third modes of being-in-common are mobilized in *Being and Time*. Whereas the first mode of the common represents extreme exteriority, the third mode represents the outer limit of interiority. The first is epitomized by Heidegger's elucidation of the inauthenticity of the they-self, while the third comes into view in his characterization of authentic being-with in terms of the historicity of Dasein as this takes shape in the destiny of a people. As such, Nancy argues that for Heidegger, we can only be together in one of two ways, neither of which are adequate for an ontological account of being-with that attends both to the singularity of Dasein and to the fact that Dasein is always already being-with. Instead, we have on the one hand the impossibility of being-with in the they-self, a self that is characterized by anonymity and isolation, and on the other, the hyper-possibility of being-with as a community within which the singular Dasein is no longer visible. In both cases, Nancy argues, neither I nor we can find ourselves in this conception of being-with.[33]

In order to develop this limit in Heidegger's thinking, Nancy considers the various moments in *Being and Time* in which Heidegger gestures toward a notion of proper being-with without clearly articulating what he means. Nancy focuses in particular on Heidegger's effort to distinguish the negative ways in which we can care for others—namely, when we are indifferent to others, against them, or when we feel isolated from them—from two positive ways in which care for another can occur. As we have already seen, Heidegger characterizes the first positive mode of caring-for-another as an inauthentic or improper way of being-with. He calls this mode "leaping in" insofar as it consists in caring for the other in her place, and relieving the other of her own care. As Nancy explains, leaping in is dis-propriative insofar as it disburdens the other of who she is. In contrast to this, Heidegger draws our attention to a second, positive mode of being-with, which he calls "leaping ahead." This mode of being-with is authentic, Heidegger argues, as it consists in getting out ahead of the other in such a way that it becomes possible to hand the other's care over to her. Whereas leaping in is keyed to a specific and exterior task, leaping ahead is a matter of being engaged in the same affair in common, which arises properly out of each existent.[34] The former may therefore be understood in terms of occupation and co-operation, whereas the latter consists in co-propriation and preoccupation in one's genuine care for the other rather than only for the task at hand.[35]

According to Nancy, the question of whether genuine care—which is to say, leaping ahead—is possible is the central question we must ask if we are to develop an ontological account of the possibilities for authentic being-with. Yet, as Nancy explains, such a notion of care for another cannot be realized for authentic Dasein as Heidegger conceives of it. Nancy maintains that Heidegger's emphasis on the *mineness* of one's own death forecloses the possibility of such a notion of genuine care. After all, Heidegger is clear that one's death is only ever one's own, since "my death is that for which no other can substitute her care for mine."[36] Thus, Nancy explains that resolving oneself for one's own most possibilities depends on encountering one's finitude in a singular and unsharable way.[37] And yet, Heidegger, in his own efforts to elucidate the with-structure of Dasein, insists that leaping ahead, or the genuine care that discloses our existential constitution as essentially being-with, is only possible when the other hands me over to my own most possibilities. Nancy thus argues that Heidegger appears to place a seemingly insurmountable limit on the possibility of authentic being-with if this possibility is thought in light of his discourse on being-toward-death. Indeed, if my own most possibilities to be are disclosed in a radically singular, inward, and unsharable confrontation with my own finitude, how could another hand over these possibilities to me?

Nancy thus contends that Heidegger is unable to account for being-with in the context of singular Dasein, leading him to turn instead to an account of being-with that is rooted in Dasein's historicity. As we have seen, Heidegger insists in §74 of *Being and Time* that Dasein, harshly isolated by its own death, has not yet risen to the height of destiny. Whereas the resoluteness of being-toward-death always occurs against the backdrop of inauthentic or improper being-with, Heidegger maintains in his analysis of Dasein's historicity that proper being-with makes possible the transformation of the inauthentic "they" into a community and the transformation of one's own possibilities into the destiny of a people. In Nancy's view, Heidegger's elucidation of the existential structure of being-with enables one's own death to be "transformed from a blow of fate into a destinal event."[38] While Heidegger does not explain how this transformation takes shape, he maintains that authentic being-with arises when a people hand down determinate possibilities, which are not the possibilities of any individual but of a larger community. In this, leaping ahead becomes possible only insofar as the possibilities of the singular Dasein are given over to the possibilities of history. While Heidegger, Nancy explains, does not specify these possibilities, he does characterize them in terms of "the message and the struggle," emphasizing a common cause for which a people must fight.[39] According to Nancy, we thus find that Heidegger does not clarify how one might genuinely care for another by handing over one's own most possibilities to be except in terms of this notion of destiny. What is thus lost, Nancy thinks, is a multiple and plural understanding of being-with, one that is characterized neither by isolation and mere contiguity nor by the collapse of the singular individual into a common, unified destiny.[40]

It is on these grounds that Nancy believes the structure of being-there-with, though essential to the existential constitution of Dasein, is passed over in *Being and Time*. He says:

> As much as Heidegger felt with peculiar acuity the necessity of the with . . . he himself erased the possibility he opened, namely, the possibility of thinking the with exactly as he had indicated, as neither exteriority nor interiority. Neither a herd nor a subject. Neither an anonymous nor a mine. Neither improper nor proper.[41]

And yet, Nancy explains that the with must determine the proximity and distinction of multiple Daseins. By Heidegger's own assertion, there must be an interweaving of the limit and continuity between Daseins, not just in juxtaposition but also in composition. "For being-with-the-there to happen," Nancy says, "there must be a contact, therefore a contagion and encroachment. . . . I can only open myself up to the there by opening at the same time onto other theres."[42] As such, Nancy argues that for being-with to be possible as a constitutive factor Dasein's existence, there can be neither a simple they-self nor a simple people, though a third possibility remains unthought in Heidegger's project.

Nancy argues that while the Western tradition has tended to make this leap from the singular individual to the destinality of community, what is called for now is an account of the middle ground between these two, or a genuine thematizing of being-together-with, where both a singular Dasein and its constitutive "with" are able to appear. Nancy believes that this is the decisive question of the modern age, one which must be addressed given the loneliness of the current times and the persistent compulsion this creates toward fascistic and totalizing forms of communal life. While Heidegger is an exemplar of this compulsion, Nancy insists that we cannot address the problem he identifies by simply condemning Heidegger for his involvement in National Socialism. In Nancy's view, there is, to be sure, a fascist element in Heidegger's treatment of what he deems to be proper being-with. This, however, must be understood as a symptom of the deeply entrenched habit of Western thinking, which has tended to leap from the fate of the individual to the communal destiny of a people. Perhaps what is most important about Heidegger, Nancy argues, is that he brings to the forefront the close connection between "the indispensable essentiality of the *with* and the dreadful destinality of community."[43] Hence, Nancy maintains that it remains for us to think the possibility of leaping ahead without doing so in terms of destiny, a task that requires us to think being-with in terms of co-constitution.[44]

NANCY'S ONTOLOGY OF THE "WE"

Nancy's own efforts to thematize the "we" are exemplified in his work *Being Singular Plural*, where he endeavors to envision authentic being-with without leaping into what he describes as "the dreadful destinality of community."[45] For Nancy, thinking this "we" depends on considering how an original exposure to alterity and difference opens up the possibility for the authentic disclosure of one's self. As we shall see, it is precisely this concern that captures a crucial problem not just in current continental thought but in modern life more generally, namely, of how to think being-with in a way that neither affirms the isolated modern subject nor succumbs to the fascistic and totalitarian possibilities of community. While Heidegger himself might have fallen short in his efforts to think these possibilities, the concern itself cannot be thought apart from his own discovery of this problem as it takes shape in his decisive insight that Dasein's native relationality does not promise immediate belonging but is instead always already vulnerable to inauthentic forms of being-with-others.

In *Being Singular Plural*, Nancy sets out to rethink the ground of social and communal life without reference to an individual subject or subjectivity. Discovering such a ground, he argues, depends on developing an ontological conception of the "with" that does not absorb difference into a totalizing collective. At stake in this project is an effort to deepen and radicalize Heidegger's notion of being-with by insisting that existence is not disclosed when we are alone in the mood of anxiety, but is instead always already made visible in the "with" that is initially present in our everyday experience of the they. This "with," he argues, is characterized by multiplicity, alterity, and inappropriability, rather than sameness, familiarity, and the purity of origin. As such, the meaning that is disclosed in and through this with is not oriented by leaping forward into a people's destiny. On the contrary, Nancy argues, the with-structure of existence makes it the case that every origin is a co-origin, every existence plural, and every appropriation a simultaneous dis-appropriation.

Nancy thus takes his task in *Being Singular Plural* to consist in developing an existential analytic that starts from the assumption that the essence of being is always co-essence, and likewise, that the essence of existence is always co-existence. In other words, Nancy wishes to make the with-structure of existence ontological in ways that he believes Heidegger never does.

As Walter Brogan has argued, Nancy can only accomplish this through a fundamental re-orientation of Western metaphysics and its emphasis on essence and unity. Nancy must develop, in contrast to this, an ontological account of being-in-common that does not destroy singularity, but rather affirms it as an ontological structure of existence. This, in turn, Brogan argues, leads Nancy to insist on the urgency of bringing the multiplicity of *praxis* and political life to bear on metaphysical inquiry. Whereas the traditional metaphysical concern for essence and unity has led to accounts of community that are oriented by nationalism and the destiny of a people, Nancy maintains that we must consider how community is possible without the notion of essence.[46] Though Heidegger ultimately falls prey to this tradition, he nevertheless sets forth a path for thinking the possibility of the with in a fundamental way. If, as Heidegger suggests, the with-structure of existence is in fact foundational, then, Nancy insists, we must think being-with without essence and unity.

This means coming to understand being-in-common not as something that stands above what it holds in common, but rather as a being-in-common that requires the singularity of each being.[47]

Nancy maintains that plurality, difference, alterity, and exposure are conditions for the possibility of asking the question of the meaning of being. Whereas Nancy takes Heidegger to insist on a notion of philosophical address that is based on a neuter, subject-less style of discourse that speaks for everyone and no one, Nancy believes that it is characteristic of human *logos* that it involves a primordial exposure that is rooted in the experience of being addressed. As Brogan says, "The task of philosophical thinking, the task of ontology, begins with a thinking by which we are in touch with ourselves and thereby know ourselves as being-addressed, as outside ourselves in relation."[48] Indeed, for Nancy we cannot think the question of the meaning of being without this ontological relationality, and, thus, fundamental ontology requires an account of the logic of the with.

In Nancy's view, the with is not an attribute of being. Rather, he says, "The *with* is the most basic feature of Being, the mark [*trait*] of the singular plurality of the origin or origins in it. . . . 'With' does not add itself to Being, but rather creates the immanent and intrinsic condition of presentation in general."[49] As we have already noted, Nancy follows Heidegger in his claim that meaning is being. Moreover, Nancy appreciates the significance of Heidegger's insight even in his early formulation of the project of fundamental ontology that there is an ontological relationship between being and the way meaning circulates through discourse (*rede*), communication (*mitteilen*), and the apophantic character of the *logos*.[50] As Heidegger argues in his elucidation of the self-showing of phenomena through our talking about them,

> Because λόγος as λεγόμενον can also mean what is addressed, as something that has become visible in its relation to something else in its "relatedness," λόγος acquires the meaning of *relation* and *relationship*. This interpretation of "apophantic speech" may suffice to clarify the primary function of λόγος.[51]

Nancy recognizes the significance of these claims as initial steps away from the prioritization of the notion of unity and essence in the history of Western metaphysics. Yet, Nancy suggests, too, that Heidegger ultimately grasps the circulation of the meaning of being in terms of historicity and destiny, overlooking the implications of his claims in his early writings for understanding the ontological status of the with. Rather than conceiving of being as an ultimate reference to which everything else variously points, Nancy maintains that coming to understand the logic of the with depends on seeing the circulation itself is primary.[52] In other words, Nancy says, "Meaning itself is the sharing of being."[53]

In Nancy's view, the presencing of being always requires a gathering of understanding, a reception that is attentive to being-in-common. As such, being-with is disclosed not after the disclosure of being, but instead in every meaning. Whereas Heidegger is led from this assertion to a notion of being-in-common that collapses singularity into unity, Nancy argues that by insisting on the relationality at stake in the philosophical address, we find that this circulation of meaning, this sharing of being, always entails an exposure to difference and alterity. We need only consider the French word *partager* to understand this. *Partager* means at once to share and to part, to participate, and to divide.[54] The same is true of the German word *mitteilen*, which means to communicate or tell, as well as to impart, to part, to participate, to break.[55] Hence, in an effort to deepen Heidegger's notion of being-with and challenge the turn he makes toward the destiny of a people, Nancy clarifies the need to examine more carefully what is entailed in the relationality that Heidegger identifies in the disclosure of being. In being shared, Nancy argues, the meaning of being is always already imparted, ruptured, and plural. It is therefore disclosed, never in terms of unity or essence, but instead as a spacing or dividing, coming to appear as what it is in this in-between. In other words, the presencing of being is always a presencing of being-with in a more genuine sense than Heidegger recognized; what therefore appears is always a co-appearance and a co-existence, always differentiated, while at the same time, together-in-common.[56]

Nancy thus wishes to show that if we take seriously the claim that the circulation of meaning is primary, then we must also concede the ontological status of being-with as always already singular-plural. In conceiving of being as co-appearance, co-essence, and co-existence, Nancy clarifies that Heidegger's effort to think meaning in terms of a pure and pre-given origin effaces the very ontological project that he sets in motion. By insisting on the relationality of the meaning of being, Nancy maintains that we must also come to terms with several further implications of the essentiality of being-with.

First, insofar as the philosophical address always entails difference, rupture, and division, there can be no single, appropriable origin. On the contrary, this origin is always being-other. In making this claim, Nancy does not wish to suggest that this other stands in opposition to meaning as something improper to the world in which we find ourselves. Rather, he says that the notion of origin is, "*alter*, that is 'one of the two.' This 'other,' this 'lowercase other,' is 'one' among many insofar as they are many . . . 'we' is always inevitably 'us all,' where no one of us can be 'all' and each one of us is, in turn . . . the other origin of the same world."[57] Indeed, the world comes to appear in its meaningfulness only from out of this co-origin. In consequence of this, Nancy argues, there is always plurality at the foundation; the origin is always irreducibly plural. This does not mean that we do not have access to the origin, but rather that we discover its truth "as many times as we are in another's presence."[58] That is to say, what is disclosed as origin is not the purity of a principle, but an exposure to "the plural singularity of the Being of being."[59] There is nothing behind this essential plurality, and, hence, it's disclosure must unfold differently than Heidegger suggests. Instead of "reaching the origin" through the appropriation or absorption of it, Nancy maintains that the disclosure of being is a matter of not missing it, of being "properly exposed to it."[60] Hence, if we take seriously the essentiality of being-with, Nancy argues that we must also concede that origin always means co-origin. This co-origin is discovered not through an appropriation of it but through an exposure to the alterity that is at stake in every meaning. This meaning itself is possible only insofar as these origins are incommensurable and irreducibly singular, while, at the same time, together.

A second implication of the claim that being-with is essential consists in the way in which we might understand the meaningfulness of the world. Whereas Heidegger begins his discussion of our relation to the world by considering what is improper to our being in it, Nancy argues that more may be done to consider how the essential with comes to appear in our everyday, average experience of the world. In Nancy's view, the genuine alterity that is at stake in the origin makes possible the appearance of a world. This world, however, is not something that I, in contrast to other beings, happen to be in. Rather, Nancy argues, the world presents itself as alterity, or, he says, as a "discrete spacing *between us*, as *between us and the rest of the world,* as *between all beings.*"[61] If existence is exposed as such by humans, then, Nancy argues, all other beings are also disclosed there. That is to say, it is not the space of the human being alone, but is instead disclosed in its worldliness by our exposure to the alterity of stones, animals, and plants, by our exposure to all that is not our own. Dasein is thus in the world insofar as the world is its own exteriority, "the proper space of its being-out-in-the-world."[62] The world is always already there in this way, as an original alterity. While Dasein may expose the world, the world itself is not disclosed as one's own as if it were appropriable and inheritable, but rather only comes to appear in its plurality and inappropriability. Yet, in just the same way as his discussion of origin, Nancy argues that this does not mean that we do not belong to the world. Quite to the contrary, for Nancy, it is only in virtue of this alterity that belonging becomes possible.

A third consequence of the assertion of the essentiality of the with comes into view in the experience of communal life. Whereas Nancy believes that for Heidegger there is either a singular existent or a they, each of which are delineated according to authenticity and inauthenticity respectively, Nancy wishes to show that the possibility for being-with depends on thinking the singular and the they together. For Nancy, any reference to a "they" is already a reference to singularity insofar as the announcement of a "they" entails the singling out of oneself in relation to others. As such, singularity constitutes a plurality, such that the one is never set apart from the multiplicity of the world in which it occurs.[63] In order to better understand this, Nancy argues that we must consider the experience of being together in terms of touch. For Heidegger, the central category for understanding ourselves and our relation is time. Though Nancy by no means wishes to undermine this decisive insight, he does believe that we must return to the notion of space in order to better understand the with-structure of existence. Nancy argues that genuine being together is always a distance, a physical in-between rather than a fusion. A symptom of the assumptions of the tradition of Western metaphysics, Nancy argues that the modern political tradition has tended to treat proximity in terms of the fusion of a collective identity or class consciousness. Yet, while we may find ourselves bound together primordially, Nancy argues that this closeness goes awry when we assume that it must take shape in terms of an absolute, whereby the other is appropriated or fused into one's self as property.[64] In contrast to this, Nancy wishes to show that genuine togetherness accomplishes proximity *through* distance. Taking the experience of touch as his point of departure, Nancy argues that this kind of proximity is possible only insofar as one is exposed to another without, at the same time, destroying her. Touch, he argues, is unmediated and, yet, the other is able to remain singular and with. In this, touch captures what Nancy means by genuine being-alongside, in which one is both exposed and together with another, both of which are fundamental to the disclosure of being.

Nancy thus wishes to upend Heidegger's notion of the average everydayness of the they in order to think being-human as being-with. Being-with must not be thought of as an attribute or property that a subject may or may not have, but instead as a fundamental attunement, responsiveness, and affective being-together-with-one-another. Whereas for Heidegger, our everyday experience is leveled down and average, Nancy argues that the ordinary is always exceptional. In Nancy's view, the world in its everydayness is not a place where we lose sight of a self that must be reclaimed through a retreat from the world. Rather, "the everyday is plural, and it is being-plural that is most proper to us all."[65] That is to say, Nancy argues "people are strange," and it is only insofar as we are originally exposed to this strangeness that meaning is disclosed. This exposure is a confrontation with alterity and, thus, those with whom we share the world are characterized by an irreducible strangeness. Beyond this, however, it is precisely these strangers on whom we depend from the outset for our own singularity. Whereas Heidegger sets the they-self apart from the singular individual, Nancy insists that being one's own self is only possible insofar as we are always already facing another, touching and being touched, acting and being acted upon, always already together as strangers. Whereas Heidegger conceives of being-together either in terms of the they-self or in terms of the destiny of a people, Nancy insists that as a people, every person is already unique, constituted by a plurality of inappropriable origins.

For Nancy, then, both the notion of the world and the notion of a people echo an irreducible multiplicity. Whereas traditional political philosophy either posits a society of atomized individuals or represses the singular in the name of the common, Nancy wishes to illustrate that neither of these options are ontologically salient. Instead, it is only when community is conceived of as singular plural that the ontological force of the with comes into view.

RELATIONALITY AND THE PLURAL EVENT

We thus find in Nancy an effort to conceive of the with-structure of existence in a way that is responsive to Heidegger's insights into the problem that Dasein's native relationality poses but that takes a step further in refining Heidegger's original ontology of being-with. In this, we might interpret Nancy as one among many who are concerned to address the problem of Dasein's peculiar loneliness in a way that promises an authentic possibility for communal life, one that neither falls prey to the anonymity of the they-self nor dissolves the singularity of the other into a unity. This concern for thinking the with-structure of existence more originally is also apparent in the recent work of Andrew Benjamin, who, in *Towards a Relational Ontology: Philosophy's Other Possibility*, is similarly concerned to develop a relational ontology that is predicated on what he describes as "the plural event" and "anoriginal relationality."

The central question with which Benjamin is concerned is the question of what it means to be in relation. Yet, answering this question, he says, depends first on understanding that "the truth of relationality inheres in what is always at work within relations, namely, the effective presence of a founding and irreducible plurality."[66] Benjamin insists that singular relations are always secondary, "pragmatic occurrences."[67] More originary, the very thing on which these relations always depend, is "the presence of an original form of multiplicity or plurality."[68] Understood this way, Benjamin argues that relationality is always primary even when philosophical inquiry does not recognize this primacy. Turning to Descartes, Kant, Fichte, Hegel, and Heidegger, Benjamin attempts to locate in each of these thinkers the operative presence of the plural event as well as anoriginal relation, or a notion of relationality in which the presumption of a singular origin is always already grounded. It is Benjamin's view that this relationality is at stake in every inquiry and intellectual undertaking, no less than in our everyday dealings with things and others. In this, Benjamin says, "Relationality is not a lost possibility to be viewed nostalgically. It can be recovered. . . . Not only can relationality be recovered from within the context of this overall argument, but relationality also is there as philosophy's other possibility."[69]

In his efforts to demonstrate the original presence of relationality, Benjamin, like Nancy, attempts to unsettle the tendency to efface relationality in the service of what is presumed to be a more foundational singularity. This tendency to give primacy to an original singularity, he thinks, is no less apparent in the Cartesian notion of subjectivity than it is in Heidegger's notion of authentic Dasein. Yet, Benjamin argues that such singularity is only an aftereffect of a "plural event," an event that he believes makes possible singularities. Benjamin explains that because this singularity is the aftereffect of the plural event, what has come to be recognized as most foundational is not this original relationality, but rather a singularity that is taken to be original and founding. Benjamin thus insists that what must be theorized is not only this plural event, but also something that is more original than the presumed originality of a singular presence, which he calls anoriginal relationality. By excising this anoriginal relationality, Benjamin attempts to demonstrate the plural that is always at stake in the appearance of the singular no less than the singular that is always already at stake in the generality or universal that is so often thought to absorb the singular.[70]

Though inquiry into relationality is by no means absent from the Western tradition, Benjamin suggests that it tends to open from a generality. Acknowledging that this has been the starting point for much of the Western metaphysical tradition, Benjamin argues, is therefore a crucial first step for thinking relationality in a more fundamental way. Yet, he maintains too that from the recognition of this typical point of departure, there is also a need to move from a concern for the general, which is always understood as the relationship between universal and particular, to a preliminary understanding of the meaning of anoriginal plurality and a plural event. In making this move, Benjamin wishes to interrupt the hold that the oscillation between the universal and the particular, the abstract and the empirical, has had on philosophical inquiry, an oscillation that he believes has obscured the disclosure of any ontology of relation, and, with this, any adequate account of the common or shared.[71]

What is thus called for is another beginning, another starting point, one that favors neither the universal nor the particular, but that instead counters this oscillation altogether by putting into relief the relationality that is always already present in this oscillation. It is only by means of this countermeasure, Benjamin argues, that we come to see that no instances in their radical differentiation can be affirmed through the universal or the particular alone, but rather require greater philosophical dexterity. This, he explains, is because "the recovery of relationality is the recovery of a sustained possibility, a potentiality, that, while having an exacting reality, is not addressed in any direct way."[72] As such, relationality can never lend itself to a process of universalization or have a generalized abstract presence. While it has been endemic to the history of Western philosophy to make such a move in regard to relationality, it is precisely this move that has not only proven impossible to make, but that is also premised on the elimination of relationality and plurality.[73] For Benjamin, however, this does not mean that the history of Western thought was not itself always already announcing a relation; rather, he argues that every time thought is deployed in a single statement—in other words, when the particular appears—a relation is present. In this, Benjamin argues, relationality is always an insistent presence, one that demands that we think both the relation and its originality in a fundamental way. This further requires that we always think relationality in terms of plurality, which is to say, never as a unity, but always in terms of difference.

This ontology of relation has a number of implications. For one, Benjamin argues, once relationality is understood as original, it becomes possible to begin thinking the relationality that is already present in the history of Western thought so that we might begin to undertake the task of philosophy anew. Benjamin argues, too, that this also means that ontology must be understood as prior to and grounding for ethics and politics insofar as existence is originally relational. These relations always have specific determinations—for instance, the determinations of self and other—and thus constitute networks that are always being reworked through the continuity of always coming into relation.[74] As such, anoriginal relation always furnishes the ground for any ethical or political judgment no less than any notion of agency. Finally, and perhaps most significantly for the purposes of this work, Benjamin's conception of relationality has implications for the notion of commonality. Whereas the history of Western thought has tended to conflate the common and the shared, Benjamin attempts through his notion of anoriginal plurality to complicate this identification. While these terms do point to the centrality of commonality and relationality, they do not acknowledge relationality or commonality as an original position. In his analysis of Fichte, Benjamin argues that we see the way in which philosophy has deployed the common in terms of an abstract universality, treating this commonality as something that precedes citizenship. This, in turn, produces an abstract a notion of citizenship that ultimately consists in being a member of a particular nation, thereby yielding "a philosophical basis of nationalism."[75] If, in contrast to this, commonality is understood in terms of anoriginal relation—anoriginal relation that becomes visible as a plural event—then we find that relationality creates the very conditions under which it becomes possible to reject a notion of nationhood grounded in a commonality that does violence to the singular.

Significantly, Benjamin recognizes something that is quite close to Heidegger's analysis of the they-self. He argues that while an ontology of relation conditions the refusal of such an identification, we also find in this relationality the tendency toward dangerous and reductive forms of being-in-common. He explains that anoriginal relationality is always being-in-common and being-in-place in a non-determined way. Yet, the aftereffect of this relation is origin, something that occurs after the plural event and that takes the form of a founding singularity. While the attribution of an origin is thus effacing of anoriginal plurality, it is also from out of this native relationality that a common origin can be posited, an origin, moreover, that can only ever be myth and that requires constant and desperate affirmation in order to remain meaningful. Hence, he says, "Place, in losing its quality as defined by the continuity of the yet-to-be-determined, becomes as a consequence the land of a 'people.'"[76] While this notion of a people is always predicated upon non-determined states of being-in-place, the ambivalence and undetermined nature of a founding moment quickly bring about the refusal of the non-determined and, with this, the refusal of plurality, possibility, and difference.

In view of this, Benjamin argues that we are called upon by the original plurality that is always at stake in every presumed national, ethnic, or communal origin, to reject the idea that plurality and community are antithetical to one another. Rather, he insists that "being-in-place" and "being-in-relation" must be understood as a holding open of the continuity of the yet-to-be-determined, as they are the sites in which "differing and incompatible determinations may obtain."[77] To be sure, it is precisely from out of this anoriginal relationality that racism and nationalism so easily follow. It is because these sites are yet-to-be-determined that the impulse to define the nation in terms of a mythical origin and unity is a great risk. Upon turning to Hegel's *Philosophy of Right*, Benjamin insists that it is precisely from out of the impulse toward unity, toward universalization, that we also discover the anxiety that arises among political subjects in consequence of being ascribed rights. Insofar as these rights are grounded in an abstract universality, they produce what Benjamin describes as anonymity and fear. He says, "Granting, dispensing, and conceding rights creates an economy that has a necessary externality. An externality that is, of course, formed by and thus held in place by the economy of abstraction. Fear is the consequence of the reality, be it real or imaginary, of that withdrawal. What is created is a withdrawal of anonymity."[78] This fear has a determining effect on the subject because it is an inherent part of the process of the universality of rights, one that arises from feeling the impossibility of being a part of the whole. The fear of the withdrawal of the "who" thus holds itself in place, leading to a desperate affirmation of the whole even if this affirmation requires the sacrifice of one's own singularity.

In much the same way as Heidegger, then, Benjamin recognizes the ways in which our ontological relationality does not promise immediate homecoming but rather contains within it the possibility of reductive and inauthentic forms of togetherness, ones that are either fundamentally lonely or dangerously totalizing and reductive of human plurality. It is clear from this, he argues, that what must now be thought is anoriginal relationality and the plural event, which he believes underlie these impulses but which also call on us to think our starting point for communal life anew. In this, Benjamin argues that what is called for is not a politics or ethics of actuality, but rather "a conception of the political that wants to maintain a continual opening to the intimate; an opening in which the disarming effect of the unwilled enters into relation."[79] An ontology of relation demands the opening for this kind of political or ethical project, one that does not determine in advance place, origin, relation, and the like but that makes possible "openings to the future [that] are held in place by the potentiality inherent in any network and the potentiality always already at work in the continual presence of the yet-to-be-determined."[80]

THINKING THE COMMON POLITICALLY

As we have seen, the question of Dasein's peculiar loneliness, a question that Heidegger makes visible through his discourse on being-with, has had a long legacy within continental thought. Whether this problem takes shape in terms of what Jaspers calls "anonymous responsibility" or in terms of the fear and anonymity that Benjamin believes is produced by the notion of universal human rights, we see in each case that there is a concern to think the possibilities for authentic being-with anew. These figures thus take seriously the problem of communal life that Heidegger identifies.

Beyond this, we see each attempting to envision from out of this authentic forms of communal life that are neither alienating of our native relationality nor reductive of our radical singularity. This is as apparent in Gadamer's effort to envision anew the notions of solidarity and friendship, as it is for Nancy in his effort to thematize the "we" ontologically. In what follows, my aim will be to add a new voice to these discourses by turning to the work of political philosopher Hannah Arendt, whose concern for the destruction of the political sphere in the modern age adds a further dimension to the question of problem of our peculiar loneliness. By turning to the significance she attributes to the political sphere of human existence and by considering her analysis of the loneliness that has arisen as a result of its destruction, we find that she is able to open new paths to thinking the possibilities for authentic communal life in light of the political climate of the day.

NOTES

1. Jean-Luc Nancy, "The Being-with of Being-there," *Continental Philosophy Review*, 41 (2008): 1–15, 5.

2. See Jean-Luc Nancy, *Being Singular Plural* (Stanford: Stanford University Press, 2000), 6, and Andrew Benjamin, *Towards a Relational Ontology: Philosophy's Other Possibility* (Albany: SUNY Press, 2015), 2.

3. Though the question of which of these figures influenced the other is a source of much scholarly debate, it is beyond the scope of the present inquiry to consider that here. Even so, it is worth noting the striking similarities between Jaspers and Heidegger in their respective diagnoses of the condition of modern mass society. It is perhaps worthy of attention, too, that upon diagnosing what I have been calling the peculiar loneliness of the current age, both of these figures take radically different paths in response to it. More than a mere personal quarrel stemming from Heidegger's decision to support the Nazi party in 1933, we might interpret their respective responses to this diagnosis as epitomizing both the promise and risk that I have suggested is inherent in this peculiar loneliness. For an especially relevant account of this relationship for the present inquiry, see Antonia Grunenberg and Adrian Daub, "Arendt, Jaspers, and Heidegger: Thinking through the Breach in Tradition," *Social Research: Hannah Arendt Centenary: Political and Philosophical Perspectives*, 74.4.II (Winter 2017): 1003–1028.

4. Karl Jaspers, *Man in the Modern Age*, trans. Eden and Cedar Paul (New York: Routledge, 2010), 21.

5. Ibid., 23.
6. Ibid., 37.
7. Ibid., 47.
8. Ibid., 44.

9. Ibid., 50.
10. Ibid., 52.
11. Ibid., 56.
12. Ibid., 57.
13. Ibid., 79.
14. Hans-Georg Gadamer, "Isolation as a Symptom of Self-Alienation," in *Praise of Theory: Speeches and Essays* (New Haven: Yale University Press, 1988): 101–113, 101–102. This is based on a modified translation by Adrian Costache in "On Solitude and Loneliness in Hermeneutical Philosophy," *Meta: Research in Hermeneutics, Phenomenology and Practical Philosophy*, 5.1 (2013): 130–149, 133.
15. Gadamer, "Isolation as a Symptom of Self-Alienation," 101–102.
16. Hans-Georg Gadamer, *A Century of Philosophy: A Conversation with Ricardo Dottori*, trans. Rod Coltman with Sigrid Koepke (New York: Continuum, 2003), 23.
17. Ibid., 23 and 29.
18. See James Risser, *The Life of Understanding* (Bloomington: Indiana University Press, 2012).
19. Though this is by no means the only way to interpret Gadamer's project, it has become an important thread of recent scholarship in philosophical hermeneutics. See, for instance, Risser, *The Life of Understanding*; Donatella Di Cesare, *Utopia of Understanding: Between Babel and Auschwitz* (Albany: SUNY Press, 2012); Günter Figal, *Objectivity: The Hermeneutical and Philosophy*, trans. Theodore George (Albany: SUNY Press, 2012); Theodore George, "Are We a Conversation? Hermeneutics, Exteriority, and Transmittability," *Research in Phenomenology* 47 (2017): 331–350; and Darren Walhof, "Friendship, Otherness, and Gadamer's Politics of Solidarity," *Political Theory*, 34.5 (2006): 569–593.
20. Nicholas Dungey, "(Re)turning Derrida to Heidegger: Being-with-Others as Primordial Politics," *Polity* 33.3 (Spring 2001): 455–477, 461.
21. Dungey, 461.
22. Ibid.
23. Ibid., 465.
24. Ibid., 472. See also Jacques Derrida, "Force of Law: The 'Mystical Foundations of Authority,'" in *Deconstruction and the Possibility of Justice*, ed. Drucilla Cornell, Michael Rosenfeld, and David Gray Carlson (New York: Routledge, 1992): 3–67, 14–15.
25. Beata Stawarska, "Reversability and Intersubjectivity in Merleau-Ponty's Ontology," *Journal of the British Society for Phenomenology*, 33.2 (2002): 155–166, 155.
26. See Chantal Bax, "Otherwise than Being-With: Levinas on Heidegger and Community," *Human Studies*, 3 (2017): 381–400, 384.
27. See Judith Butler, "Precarious Life, Vulnerability, and the Ethics of Cohabitation," *Journal of Speculative Philosophy*, 26.2 (2012): 134–151.
28. See Mariana Ortega, "*In-Between: Latina Feminist Phenomenology, Multiplicity, and the Self*" (Albany: SUNY Press, 2016).
29. My discussion of Nancy will be keyed primarily to *Being Singular Plural*, though I will begin with his analysis of the limits of Heidegger's notion of being-with in his 2008 essay, "The Being-with of Being-there," *Continental Philosophy*

Review, 41 (2008): 1–15. While the former pre-dates the latter, the critique he lays out in this essay sets the stage nicely for his conception of the "we."

30. Nancy, "The Being-with of Being-there," 4.
31. Ibid., 5.
32. Ibid., 4.
33. Ibid., 10.
34. Ibid., 7. See also Heidegger, *Being and Time*, 118–119.
35. Nancy, "The Being-with of Being-there," 8.
36. Ibid. See also Heidegger, *Being and Time*, 230.
37. Nancy, "The Being-with of Being-there," 8.
38. Ibid., 9.
39. Ibid. See also Heidegger, *Being and Time*, 336. I have used Nancy's translation of "Mitteilung" here as "message," while the English translation upon which I have relied translates this word as "communication." The original German sentence reads as follows: "In der Mitteilung und im Kampf wird die Macht des Geschickes erst frei." See Martin Heidegger, *Sein und Zeit* (Tübingen: Max Neimeyer Verlag, 2006), 384.
40. Nancy, "The Being-with of Being-there," 12.
41. Ibid., 11.
42. Ibid., 10.
43. Ibid., 12.
44. Ibid., 13.
45. Ibid., 12.
46. Walter Brogan, "The Parting of Being: On Creation and Sharing in Nancy's Political Ontology," *Research in Phenomenology*, 40 (2010): 295–308, 295.
47. Brogan, 296.
48. Ibid., 297.
49. Jean-Luc Nancy, *Being Singular Plural* (Stanford: Stanford University Press, 2000), 62.
50. See Heidegger, *Being and Time*, §7 and §34.
51. Heidegger, *Being and Time*, 32.
52. Brogan, 298.
53. Nancy, *Being Singular Plural*, 2.
54. Ibid., 61. See also Brogan, 298.
55. Brogan, 298.
56. Nancy, *Being Singular Plural*, 59.
57. Ibid., 11.
58. Ibid., 13.
59. Ibid.
60. Ibid.
61. Ibid., 19.
62. Ibid., 18.
63. Ibid., 8.
64. Brogan, 302.
65. Brogan, 304.
66. Andrew Benjamin, *Towards a Relational Ontology: Philosophy's Other Possibility* (Albany: SUNY Press, 2015), 2.

67. Benjamin, 3.
68. Ibid., 2.
69. Ibid.
70. Ibid., 5.
71. Ibid., 5–6.
72. Ibid., 10.
73. Ibid., 218.
74. Ibid., 219.
75. Ibid., 90.
76. Ibid., 91.
77. Ibid., 93.
78. Ibid., 144.
79. Ibid., 215.
80. Ibid., 183.

3

The Politics of Being-With: Hannah Arendt on the Space of Appearance

To this point, I have attempted to bring into focus the centrality of the problem of our peculiar loneliness for the main currents of continental thought. Turning to Heidegger's discourse on the they-self in *Being and Time*, I have suggested that he makes visible the philosophical significance of this problem through his efforts to displace the isolated modern subject with the relational structure of being-in-the-world. Though we might expect Heidegger to be led from this discovery to insist on Dasein's immediate belonging, he does not. Instead, Heidegger suggests that it is precisely because Dasein is not an isolated subject surrounded by objectively present things, but rather constituted by care, that it finds itself always already reaching out and bringing nearer the world into which it has been thrown. This tendency toward nearness, this longing to make more proximate and familiar the world into which it has been thrown, is the same tendency that leads us to reduce each other to the metrics of utility, to make one another more familiar and accessible while at the same time covering over the excessive possibility of those with whom we share the world. A crucial if underappreciated insight of *Being and Time*, Heidegger thus discovers at the ground of Dasein's being a way of being in relation that leaves Dasein hidden, isolated, and shrouded in anonymity. That is to say, Heidegger makes visible as a philosophical problematic a peculiar loneliness to which Dasein, in its native relationality and excess of possibility, is always already vulnerable.

The question thus arises as to how we might envision authentic forms of communal life from out of this loneliness. Though scholars have challenged the extent to which Heidegger is able to answer this question in *Being and Time*, the question itself has nevertheless remained central. Its legacy has reverberated through the main currents of continental thought, leading scholars to consider how we might envision ways of being together, ways of thinking the shared and the common, that are neither alienating of our interrelatedness nor reductive of our radical singularity. Whereas the former only perpetuates this peculiar loneliness, the latter opens the possibility for dangerously totalizing forms of communal life. Hence, the task within these discourses has been to envision possibilities for communal life that are grounded in an exposure to alterity, exteriority, and difference.

In what follows, I wish to suggest that we might open new inroads within this discourse by developing the problem of the peculiar loneliness of the current age in a political register. After all, this loneliness—or the fact that we find ourselves more hyperbolically connected and yet more alienated and isolated from one another than ever before—is perhaps no more pronounced than in political life today. Citizens in liberal and allegedly open societies struggle not simply to converse, but even to see themselves as belonging to the same reality. While we may have greater access to one another and to the events of the world than ever before, we use this access to build echo chambers rather than spaces for genuine discourse and find that we can barely recognize the humanity of those whose worldviews differ from our own. In view of this, it will be the goal of this chapter and those that follow to interpret this problem in its political significance, treating this loneliness as a symptom of the destruction of the political sphere of our lives in the modern era.

To this end, I turn to the work of Hannah Arendt, who adds a new voice to these discourses in the novel critical perspective she offers on the liberal political tradition. Though Arendt develops her concerns in relation to the rise of European totalitarianism at the beginning of the twentieth century, I maintain that her insights provide an important platform for considering the loneliness of citizens in Western liberal democracies today and the increasing vulnerability of these societies to right-wing nationalism and populism.

Jill Stauffer has carved out a space to begin thinking the problem of loneliness in a political register in her recent work *Ethical Loneliness: The Injustice of Not Being Heard*. Stauffer conceives of loneliness as a symptom of the unwillingness, often on the part of just-minded people, to listen to those who have suffered injustice.[1] In this, she emphasizes those who find themselves cast out from the dominant discourse and for whom the inability to be heard produces a profound and abiding loneliness. My aim in the chapters that follow will be to take the next steps in advancing this discourse. Whereas Stauffer frames the problem of loneliness in terms of the ethical responsibility we have to listen to those who have historically been excluded from liberal democratic spheres of political discourse, my aim in turning to Arendt is to emphasize the peculiar loneliness that is already at work in the forms of subjectivity that these spheres produce. In this, my goal is not to deny the importance of the loneliness that Stauffer identifies, but rather to approach this problem from a different vantage point, considering the ways in which the peculiar loneliness of the current age is affirmed and reproduced by the very structures that organize liberal societies today.

In view of this, I turn to Arendt to suggest that the political structures we have inherited from the liberal tradition—such as the emphasis on representation rather than deliberation and the prioritization of the right to pursue one's private self-interest as far as possible—have eroded the space of politics, leaving even those endowed with the full rights of liberal citizenship hidden from one another, unable to see themselves as belonging to a common world. By turning to Arendt, I will argue that it is precisely this loss of a world—a loss that arises from the destruction of the political sphere—that renders human beings lonely. Drawing on Arendt's characterization of totalitarianism as "organized loneliness," I maintain that the consequences of this experience are as dire as they are urgent.[2] Whereas we might take for granted the liberal political structures that organize modern life and even call for their expansion in the service of ending political alienation and exclusion, I wish to suggest that these structures do not promise such an end; quite to the contrary, they reproduce the very loneliness that makes modern individuals vulnerable to totalitarian domination.

This argument will unfold over the next three chapters. As we shall see, Arendt offers a prescient critical perspective on the liberal tradition, one that uncovers the possible risks for totalitarianism and populism in the loneliness that she believes is produced by liberal notions of subjectivity. Yet, understanding this critical perspective depends first on turning to the significance that she attributes to the political sphere of human existence. To this end, I will trace Arendt's critical appropriation of Heidegger's fundamental ontology and the groundwork this provides for the development of her own political ontology. Arendt treats the political as the site of both self and world disclosure, or that space in which human beings are able to appear to one another in their irrevocable interdependence and irreducible singularity. I will therefore argue that her conception of the political might be interpreted as an answer to the question of how we might think the possibilities for authentic communal life from out of the peculiar loneliness that Heidegger diagnoses in *Being and Time*.

Arendt's critical perspective on Heidegger is often taken to center on his disavowal of the public in Division I of *Being and Time*. Though it is true that Arendt is concerned throughout much of her work with overturning the age-old philosophical prejudice against *praxis*, even her earliest critical engagement with Heidegger cannot be reduced to this. By considering the emphasis Arendt places on Heidegger's analysis of the self in his discourse on authentic Dasein, I argue that she is not critical of his discourse on the publicness of average everyday Dasein per se; rather, she wishes to bring into focus the implications of this analysis for understanding the depravity of political life in the modern age. Arendt, for her part, follows Heidegger in conceiving of the human being in terms of its native relationality and excessive possibility. She also agrees with him that we find ourselves originally and for the most part indwelling our relations with others in ways that are leveled down and reductive, leaving us hidden from one another and shrouded in anonymity. Yet, whereas Heidegger is led from this to envision Dasein's escape from the loneliness of the they-self through its displacement from the world in the mode of authenticity, Arendt suggests that the they-self must be interpreted as a symptom of the destruction of the political sphere in the modern age, calling instead for its rehabilitation.

We might therefore read Arendt as taking issue with Heidegger's inability to recognize that his critique of the isolated modern subject is in fact a critique of notions of subjectivity inherited from the liberal political tradition. In the chapters that follow, I will suggest that this, in turn, leads Arendt to suggest that what is called for in response to the peculiar loneliness of the current age is not a destruction of the history of Western metaphysics, but rather a destruction of the history of Western politics. In so doing, Arendt suggests we find that the liberal tradition, in adopting the credo that "freedom begins where politics ends," has fundamentally obscured the meaning of freedom, leaving human beings unable to appear in their radical singularity as belonging to a common world. I therefore turn in this chapter to the significance she attributes to the political sphere of human existence to illustrate a further danger of modern subjectivity that Arendt recognizes, one that is born out of the liberal political tradition and that offers a distinctive vantage point from which to view the modern subject's vulnerability to the peculiar loneliness of the current age.

ARENDT'S CRITICAL APPROPRIATION OF HEIDEGGER

Arendt's intellectual engagement with Heidegger began in the fall of 1924 when she traveled to Marburg to attend his 1924–1925 winter semester lecture course on Plato's *Sophist*. This period was, for Heidegger, perhaps the most creative and decisive of his career. In 1919, he began giving a series of lecture courses in Freiburg and Marburg that would provide the basis for his 1927 masterwork *Being and Time*.[3] Among the most notable of these was the 1924–1925 winter semester lecture course that Arendt attended on Plato's *Sophist*. As Jacques Taminiaux explains, Heidegger was able to underscore in this lecture course his central argument in *Being and Time* that "philosophy in its cardinal form, which is metaphysics, is not a doctrine, but rather a form of existence."[4] With this, he outlines the existential structure of Dasein as being-in-the-world, developing the implications of this in his discourse on the Greek conception of truth as *aletheia* or unconcealment in order to give contour to his radical assertion that truth is "a determination of the being of Dasein itself."[5] This, in turn, sets the stage for his claim in *Being and Time* that Dasein's relation to the world is never indifferent or passive; instead, insofar as being-in means dwelling, being amid, and being together with the things in the world, Heidegger insists that Dasein is primordially concerned about the things and others with which it is involved. That is to say, Dasein is oriented toward the world in an original way by its care (*sorge*) for things and others and, hence, cannot be thought apart from this native relationality and involvement.[6]

These insights remain central to Arendt's corpus throughout. Yet, Arendt, in much the same way as figures like Nancy, also perceives in Heidegger a failure to realize fully the communal and political implications of his own account of being-in-the-world. While contemporary commentators have focused on Arendt's treatment of Heidegger's disavowal of the public in *Being and Time*, perhaps more important is her concern for the way in which his treatment of authentic Dasein appears to leave intact the isolated modern subject that Heidegger himself insists on dismantling through his notion of care. The communal and political possibilities of Heidegger's project were salient in his 1924–1925 lecture course, particularly in his efforts to appropriate Aristotle's notion of *phronesis* in an existential register.[7] Yet, Arendt interprets Heidegger's treatment of authenticity in *Being and Time* as a missed opportunity to elucidate the importance of the communal and relational context within which his existential interpretation of *phronesis* becomes possible. In placing being-toward-death at the center of his analysis, Arendt believes that Heidegger poses his notion of authenticity in direct opposition to Dasein's engagement in the world, equating one's publicly interpreted self with the "they-self" or the leveled down, average everydayness of inauthentic Dasein.[8] With this, Heidegger stresses in *Being and Time* that authenticity reaches its apex through the accomplishment of a certain kind of care of the self, one that takes shape at a distance from Dasein's normal course of existence as being-in-the-world. Arendt sees in this a betrayal of the very interrelatedness that he so radically insists is constitutive of human existence, a betrayal that she believes leads Heidegger to implicate himself in the very notion of subjectivity that he wishes to upend.[9]

These concerns begin to coalescence as early as Arendt's dissertation *Der Liebesbegriff bei Augustin*, which she completed in 1929 under the direction of Karl Jaspers.[10] Though her engagement with Jaspers proved crucial for the trajectory of her thinking, Heidegger is far from absent in Arendt's earliest philosophical writings. As Roy Tsao explains, "[*Der Liebesbegriff bei Augustin*] attests to Heidegger's influence on every page . . . the questions posed, the inferences drawn, and the distinctions insisted upon all lie within the ambit of Heidegger's fundamental ontology, and conform with exactitude to its protocols."[11] Yet, even in these early years, Arendt's work is distinguished not just by its proximity to Heidegger but also by her critical approach to his early formulation of the project of fundamental ontology.[12] In her dissertation, Arendt reinterprets Heidegger's conception of care in terms of Augustine's notion of *caritas* or neighborly love in order to put into relief the importance of the neighborhood or community for human existence.[13] She, like Heidegger, argues that it is native to care to reach out beyond itself. Yet, whereas Heidegger's emphasis on death leads him to suggest that care reaches its summit through the self-relation achieved in anticipatory resoluteness, Arendt tarries on the fact that in reaching out, Dasein finds itself exposed to more than it can grasp—an exteriority, alterity, and otherness—that is fundamental to who it is. In contrast to *cupiditas*, which Augustine characterizes in terms of self-love, private desire, and an attraction to temporary things that can be lost against one's will, *caritas* is the love of things that are larger and more enduring than one's own existence, such as one's neighbor and community, the objects of knowledge, and God. In this, the objects of *caritas* are not only more permanent but also able to be shared in common, promising the possibility of belonging to a common world that is never available to *cupiditas*. In her existential interpretation of *caritas*, Arendt thus emphasizes that the self-love involved in *cupiditas* leaves the human being hidden and alone, while neighborly love or *caritas* enables us to belong to a common world with others. Arendt's interpretation of Augustine's notion of *caritas* in this early work may therefore be seen as an effort to show that the responsibility to care is not first and foremost a matter of care for the self, as Heidegger suggests, but rather a matter of care for the world and the plurality that constitutes it. She thus interprets care as reaching its summit, not through the silent and inward call of conscience, but rather through the visible and audible call of human plurality.[14]

This concern for loving the world is deeply formative for Arendt's own political project, offering a counterpoint to the self-relation that she believes Heidegger emphasizes in his discourse on authentic Dasein. Yet, while Arendt begins to develop her critique of Heidegger as early as her dissertation, her concern for the political does not become explicit until Hitler's rise to power in 1933. She identifies February 27, 1933—the day the Reichstag was burned—as the definitive event in her memory that dated her turn toward the political.[15] Reflecting on this period in her acclaimed 1964 interview with Günter Gaus, she says:

> The year 1933 made a lasting impression on me. . . . The problem, the personal problem, was not what our enemies might be doing, but what our friends were doing. This wave of cooperation . . . made you feel surrounded by an empty space, isolated. . . . I came to the conclusion that cooperation was, so to speak, the rule among intellectuals, but not among others. And I have never forgotten that.[16]

Upon witnessing the illegal arrests of people, who, under the guise of protective custody, were sent to Gestapo cellars and concentration camps, Arendt decided that "indifference was no longer possible" and, for a time, resolved to disavow the intellectual tradition in which she had been raised.[17] Upon fleeing Germany in 1933 and living in exile for the next eighteen years, Arendt explains that she decided to resist all forms of worldless contemplation, developing a project instead that centered on political judgment, action, and communal responsibility.

It was, of course, in April of the same year that Heidegger accepted the rectorship at Freiburg University, and only days later, on May 1, 1933, joined the Nazi Party. Though there is much to be said about Heidegger's involvement in National Socialism, no less than Arendt's reaction to his decision, what is especially interesting is that she comes to identify the limits and political dangers of his project in his discourse on authentic Dasein. She offers perhaps her clearest statement of this in her 1946 essay "What Is Existential Philosophy?" where she argues that Heidegger's notion of Dasein in *Being and Time* devolves from a being that is constituted by being-in-the-world to an isolated self whose "absolute self-ness" makes its relation to the world and others irrelevant. She insists in this essay that Heidegger's notion of "being-toward-death" motivates this self-oriented Dasein, while anticipatory resoluteness offers "the opportunity to devote myself exclusively to being-a-Self . . . and to free myself once and for all from the world that entangles me."[18] In view of this, Arendt explains that by Heidegger's own lights, "Dasein could be truly itself only if it could pull back from its being-in-the-world into itself, but that is what its nature can never permit it to do."[19] Unable to be itself with others, Dasein must avail itself of its singularity in order to return to the world. The community, for

Heidegger, thus serves not as a space for the appearance of one's own most possibilities, but as something that forecloses any sense of belonging in this irreducible and excessive possibility.

Though Heidegger insists that the world and others are never at the margins, Arendt explains that in placing death at the center of his analysis, he is left with nothing but an isolated self. She says:

> The crucial element of man's being is its being in the world, and what is at stake for his being is quite simply survival in the world. That is the very thing that is denied man, and consequently the basic mode of being-in-the-world is alienation, which is felt both as homelessness and anxiety.[20]

Dasein can only be a self by pulling back from its very nature as being-in-the-world through the anticipation of the most radical separation from others and the world, namely, death. Thus, Arendt says, "The essential character of the Self is its absolute self-ness, its radical separation from all its fellows."[21] Arendt explains that for Heidegger, Dasein thus finds itself faced with an irreconcilable fate; it must either surrender its being-in-the-world for itself or it must surrender itself for its being-in-the-world, both of which are fundamentally alien to its nature.[22]

No longer grounded in a Christian God or a humanistic moral law, Arendt believes that Heidegger's existential orientation toward becoming a self generates a notion of selfhood that is especially dangerous. As Arendt explains,

> What emerges from this absolute isolation is a concept of the Self as the total opposite of man. . . . If Kant's categorical imperative insisted that every human act had to bear responsibility for all of humanity, then the experience of guilty nothingness insists on precisely its opposite: the destruction in every individual of the presence of all humanity. The Self in the form of conscience has taken the place of humanity, and being-a-self has taken the place of being human.[23]

It is in virtue of this, Arendt argues, that Heidegger is led to appeal to such concepts as "folk" and "earth" to "supply his isolated Selves with a shared, common ground to stand on."[24] As she explains,

> If it does not belong to the concept of man that he inhabits the earth together with others of his kind, then all that remains for him is a mechanical reconciliation by which the atomized Selves

are provided with a common ground that is essentially alien to their nature. All that can result from this is the organization of these Selves intent only on [transforming] themselves into an Over-self in order somehow to effect a transition from resolutely accepted guilt to action.[25]

The language in this passage resonates with the language of atomization and isolation that Arendt uses to describe the vulnerability of modern mass society to totalitarianism in many of her essays throughout the 1940s. It is also characteristic of the language she employs in her famous discourse on ideology and terror in her 1951 text *The Origins of Totalitarianism*, which I will discuss at length in the chapters that follow.[26] Perhaps most importantly, we find in these passages not a critique of Heidegger's discourse on the publicness of the they-self, but rather a concern for his response to the alienation and isolation that he rightly identifies in his analysis of the they-self. This response, she thinks, turns not on considering how such conditions might have become possible but rather on developing a worldless notion of authentic Dasein that is able to escape these conditions.

In view of this, we might read Arendt's positive political project not as a rejection of Heidegger's critique of publicness per se, but rather as a response to what she perceives as a failure on his part to recognize that the hiddenness and isolation of modern life is symptomatic of the loss of the political sphere. The significance that she attributes to political life may therefore be interpreted as a response to the peculiar loneliness that Heidegger identifies but that Arendt believes he fails to acknowledge as a symptom of the destruction of the political sphere in the modern era.

THE POLITICS OF TECHNO-SCIENTIFIC RATIONALITY

Arendt's conception of the political comes into view perhaps most clearly in her seminal 1958 work *The Human Condition*. Heidegger is certainly in the background of this project as is evidenced by a letter that Arendt sent to him with a copy of the German edition of this text. She says:

> You will see that the book does not contain a dedication. If things had ever worked out between us—and I mean *between*, that is, neither you nor me—I would have asked you if I might dedicate it to you; it came directly out of the first Freiburg days and hence

owes practically everything to you in every respect. As things are, I did not think it was possible, but I wanted at least to mention the bare fact to you in one way or another.[27]

Even in this brief remark, we see the decisive influence that Heidegger had on Arendt's political project. Beyond this, however, we also see her concern for the "between, that is, neither you nor me." Though she is, of course, referring to her personal relationship with Heidegger, Ronald Beiner has argued that we might also interpret this as a gesture toward her deeper concern for plurality, or the with-structure of human existence, which she believes Heidegger is never able to give full articulation to in his own account of authentic Dasein.[28] Whereas she perceives in Heidegger an emphasis on the self that is dangerous insofar as it reproduces an isolated subject, it is crucial to Arendt that the "in-between" be thought authentically, as it is only in this in-between that our native relationality and radical singularity can make itself felt in the world. Arendt thus conceives of the political as this in-between, an in-between that she believes makes it possible for human beings to see themselves in their irreducible possibility as belonging to a common world. That is to say, the political, for Arendt, is the condition for the possibility of authentic communal life, a condition that Heidegger himself failed to recognize as the very thing that can address the peculiar loneliness of the they-self.

As distinctive as Arendt's treatment of the political is, it is significant for our purposes that the prologue of *The Human Condition* is oriented by a familiar set of concerns regarding the impact of the ascendance of scientific and technical rationality on modern life. She begins her analysis by turning to the year 1957, when, she says, Sputnik was completed and the first earth-born object was launched into the universe. An event that Arendt describes as second in importance to no other, she says that those who bore witness to it were moved not by the joy of triumph but rather by a sense of relief about accomplishing "the first 'step toward escape from men's imprisonment to the earth.' "[29] Arendt argues that this longing to escape our imprisonment on the earth is at the same time a longing to escape the human condition. It is the same desire, she thinks, that is "manifest in the attempt to create life in the test tube, in the desire to mix 'frozen germ plasm from people of demonstrated ability under the microscope to produce superior human beings' and 'to alter [their] size, shape and function.' "[30] This wish to escape the human condition, this totalizing rebellion against human existence, is what modern techno-scientific rationality promises to achieve.

Arendt maintains, too, that we have as little reason to doubt that science can accomplish the exchange of human existence for the technical and scientific mastery of the world. Yet, despite how vast the reach of modern science has been, she says that we must still wonder "whether we wish to use our new scientific and technical knowledge in this direction." [31] Arendt is clear that the answer to this question cannot be decided by scientific "know-how." Rather, she says, "It is a political question of the first order and therefore can hardly be left to the decision of professional scientists or professional politicians."[32] Whereas it is in the nature of scientific and technical advancement to continue pursing knowledge without thinking its consequences, she explains that the task before us now is "to think what we are doing."[33] She says:

> If it should turn out to be true that knowledge . . . and thought have parted company for good, then we would indeed become the helpless slaves, not so much of our machines as of our know-how, thoughtless creatures at the mercy of every gadget which is technically possible, no matter how murderous it is.[34]

A point of departure that should remind us of similar concerns raised by Heidegger and Jaspers, no less than those who follow these figures, it is significant that Arendt is led from this to the political. She explains that thinking what we are doing depends on speech, which, she says, "is what makes man a political being."[35] Whereas modern science and technology must adopt a "language" of mathematical symbols, this language "in no way can be translated back into speech."[36] In order to think what we are doing, Arendt argues that we must recognize that we cannot defer to the political judgment of scientists, not because they are not wise, but "because they move in a world where speech has lost its power."[37] Instead, Arendt explains that "whatever men do or know or experience can make sense only to the extent that it can be spoken about."[38] With this, she argues that while there may be truths beyond speech, these truths are only of great relevance to man in the singular, "which is to say, Man insofar as he is not a political being, whatever else he may be."[39] Yet, for Arendt, one's humanity is keyed to the fact that human beings are not atomized, self-contained entities who can be understood within the purview of modern subjectivity. That we have speech, that we are political beings, is at the same time an affirmation of human plurality, or the fact that we are always already born into a world with others. Because of this, she says, "Men in the plural, that is, men in so far as they live and move and act in this world, can experience meaningfulness only because they can talk with and make sense to each other and to themselves."[40] That speech has lost its power, Arendt argues, is among the greatest crises of our times, one that not only runs the risk of foreclosing the possibility for meaningful engagement in what we are doing but that also threatens our very ability to appear to one another in our humanity.

No less threatening, she explains, is the advent of automation. "Here, too," she says, "a fundamental aspect of the human condition is at stake."[41] Though human beings for centuries have fought for liberation from labor, Arendt argues that our times are different. While the advent of automation may make us think that we will finally be liberated from labor, Arendt says, "This is so only in appearance. The modern age has carried with it a theoretical glorification of labor and has resulted in a factual transformation of the whole of society into a laboring society."[42] Because of this, all activity in the modern world has been reduced from its meaningfulness to labor. Hence, she says, "What we are confronted with is the prospect of a society of laborers without labor, that is, without the only activity left to them."[43] Taken together, the loss of meaningful speech and meaningful action constitutes the crisis of our times, a loss that is only exacerbated by the unremitting advance of techno-scientific rationality. It is on the basis of this that she believes the task before is to "think what we are doing," lest we allow these processes to consume humanity altogether.[44]

Arendt's point of departure for this work echoes the critical perspectives we have already considered on the dangers and limits of the techno-scientific rationality of the modern age and the impact its advance has had on our communal relations and responsibilities. Yet, while Heidegger, in particular, is led from the anonymity, isolation, and inauthenticity of the they-self to a conception of authenticity that liberates Dasein from the world and the relations that constitute it, Arendt believes that this critique issues a different call. In her view, it points not to the need to retreat from the depravity of the world; instead, it issues an urgent call to rehabilitate the world and the plurality that constitutes it.

NATALITY, PLURALITY, AND THE SPACE OF APPEARANCE

In order to develop a conception of the political that challenges the reductive and alienating nature of modern mass society, Arendt argues that it is necessary to recover a notion of the *vita activa* or the fundamental activities of human life. In so doing, she thinks that it is possible to remind ourselves of what makes us human so that we might call into question the way in which the techno-scientific ordering of modern life seeks to liberate us from our humanity. The *vita activa*, Arendt explains, may be characterized in terms of the three fundamental activities of human life: labor, work, and action. These activities are fundamental because "each corresponds to one of the basic conditions under which life on earth has been given to man."[45] Labor corresponds to the cyclical biological processes of production and consumption, the spontaneous growth, metabolism, and eventual decay of the human body that is the condition of life itself.[46] Work is the activity that corresponds to the "unnaturalness of human existence," or the process by which we erect an artificial world of things that have permanence and endure in spite of the cyclical processes of nature. In this, she explains that work is what makes possible a world, and for this reason corresponds to the human condition of worldliness.[47]

In contrast to labor and work, Arendt argues that action distinguishes itself insofar as it is "the only activity that goes on directly between men without the intermediary of things or matter."[48] Action, she explains, corresponds most closely to the human conditions of natality and plurality, conditions that make action "the political activity par excellence."[49] She says, "Action would be an unnecessary luxury, a capricious interference with general laws of behavior if men were endlessly reproducible repetitions of the same model, whose nature or essence was the same for all and as predictable as the nature of essence of any other thing."[50] Yet, Arendt insists that this is not the case. Rather, because human beings are conditioned by natality and plurality, they are irreducible in this way, and, because of this, are always in need of the political sphere in order to appear to one another in their humanity.

The human condition of natality arises from the fact that we are each born into the world anew. To the extent that we are born into a world that we neither choose nor control, left without recourse to a pre-given essence, natality can be understood as Arendt's interpretation of Heidegger's notion of thrownness or facticity. Yet, while

Arendt recognizes both birth and death as existential conditions of human existence, she says, "Natality and not mortality may be the central category of the political, as distinguished from metaphysical thought."[51] In being born, Arendt argues, we are always already radically unique, appearing in the world as something entirely unexpected and natively capable of acting against the overwhelming odds of statistical laws and their probability.[52] From birth, we are thus marked with the capacity for new beginnings, or the ability to introduce something into the world that has never before been seen and that could never have been predicted. That is, she says, "With the creation of man, the principle of beginning came into the world itself, which, of course, is another way of saying that the principle of freedom was created when man was created but not before."[53] Human freedom thus arises from the infinite improbability that accompanies the character of human existence insofar as we find ourselves conditioned by natality.

Natality comes to appear in the world through action, which Arendt identifies with the native human capacity to initiate something into the world that has never before been seen and that could never have been predicted. She says, "To act, in the most general sense means to take initiative, to begin (as the Greek word *archein*, 'to begin,' 'to lead,' and eventually 'to rule,' indicates), to set something in motion (which is the original meaning of the Latin *agere*)."[54] It is therefore only in being conditioned by natality that one is able to bring something new into the world. Through action, individuals enact their capacity to intervene in the necessary processes that govern ordinary existence, a capacity that arises from the fact of our birth. Arendt explains, "The fact that man is capable of action means that the unexpected can be expected from him, that he is able to perform what is infinitely improbable. And this again is possible only because each man is unique, so that with each birth something uniquely new comes into the world."[55] The ability to introduce something new to the world is concomitant with the ability to be free, or the ability to exceed the automatic processes of everyday life. That is, she says:

> The new beginning inherent in birth can make itself felt in the world only because the newcomer possesses the capacity of beginning something anew, that is, of acting. In this sense of initiative, an element of action, and therefore of natality, is inherent in all human activities.[56]

For this reason, she argues, action is the political activity par excellence.[57] It is only in virtue of the singularity of our experience in the world, or the fact that every human being can introduce something new to it, that we can appropriate the world we have inherited in such a way that it becomes meaningful. Whereas the sphere of labor is governed by the necessity of the life processes, and the sphere of work by the yardsticks and measurements of utility, Arendt is clear that action, insofar as it is conditioned by natality, is the only human activity that is free, and, because of this, most proper to sphere of politics.

She explains, however, that we are only radically unique and able to appear in our natality to the extent that we also find ourselves always already in relation to others. She thus turns to the human condition of plurality, or the fact that "men, not Man, live on the earth and inhabit the world."[58] We cannot enact our natality in isolation, as "to be isolated is to be deprived of the capacity to act."[59] As such, she explains that action is conditioned by natality insofar as it is also conditioned by natality or the fact that "we are all the same, that is, human in such a way that nobody is ever the same as anyone else who ever lived, lives, or will live."[60] Whereas natality is the condition by which we initiate something new in the world, the human condition of plurality makes its appearance through speech, or the ability to announce to others that we are the authors of our action.[61] As Arendt explains, "If action as beginning corresponds to the fact of birth, if it is the actualization of the human condition of natality, then speech corresponds to the fact of distinctness and is the actualization of the human condition of plurality, that is, of living as a distinct and unique being among equals."[62] This ability to announce ourselves to one another in our diversity is a distinctly human capacity. For this reason, action is only possible insofar as it is accompanied by speech. She says:

> Without the accompaniment of speech, at any rate, action would not only lose its revelatory character, but, and by the same token, it would lose its subject, as it were; not acting men but performing robots would achieve what, humanly speaking, would remain incomprehensible. Speechless action would no longer be action because there would no longer be an actor, and the actor, the doer of deeds, is possible only if he is at the same time the speaker of words.[63]

Therefore, in addition to action, speech—or the ability to announce that I am the author of my action—is required if I am to appear fully in my singularity among others. Taken together, then, speech and action are disclosive of being human, allowing individuals to become visible to one another in their plurality and natality. She says:

> In acting and speaking, men show who they are, reveal actively their unique personal identities and thus make their appearance in the human world, while their physical identities appear without any activity of their own in the unique shape of the body and sound of the voice. The disclosure of "who" in contradistinction to "what" somebody is . . . is implicit in everything somebody says and does.[64]

By the same token, if one loses the ability to speak and act, the fullness of one's humanity remains hidden. In contrast to the life of labor and that of work, Arendt says, "A life without speech and without action . . . —and this is the only way of life that in earnest has renounced all appearance . . . is literally dead to the world; it has ceased to be a human life because it is no longer lived among men."[65] We thus insert ourselves into the world through word and deed and, in so doing, undergo what she describes as a kind of second birth that is tantamount to the enactment of freedom and the appearance of one's humanity.[66]

To the extent that speech and action are tied to the human capacity for freedom, Arendt takes these activities to be distinctly political. The political, Arendt explains, is where we speak and act with others in order to introduce new meaning to the world, saving it from "its normal 'natural' ruin," or the necessity that governs ordinary life.[67] In other words, it is the space for the appearance of human freedom and, thus, she says, "the *raison d'être* of the political is freedom and its field of experience is action."[68] Only in this space are we able to appear, not as interchangeable entities, but as always already capable of acting against the overwhelming odds of statistical laws and probability.[69] Only here, Arendt argues, do the reductive metrics of utility lose their relevance, disclosing a more authentic possibility for human action, one that enables a common world constituted by the irreducible singularity and plurality of its actors to appear.

It is only in the context of political life that individuals come together for the sake of initiating something new in the world and, in so doing, transcend the finitude of their particular existence in order to engage in what we might call authentic being-with. She thus describes the political as "the space of appearance in the widest sense of the word, namely, the space where I appear to others as others appear to me, where men exist not merely like other living or inanimate things but make their appearance explicitly."[70] Arendt thus attempts to illustrate that each newcomer who enters the world is at once irreducibly singular while, at the same time, irrevocably embedded within the fabric of communal life. With this, she insists that there is no self without the relations that constitute it and no disclosure without the political—or that space in which I appear to others as they appear to me, not as endlessly reproducible entities but as radically unique.[71]

Arendt is clear, however, that this space of appearance does not always exist, but rather comes into existence through speaking and acting together. It is a space that requires no government or formal constitution, nor can it be guaranteed by these mechanisms.[72] Rather she says, "It is the organization of the people as it arises out of acting and speaking together, and its true space lies between people living together for this purpose, no matter where they happen to be."[73] Yet, while the political constitutes a space that makes possible the appearance of human plurality and natality, enabling us to become visible to one another in our humanity, it is also a fragile space, one that is always at risk of going out of existence as quickly as it came into existence. The stakes of the loss of this space are high; without the political, Arendt argues, human beings lose the ability to see one another in the fullness of their humanity. They become hidden and isolated, vulnerable to being reduced in their radical singularity and plurality to repeatable and replaceable entities, unable, in turn, to intervene in the necessary processes that govern ordinary life. A space that is as important as it is fragile, Arendt is clear that it must be held open if we are to envision possibilities for communal life that are neither alienating of our relations nor reductive of our difference. Yet, she is clear that it is precisely this space that has fallen into decay in the modern era, a symptom, she thinks, of the tendency within the liberal political tradition to elevate the right to pursue one's private self-interest to the highest aim of politics.

THE POLITICS OF MODERN SUBJECTIVITY

It is this tendency and its impact on the space of appearance that Arendt believes Heidegger failed to see. While she follows Heidegger in a number of ways, she suggests that his own notion of authenticity, no less than the idea of freedom that accompanies this, remains indebted to notions of subjectivity inherited from the liberal tradition. We might therefore read her as interpreting Heidegger's own analysis of the they-self as symptomatic of the destruction of the political sphere in the modern era. Whereas Heidegger turns to Dasein's displacement from the world in the mode of authenticity, Arendt turns to the political, treating the loneliness of the they-self as symptomatic of its destruction. With this, she reformulates his notion of freedom, asserting that freedom comes to appear, not through a retreat from the world and the relations that constitute it, but rather through speaking and acting with others in the space of politics.

The consequences of this are significant for Arendt's project. As Dana Villa has argued, Arendt follows closely from Heidegger in her efforts to envision anew the constitution of the human being not in terms of a pre-given essence but rather in terms of the possibilities that arise from the fact of its existence. In existing, Arendt, like Heidegger, believes that we always already find ourselves involved in a world or context of meaning that is not our own. Yet, in having one's constitution in existence rather than a pre-given essence, one does not simply find oneself in this context of meaning as an indiscriminant being among many. Instead, for Arendt and Heidegger alike, it is only in virtue of "being-in" that one's radical individuation becomes possible. For both, then, freedom is not an inner disposition of the human being that can be realized through a retreat from the world, nor is the kind of freedom to which this gives birth "a free-floating potentiality of being in the sense of the 'liberty of indifference.'"[74] Rather, both treat freedom as an event of appropriation, whereby Dasein comes to appear upon seizing those possibilities that are given to it by its thrownness. That is, as Dana Villa explains, "What matters, in short, is the *event* of authentic disclosedness, an event that, in both Arendt and Heidegger, signifies a wrenching free of everydayness and its illumination through the unpredictable uncovering of the new. Through such disclosive spontaneity, the world is revealed in its worldliness."[75]

Yet, Arendt is clear that Heidegger's notion of the self in *Being and Time* overlooks the importance of the political for holding open a space in which Dasein's freedom of possibility might be realized. Though Heidegger envisions a new kind of existential freedom, his emphasis on Dasein's displacement from the world in anticipatory resoluteness nevertheless reiterates a familiar trope in the Western metaphysical tradition of upholding the individual over and against the plural. In her 1954 essay "Concern with Politics in Recent European Thought," Arendt says, "The old hostility of philosophy towards the *polis* [is] in Heidegger's analysis of average everyday life in terms of *das Man* (the 'they' or the rule of public opinion, as opposed to the 'self') in which the public realm has the function of hiding reality and preventing even the appearance of truth."[76] Arendt acknowledges the importance of Heidegger's concern for the pitfalls of modern life as this takes shape in his critique of publicness in *Being and Time*. Yet, she argues that in retaining an age-old hostility toward *praxis*, he is unable to envision the possibilities for authentic forms of communal life that his own existential analytic of Dasein demand.

Arendt explains that it is in consequence of this that Heidegger is only able to turn to Dasein's historicity in his analysis of authentic being-with, which, she says, "despite its obvious closeness to . . . always misses the center of politics—man as an acting being."[77] This, she argues, is the perennial problem of the Western philosophical tradition of which Heidegger is a final and perhaps especially radical exemplar. She says, "The more pertinent question of political science, which, in a sense, are more specifically philosophic—such as, What is politics? Who is man as a political being? What is freedom?—seem to have been forgotten altogether."[78] The problem is not simply that Heidegger neglects the political; beyond this, in failing to see the peculiar loneliness he diagnoses as a symptom of the decay of political life, he leaves untouched the liberal political structures that Arendt believes have led to the closure of the political and the loneliness of modern life.

While Arendt certainly discovers in Heidegger's project what she takes to be an impulse toward totalitarianism, I will argue in the chapters that follow that she believes this path of thinking owes its trajectory less to the principles of fundamental ontology and more to the liberal political structures that have produced and sustained lonely forms of subjectivity. In Arendt's view, Heidegger remains too wedded to the history of Western metaphysics, which has never been able to see the political, or that space that she believes is most proper to human plurality. Instead, in its emphasis on "the one," it is only able to see the individual. Arendt suggests as much in a 1951 letter to Karl Jaspers:

> The Western tradition is suffering from the preconception that the most evil things human beings can do arises from the vice of selfishness. Yet . . . it seems to me to have something to do with the

following phenomenon: making human beings as human beings superfluous. This happens as soon as all unpredictability—which in human beings is the equivalent of spontaneity—is eliminated. And all this in turn arises from—or, better, goes along with—the delusion of the omnipotence (not simply the lust for power) of the individual man. If man qua man were omnipotent, then there is in fact no reason why men in the plural should exist at all. [79]

We may read her concern for "the one" as a concern for what must arise from the presumption that individuals are isolated, self-contained subjects who stand in an indifferent and distant relation to the world. Yet, in the next lines she makes clear, not just why this presumption is problematic, but why philosophical thinking has found itself unable to see its own vulnerability to this presumption. She says:

> I suspect that philosophy is not altogether innocent in this fine how-do-you-do. Not, of course, in the sense that Hitler had anything to do with Plato. . . . Instead, perhaps in the sense that western philosophy has never had a clear concept of what constitutes the political, and couldn't have one, because, by necessity, it spoke of man the individual and dealt with the fact of plurality tangentially. [80]

In view of this, Arendt insists that if we are to understand the pitfalls of modernity we must turn not to the history of being, as Heidegger did, but rather to the history of the political. In so doing, we find that Heidegger's project may be located at the extreme end of a history of error in Western thought, which she believes has yet to deal with the fact of human plurality, a fact that is intimately bound up with the political sphere of human existence. In what follows, I will consider how Arendt develops this history through her account of the transformation of the idea of freedom from a political phenomenon to a property of thought or the will. In so doing, we shall see that she interprets the isolated modern subject not as a symptom of the forgetfulness of being, but instead as a symptom of the loss of the political sphere of human existence in the modern age.

NOTES

1. Jill Stauffer, *Ethical Loneliness: The Injustice of Not Being Heard* (New York: Columbia University Press, 2015), 1.

2. Hannah Arendt, *The Origins of Totalitarianism* (New York: Harcourt Inc., 1974), 477.

3. Jacques Taminiaux, *The Thracian Maid and the Professional Thinker: Arendt and Heidegger*, trans. Michael Gendre (Albany: SUNY Press, 1997), 4.

4. Ibid., 5. See also Martin Heidegger, *Plato's Sophist*, trans. Richard Rojcewicz and Andre Schuwer (Bloomington: Indiana University Press, 1997), 22.

5. Heidegger, *Plato's Sophist*, 23.

6. Richard Polt, *Heidegger: An Introduction* (New York: Routledge, 1999), 79.

7. Arendt arrived in Margbug in the fall of 1924 immediately after Heidegger had given his summer semester lecture course on the basic concepts of Aristotelian philosophy. Heidegger's lectures on Aristotle in that course, as well as in the 1924–1925 lecture course, *Plato's* Sophist, proved decisive, not only for his development of *Being and Time* but also for Arendt's political appropriation of his work. See Taminiaux, 3. See also Elizabeth Young-Bruehl, *Hannah Arendt: For Love of the World*, second edition (New Haven: Yale University Press, 2004), 44.

8. See Dana Villa, *Arendt and Heidegger: The Fate of the Political* (Princeton: Princeton University Press, 1995), 212–213.

9. See Dana Villa, *Politics, Philosophy, Terror: Essays on the Thought of Hannah Arendt* (Princeton: Princeton University Press, 1999), 67. Arendt offers this criticism of Heidegger in her essay "What Is Existential Philosophy?" in *Essays in Understanding 1930–1954: Formation, Exile and Totalitarianism* (New York: Random House, Inc., 1994): 176–181.

10. Roy Tsao, "Arendt's Augustine," in *Politics in Dark Times: Encounters with Hannah Arendt*, ed. Seyla Benhabib (New York: Cambridge University Press, 2008): 39–57, 40.

11. Ibid., 42.

12. See Young-Bruehl, 76. While scholars have turned to *Love and Saint Augustine* to develop Arendt's conception of "amor mundi" or love of the world, this text is often taken to mark the beginning of a radical departure from Heidegger's project of fundamental ontology. One aim of this chapter is to shift the orientation of these debates by suggesting that Arendt does not abandon Heidegger's project in this early work, but recognizes, perhaps more fully than he does, the stakes of his project for understanding our communal relations and responsibilities. For recent works on *Love and Saint Augustine*, see Lucy Tatmen, "Arendt and Augustine: One More Kind of Love," *Sophia*, 52.4 (2013): 625–635; Siobhan Kattago, "Why the World Matters: Hannah Arendt's Philosophy of New Beginnings," *The European Paradigm: Toward New Paradigms*, 18.2 (2013): 170–184; Antonio Calcagno, "The Role of Forgetting in Our Experience of Time: Augustine of Hippo and Hannah Arendt," *Parrhesia*, 13 (2011): 14–27; and Barry Clark and Lawrence Quill, "Augustine, Arendt, and Anthropy," *Sophia*, 48.3 (2010): 253–265.

13. See Hannah Arendt, *Der Liebesbegriff bei Augustin: Versuch einer philosophischen Interpretation* [1929], ed. Ludger Lütkehaus (Berlin: Philo, 2003), and Hannah Arendt, *Love and Saint Augustine*, ed. Joanna Vecchiarelli Scott and Judith Chelius Stark (Chicago: Chicago University Press, 1996). It is impor-

tant to note that the English translation of Arendt's dissertation, *Love and Saint Augustine*, is not a direct translation of her original 1929 dissertation *Der Liebesbegriff bei Augustin*, but is instead based on an unfinished revision of her dissertation that she translated into English in the early 1960s. Though the spirit of the original is retained, there are especially interesting changes that reflect Arendt's mature thought in works such as *The Origins of Totalitarianism* and *The Human Condition*, particularly with respect to the concept of natality. For more on the differences between the two versions of her dissertation, see Stephan Kampowski, *Arendt, Augustine, and the New Beginning: The Action Theory and Moral Thought of Hannah Arendt in Light of Her Dissertation on St. Augustine* (Grand Rapids: Eerdmans, 2008), 13–24. See also Roy Tsao, "Arendt's Augustine," in *Politics in Dark Times: Encounters with Hannah Arendt*, ed. Seyla Benhabib (New York: Cambridge University Press, 2008): 39–57, 41.

14. Arendt, *Love and Saint Augustine*, 58, 264–269.

15. Hannah Arendt, "What Remains? The Language Remains," in *Essays in Understanding, 1930–1954: Formation, Exile, and Totalitarianism*, ed. Jerome Kohn (New York: Schocken Books): 1–23, 4.

16. Ibid., 10–11.

17. Ibid., 4–5.

18. Hannah Arendt, "What Is Existential Philosophy?" in *Essays in Understanding 1930–1954: Formation, Exile and Totalitarianism* (New York: Random House, Inc., 1994): 176–181, 181.

19. Arendt, "What Is Existential Philosophy?" 179.

20. Ibid.

21. Ibid., 181.

22. Ibid., 179.

23. Ibid., 181.

24. Ibid.

25. Ibid.

26. Hannah Arendt, "On the Nature of Totalitarianism: An Essay in Understanding," in *Essays in Understanding 1930–1954: Formation, Exile, and Totalitarianism*, ed. Jerome Kohn (New York: Schocken Books, 1994): 328–360, 358. See also Hannah Arendt, *The Origins of Totalitarianism*, 471.

27. Hannah Arendt and Martin Heidegger, *Letters 1925–1975*, ed. Ursula Ludz (Orlando: Harcourt, 2004): 123–124. See also Ronald Beiner, "The Presence of Art and the Absence of Heidegger," *Arendt Studies*, 2 (2018): 9–15, 9.

28. See Beiner, "The Presence of Art and the Absence of Heidegger," 9–15, 9.

29. Hannah Arendt, *The Human Condition* (Chicago: University of Chicago Press, 1998), 1.

30. Ibid., 2.

31. Ibid., 3.

32. Ibid.

33. Ibid., 4.

34. Ibid., 3.

35. Ibid.

36. Ibid., 4.

37. Ibid.
38. Ibid.
39. Ibid.
40. Ibid.
41. Ibid.
42. Ibid., 4–5.
43. Ibid., 5.
44. Ibid.
45. Ibid., 7.
46. Ibid.
47. Ibid.
48. Ibid., 8.
49. Ibid., 9
50. Ibid., 8.
51. See Jeffrey Andrew Barash, "Martin Heidegger, Hannah Arendt, and the Politics of Remembrance," *International Journal of Philosophical Studies*, 10.2 (2002): 171–182, 178.
52. Arendt, *The Human Condition*, 178.
53. Ibid., 177.
54. Ibid.
55. Ibid., 178.
56. Arendt, *The Human Condition*, 9.
57. Ibid., 9.
58. Ibid., 7.
59. Ibid., 188.
60. Ibid., 8.
61. Ibid., 178.
62. Ibid., 180.
63. Ibid., 179.
64. Ibid.
65. Ibid., 176.
66. Ibid., 177.
67. Ibid., 247.
68. Hannah Arendt, "What Is Freedom?" in *Between Past and Future*, ed. Jerome Kohn (New York: Penguin Books, 2006): 142–169, 145.
69. Arendt, *The Human Condition*, 178.
70. Ibid., 198–199.
71. Ibid., 178.
72. Ibid.
73. Ibid., 198.
74. Heidegger, *Being and Time*, 139.
75. Villa, *Arendt and Heidegger*, 139.
76. Arendt, "Concern with Politics in Recent European Thought," in *Essays in Understanding 1930–1954: Formation, Exile, and Totalitarianism*, 432.
77. Ibid., 430.

78. Ibid.
79. Arendt to Jaspers, March 4, 1951, in *Hannah Arendt, Karl Jaspers: Correspondence, 1926–1969*, ed. Lotte Kohler and Hans Saner, trans. Robert and Rita Kimber (New York: Harcourt Brace & Company, 1992): 504–505, 165.
80. Ibid., 166.

4

Loneliness and Liberty: Arendt's Critique of Liberal Subjectivity

Arendt departs from Heidegger in her suggestion that the political must be held open if human beings are to appear together in their freedom of possibility. The public realm, she explains, illuminates the affairs of human beings, enabling them to appear in the fullness of their humanity through speech and action. In so doing, the political creates a space for individuals to come together in order to appropriate the world anew and disclose new ways of seeing. Beyond this, she takes the political to constitute the ground for the possibility of authentic communal life, a space in which human beings become visible to one another in their singularity, without demanding of this singularity that it alienate itself from the relations that constitute it. In this, Arendt deepens and challenges Heidegger's own response to the peculiar loneliness of the they-self, putting into relief the ways in which the political might work against this experience.

And yet, as significant as Arendt takes this sphere of human existence to be, she is clear that the political is precisely what has been lost in the modern era. Arendt treats this loss as a symptom of the emphasis within the liberal tradition on the expansion of rights and liberties in the private sphere and the elevation of the security of these rights to the paramount aim of politics. Though Arendt takes it to be a pillar of all civilized governments to protect the private rights and liberties of individual citizens, she argues that the liberal political tradition has transformed this into the *sole* concern of politics, enabling the necessity that drives "the pursuit of 'enlightened' self-interest" and national investment in the expansion of these interests, to rule supreme.[1] In Arendt's view, the liberal credo that freedom begins where politics ends has thus had a devastating effect; it has destroyed the space of appearance, leaving behind lonely, atomized individuals, who, though pressed together into a great mass, nevertheless remain hidden, unable to appear to one another in the fullness of their humanity.

Arendt, in much the same way as figures like Nancy, takes seriously Heidegger's claim that the world and others are never at the margins but are instead always already conditioning of who we are. With this, however, she also suggests that despite Heidegger's decisive intervention in modern notions of subjectivity, he nevertheless fails to realize the political significance of the peculiar loneliness that he makes visible through his analysis of the they-self. It is in consequence of this, Arendt argues, that Heidegger is unable to thematize adequately a notion of being-with that is neither alienating of Dasein's relations nor reductive of its singularity.

By reinterpreting the modern subject in a political register, Arendt thus adds an important dimension to this critique. Whereas Heidegger attributes the ascendance of such notions of subjectivity to the forgetfulness of being, Arendt argues that this ascendance is instead a consequence of the fact that "the more pertinent questions . . . such as, What is politics? Who is man as a political being? What is freedom?—seem to have been forgotten altogether."[2] Arendt interprets the modern conception of subjectivity as a consequence of the forgetfulness of the political—which is to say, the forgetfulness of the plural—something that she believes the tradition of Western metaphysics has never been able to comprehend. Hence, rather than turning to the history of being, as Heidegger does, Arendt turns to the history of the political, and specifically, the history of the idea of freedom, to confront what modernity seems to have forgotten, namely, that "men, not Man, live on the earth and inhabit a world."[3]

In this chapter, I will develop Arendt's account of this history, which comes into view in her analysis of the transformation of the idea of freedom from a political phenomenon to a property of thought or the will. Originally conceived as something that only pertained to political life, Arendt maintains that freedom was thought in the classical world to appear when human beings left behind the necessities of their private lives in order to care for something larger than themselves, namely, the world. Understood as an activity that was accomplished with and through others in the space of politics, Arendt suggests that freedom was believed to arise when individuals acted in concert in order to introduce new meaning to the world. It was not until late-antiquity, she explains, with the fall of the Roman Empire and the decline of the political sphere, that freedom retreated inward to become a property of thought or the will. Though she believes that it has become axiomatic in the modern age to identify freedom with one's inalienable rights and liberties in the private sphere, Arendt turns to the history of Western politics to suggest that this presumption is by no means self-evident. On the contrary, it is a consequence of the loss of the political, or the destruction of those spaces that make it possible for human beings to appear in their freedom as creatures who, in virtue of their natality and plurality, are capable of intervening in the necessity that governs ordinary life.

In view of this, I argue that for Arendt, the peculiar loneliness of the current age cannot be thought apart from this loss. She suggests that the elevation of the security of one's private rights and liberties to the highest political ideal epitomizes this loss, leaving human beings atomized and hidden from one another even as they find themselves hyperbolically interconnected through the advances of modern science and technology. Arendt is clear that this transformation of the idea of freedom from a political phenomenon to an inner property of the will renders the concept of freedom itself meaningless. The consequences of this, she argues, were no more apparent than in the paradox of the Rights of Man, or those supposedly inalienable rights that were thought to justify the existence of the nation-state, that came to appear with the rise of stateless people in the period between the world wars. Upon being stripped of their citizenship and left without recourse to a space in which their actions could be effective and their opinions significant, Arendt argues that masses of stateless people were exposed to unforeseen spaces of rightlessness and dehumanization. This space of rightlessness uncovered the vacuity of enlightened liberal notions of freedom, revealing that these rights were indeed alienable and that there was nothing sacred in the bare fact of being human.

Arendt's analysis of statelessness may therefore be interpreted as the culmination of a long history of error in Western thought. In view of this, I wish to suggest that we find, on the one hand, that

Arendt's reading of statelessness can perhaps be understood as a highly refined form of the peculiar loneliness of the current age, a loneliness that is symptomatic of the very presumptions of the liberal tradition that are meant to promise universal emancipation. That is to say, the phenomenon of statelessness epitomizes one especially radical form of the loneliness of liberal subjectivity. As we shall see in the chapters that follow, however, statelessness is only one side of this history of error in Western political thought. On the other hand, Arendt suggests that the loneliness that has been produced by the notion of freedom inherited from the liberal tradition and the forms of subjectivity that this entails, in turn, renders even those endowed with the full rights of liberal citizenship hidden and atomized. Left without recourse to any sense of community or belonging, Arendt thus argues that human beings become willing to surrender their humanity to the delusional fellowship promised by totalitarianism. In view of this, we find that not only statelessness but also its photographic negative in the rise of European totalitarianism may be understood as the culmination of this history of error and an equally refined form of the peculiar loneliness of the current age. In both cases, Arendt suggests that this peculiar loneliness is a symptom, not of the forgetfulness of being, but rather of the forgetfulness of the political. Therefore, in order to envision new possibilities for communal life from out of the peculiar loneliness of the current age, Arendt argues that we must undertake a destruction, not of the history of being, but rather of the history of the political, so that we might think the possibilities for communal life in ways that do not fall prey to this history of error.

FROM POLITICAL FREEDOM TO PRIVATE LIBERTY

In order to undertake this destruction of the history of the political, Arendt suggests that we must return to antiquity to recover a more originary notion of freedom, one that is oriented by our embeddedness in the world and the relations that constitute it. In so doing, Arendt not only attempts to think the concept of freedom anew but also to recover a more originary notion of communal life that is responsive to the peculiar loneliness of the current age. Though Arendt's appeal to the Greek *polis* and the Roman *res publica* to uncover this more originary notion of freedom is sometimes regarded as nostalgic, and even Eurocentric, I wish to suggest that this is perhaps better understood as a critical appropriation of Heidegger's destruction of the history of Western metaphysics.[4] In a move that deepens and challenges Heidegger's critique of the forgetfulness of being in the modern age, we might interpret Arendt as attempting to account more fully for the origins of the peculiar loneliness that he makes visible in *Being and Time* in order to open new paths to thinking being-with authentically.

In her 1961 text "What Is Freedom?" Arendt locates the origins of the modern political sphere in late-antiquity and early Christianity, when the idea of freedom began to retreat from the world. She focuses especially on Epictetus and Augustine, who, in the face of the rise and fall of the Roman Empire, found it necessary to discover within themselves a freedom that remained untouched by the violence and decadence of the world. Whereas freedom was understood prior to this decline as a distinctly political phenomenon, making its appearance in the world through speech and action in the public sphere, Arendt argues that stoic and especially Christian notions of freedom withdrew into the self, making freedom a metaphysical question rather than a political question for the first time. No longer understood as a worldly phenomenon, freedom within this framework was achieved through a retreat from the world and the temptations contained therein. The world thus became an impediment to freedom rather than the stage for its appearance. Marking a drastic shift from political notions of freedom characteristic of classical Greek and Roman political life, this notion of freedom becomes foundational for the modern age, making freedom an internal and fixed property of the human being rather than an activity that comes to appear in the world by speaking and acting with others in the space of politics.

It is important to note that Arendt has a notoriously conflicted relation to the modern political tradition. As Seyla Benhabib has argued, Arendt rarely takes a definitive stance on the question of whether the political structures that organize Western liberal democracies can be rehabilitated in the wake of the political catastrophes of the twentieth century.[5] This tension, to be sure, remains unresolved throughout Arendt's thought, leading her at once to praise the emancipatory ideals of the Enlightenment, while, at the same time, locating the seeds of totalitarianism in the very structures on which these ideals are based. Yet, while many, including Benhabib, have been led from this tension to deemphasize Arendt's critical relation to the liberal political tradition, I maintain that this critique warrants greater attention if we are to understand her analysis of the political catastrophes of the early twentieth century, no less than her distinctive critical appropriation of Heidegger. Though Arendt may praise aspects of the modern political tradition, one aspect of it that she consistently challenges is its emphasis on the ideal of liberty. Arendt is clear that the transformation of the idea of freedom from a political phenomenon into the liberty to pursue one's private self-interest as far as possible has had "fatal consequences" for the current age.[6]

Arendt maintains that the idea of liberty is neither new nor distinctively modern. Rather, she explains that it has been central to the development of Western political theory since classical antiquity.[7] The concept of liberty found its original formulation in ancient Greece where the power of locomotion was taken to be the most important civil right, just as it is in the modern world.[8] From its inception, then, liberty has been defined in terms of the individual's liberation from unjustified restraint, consisting above all in the freedom of movement, or the freedom to undertake those activities that are necessary for living in general.[9] Yet, while securing the basic necessities of life has been understood throughout the tradition of Western political thought to form a necessary condition for freedom, liberty in the ancient Greek world was neither identical to nor sufficient for engendering freedom.[10] Such a presumption is distinctively modern, and thus, Arendt explains, the modern age distinguishes itself not so much in the significance it attributes to liberty, but rather in the identity it establishes between liberty and freedom.

Arendt argues that in the classical world, liberty and freedom, though intimately related, nevertheless pertained to two distinct realms of human affairs. Liberty concerned the freedom to satisfy the basic necessities of life through the maintenance of one's home (*oikia*) and thus pertained to the household or private realm. The life of the household realm occupied a distinct space in relation to a second, higher form of life, the *bios politikos*, which, she says, came into existence with the Greek city-state and denoted the kind of life most proper to the human being.[11] As Arendt explains, "The distinctive trait of the household sphere was that in it men lived together because they were driven by their wants and needs."[12] While having the liberty to rule as one wished in the privacy of one's home was taken to be a basic condition for citizenship, liberty itself was not identified with freedom in antiquity, as it permitted nothing more than the fulfillment of those life processes that are governed by necessity. Freedom, on the other hand, was believed to be an eruptive event that gave birth to something new in the world, thereby initiating a break from the necessary processes that characterize life in general. As Arendt says, "The realm of the *polis* . . . was the sphere of freedom, and if there was a relationship between these two spheres, it was a matter of course that the mastering of the necessities of life in the household was the condition for freedom of the *polis*."[13] Whereas the effects of liberty remained hidden away in the private realm of everyday life, freedom required a public realm where individuals, having already satisfied the basic necessities of life, could come together with their fellow citizens to engage in the task of politics.

In their capacity as citizens, individuals cast aside their concern for their particular existence in the household realm, joining together in the public realm for the sake of carrying a common world from the past into the future.[14] No longer concerned with satisfying their basic needs, individuals entered into the public realm in order to engage in a higher kind of life, namely, political life, which was distinctively human insofar as it created the conditions under which freedom could appear. By participating in political life, individuals worked together to preserve a space of human meaning that transcended the necessity of ordinary life, reminding them that their existence was not futile because they belonged to and were responsible for a world that had existed before them and that would outlast their lives in it.[15]

Arendt thus argues that in classical antiquity, freedom was thought to be a worldly phenomenon that made its appearance when individuals came together through speech and action to initiate something new. Accordingly, she says, "Freedom needed, in addition to mere liberation, the company of other men who were in the same state, and it needed a common public space to meet them—a politically organized world, into which each of the free men could insert himself by word and deed."[16] Whereas one's household life was taken to have little meaning beyond satisfying one's biological needs, *polis*-life, she argues, promised transcendence, providing human beings who had liberated themselves from the necessities of everyday life with the opportunity to actualize their freedom by acting in concert with others to initiate something new in the world.

Whereas the Greeks believed that freedom was a political phenomenon, Arendt says that in the modern age, "It has become almost axiomatic even in political theory to understand freedom not as a political phenomenon, but on the contrary, as the more or less free range of non-political activities which a given body politic will permit and guarantee to those who constitute it."[17] Arendt argues that the displacement of freedom from the political realm has transformed the structure of politics altogether, making liberty the chief political ideal in the modern era and the protection of the rights of individuals in private life the paramount aim of politics.

While this non-political notion of freedom has become the centerpiece of modern political theory, Arendt explains that its origins are in fact pre-modern, finding their earliest manifestations in late antiquity and early-Christianity. Arendt turns to Epictetus and Augustine to illustrate this, both of whom, she argues, attempt to elevate "inner freedom," or freedom of thought and the will to the highest kind of human freedom. In so doing, each reverses the predominant assumption of classical antiquity that "the experiences of inner freedom are derivative in that they always presuppose a retreat from the world."[18]

Epictetus, she explains, interprets freedom as something that is manifest neither in the accumulation of worldly possessions nor in one's mastery over other men, as these sorts of things reside in the exterior world over which we have no control. Instead, Epictetus suggests that freedom arises when we limit ourselves to what is within our control, namely, our thoughts and dispositions toward the world in which we find ourselves.[19] As Arendt explains,

> According to ancient understanding, man could liberate himself from necessity only through power over other men, and he could be free only if he owned a place, a home in the world. Epictetus transposed these worldly relationships into relationships within man's own self, whereby he discovered that no power is so absolute as that which man yields over himself, and that inward space where man struggles and subdues himself is more entirely his own, namely, more securely shielded from outside interference, than any worldly home could ever be.[20]

Epictetus thus introduces a notion of freedom that could be realized through a retreat into the internal domain of thought where it becomes possible to master one's desires and judgments, or those states that seem to be untouched by the exterior world.

Like Epictetus, Arendt argues, Augustine similarly divorces freedom from the world, insisting that human beings are powerless to influence their surrounding environment and powerful only insofar as they are the arbiters of their will.[21] While Arendt is taken in her early writings by Augustine's notion of love, she nevertheless problematizes this idea of freedom and its pervasive influence on early Christian thinking. Understood in terms of the free choice of the will, Augustine's conception of freedom arises only when one retreats into "the 'inner dwelling' of the soul and the dark 'chamber of the heart,'" a space permanently protected from the coercion of bodily desire.[22]

In tying freedom to the will, Arendt argues that the early Christian tradition sought to distance freedom from the contingencies of the world, transforming it in ways that proved decisive for the modern tradition. No longer a political concept, freedom became something "other-wordly" such that it was thought not to effect change in the world, but rather to liberate us from it.[23] Such a notion of freedom, Arendt argues, is most fully realized in solitude, never appearing in the phenomenal world but instead remaining hidden in the interior dwelling of the soul.[24] In identifying freedom with the capacity of the will, Arendt maintains that the early Christian tradition simultaneously divorced freedom from action; in suggesting that the exercise of free will is possible only in solitude, freedom comes to be associated with the ability to prohibit oneself from giving into the temptations of the exterior world. This, Arendt argues, had a paralyzing effect, giving birth to a notion of freedom that inhibited action by creating a conflict between the willing and performing self.[25]

While this way of conceiving of freedom is undoubtedly formative for the tradition of Western metaphysics, providing the basis for Descartes's epistemology and the representational problematic it creates for thinkers from Kant to Husserl, Arendt believes that its most dramatic consequences are felt in the context of politics.[26] She argues that neither Epictetus nor Augustine were especially concerned with applying their respective conceptions of freedom to the political. Rather, working against the backdrop of a decaying and hostile political realm, both wished to establish a new ground for human freedom in a world in which political life was in decline.[27] For this reason, Arendt says, "Neither the philosophical conception of freedom as it first arose in late antiquity, when freedom became a phenomenon of thought by which man could, as it were, reason himself out of the world, nor the Christian and modern notion of free will has any ground in political experience."[28] And yet, it is precisely this notion of freedom that ultimately took center stage in politics at the beginning of the seventeenth century, transforming freedom into self-liberation and security into the highest political ideal.

LIBERTY AND THE POLITICAL EMANCIPATION OF THE BOURGEOISIE

In much the same way as their pre-modern counterparts, Arendt explains that political theorists in the modern age do carry on the tradition of distrusting the world around them. Yet, unlike Augustine and Epictetus, Arendt suggests that these modern thinkers ultimately reformulate the task of politics in terms of this distrust. In so doing, she argues that they are led to suggest that politics consists in guaranteeing freedom from political life, or freedom from the unjustified restraint of government.[29] A new political infrastructure thus emerges in the modern age, predicated above all on the idea that "freedom begins where politics ends."[30] With this transformation in the idea of freedom, Arendt argues that the political ceases to constitute a space where freedom can appear and instead becomes a mechanism for ensuring the security of private liberties. "Security," she says, "made freedom possible, and the word 'freedom' designated a quintessence of activities which occurred outside the political realm."[31]

Arendt takes Thomas Hobbes to be the most emblematic thinker for understanding the birth of the modern political tradition, introducing a framework for government organized according to the delegation of power rather than political rights. In taking the purpose of the political to consist in providing conditional protection from being killed in exchange for absolute obedience, Hobbes conceives of the law and government in terms of security rather than freedom. While Hobbes no doubt championed absolutism and monarchical government, Arendt suggests that he nevertheless lays the theoretical foundations for the rise of bourgeois liberalism, giving clearer articulation to the structures of liberal politics than any other modern political theorist.

Hobbes, she explains, is the only political theorist who does not insist that the state of nature has its basis in divine law or natural law and, furthermore, dismisses the idea that it provides the ground for a social contract. Instead, Hobbes conceives of the state of nature in such a way that the law can only be understood in terms of individual interests themselves. For this reason, Arendt argues, Hobbes, even more than figures like Locke or Smith, is "the only great philosopher to whom the bourgeoisie can rightly and exclusively lay claim."[32] In identifying the task of politics with security rather than action, Arendt explains that political theory in the modern age, taking its point of departure from Hobbes, transformed government into "the appointed protector not so much of freedom as of the life process, the interests of society and its individuals."[33] Therefore, upon divorcing freedom from the political, the realm of politics that had once served to contravene the automatic processes that characterize life in general, became a vehicle for upholding and guaranteeing them.

In order to demonstrate how this internal, stoic-Christian notion of freedom entered the political structures that organize Western liberal democracies, Arendt turns to what she describes as the political emancipation of the bourgeoisie beginning in the seventeenth century.[34] It was the ascendance of this group of otherwise politically neutral capitalists to political power that brought the ideal of liberty to bear on the structures of modern government. It was also this group, she argues, that revealed the political dangers of the seemingly emancipatory ideals of classical liberalism. Operating according to the principle of enlightened self-interest, Arendt explains that the bourgeoisie saw that it had to obey the law of expansion inherent in capitalist production. This, in turn, made clear that it was necessary to impose this law on the structure of the political so as to foster economic growth beyond national borders.[35] For this reason, Arendt says, national governments began transforming in the seventeenth century, making expansion the principal aim of all foreign policy.[36] As the capitalist interests of the bourgeoisie became increasingly intertwined with the affairs of national governments, these governments became increasingly concerned with exporting mechanisms of power and violence abroad for the sake of dominating foreign peoples and resources. The law thus became a vehicle for protecting national governments' stake in the wealth that these enterprises generated rather than something that served to support and ensure the continuation of the political realm.

Arendt argues that as business interests and politics coalesced, private life was raised to the "one publicly honored political principle."[37] The body politic that had once served to defend itself and its citizens against the recklessness that prevailed in the private realm became a national government concerned with maintaining its imperial enterprises and protecting the private interests of those living outside its national borders.[38] As Arendt explains, the outcome of this imperial enterprise was "the destruction of all living communities, those of the conquered people as well as of the people at home. . . . Power became the essence of political action and the center of political thought when it was separated from the political community which it should serve."[39] Through imperial expansion, the interests of the bourgeoisie generated a new kind of government, one that promised security but not political rights, serving above all to preserve those automatic life processes associated with the private realm.[40] No longer guided by a concern for political freedom, the public realm where individuals "could show who they really and interchangeably were" became increasingly hidden, enabling national governments guided by the interests of the bourgeoisie to demand obedience and blind conformism with regard to political affairs.[41] Arendt thus argues that the notion of selfhood and political subjectivity that these structures produced could be characterized by worldlessness. Arendt says:

> Deprived of political rights, the individual, to whom public and official life manifests itself in the guise of necessity, acquires a new and increased interest in private life and his personal fate. Excluded from participation in the management of public affairs that involve all citizens, the individual loses his rightful place in society and his natural connection with his fellow men.[42]

Even at this early stage, Arendt draws our attention to the emergence of a peculiar loneliness. While we might expect this expansion of national interest and wealth to generate greater connection and opportunity for belonging, Arendt is clear that it did not. Quite to the contrary, it generated the loss of a sense of having a place in one's society and the destruction of one's natural connection with others.

Arendt explains that this over-accumulation of capital and power reached its height by the beginning of the twentieth century once local political communities had been transformed into states governed by unprincipled power politics. As expansion became an automatic and seemingly unending process, these so-called national governments simultaneously produced mobs whose actions were guided not by political principles such as freedom and equality, but rather by blind submission to the project of imperialism.[43] By the late nineteenth and early twentieth centuries, Arendt explains that these mobs were fueled by racist propaganda that served to justify expansion, which she describes as "the main ideological weapon of imperialist politics."[44] While the liberal tradition grounded its promise of universal emancipation in liberty, elevating it to the highest political ideal, she suggests that this ultimately gave rise to a political structure that made freeing oneself from the automation of the life processes impossible.

Arendt is clear that while a bright line must be drawn between the period of European imperial expansion and the era of the concentration camps, the bureaucratic political infrastructure of European imperialism, one ultimately built on power, obedience, and necessity, set the stage for the political catastrophes that unfolded in Europe at the beginning of the twentieth century.[45] By considering Arendt's analysis of the transformation of the notions of freedom and liberty throughout the history of the Western political tradition, we find that she discovers a contradiction internal to the tradition of enlightened liberalism that culminates in crisis after World War I. In the effort to liberate human beings from the constraints of government, the liberal political structures of modern life ultimately produced and reinforced the existence of atomized and isolated subjects who had no place to appear in the world. Arendt's prescient analysis of the rise of stateless people in the period between the world wars, and her critique in light of this of the eighteenth-century declarations of the Rights of Man for failing to protect those who found themselves without any community to protect them, brings the dangers and limits of liberal conceptions of freedom into focus.

As we have seen, Arendt believes that we should not take for granted the presumption in the modern liberal political tradition that liberty is the highest aim of politics. In her view, this presumption, though taken to promise universal emancipation, is in fact a symptom of the decay of the political sphere of our lives, or that space in which we can appear to one another, not as reproducible entities, but as irreducibly unique and capable of acting against the overwhelming odds of statistical law and probability.[46] In emphasizing the expansion of rights and liberties in the private sphere, Arendt argues the liberal political structures that organize modern life reinforce the destruction of the political sphere and the possibility for freedom. With this, she argues that it has transformed human beings into isolated, atomized, and superfluous subjects who are unable to appear to one another in the fullness of their humanity.

FATAL CONSEQUENCES: LIBERTY AND STATELESSNESS

Arendt explains that the consequences of the elevation of liberty to the highest aim of politics come into view perhaps most clearly in the rise of stateless people in the period between the world wars. In turning to Arendt's prescient critique of the eighteenth-century Rights of Man and their failure to protect stateless people against all manners of dehumanization, we find that she not only brings into focus a contradiction inherent in the structure of the nation-state but also identifies the worldlessness of the forms of subjectivity that have been produced and sustained by the liberal political structures that organize modern life. In this, it becomes clear that her analysis of statelessness, in much the same way as her critique of Heidegger, may be situated at the extreme end of a history of error in Western political thought, one that has failed to thematize adequately human plurality and that has, in turn, given rise to the presumption that human beings are isolated, self-contained entities who stand at a distant and indifferent relation to the world.

In her account of the rightlessness of stateless people in *The Origins of Totalitarianism*, Arendt suggests that the phenomenon of statelessness ultimately revealed a contradiction inherent in the structure of the nation-state that turned on its inability to make good on the Enlightenment promise of universal emancipation. The eighteenth-century formulations of the Rights of Man promised this emancipation on the grounds that all people were born with inalienable rights that required no special law to guarantee them. That is, rather than being guaranteed by God or a king, the Rights of Man were taken to be guaranteed by man himself, who, in his sacredness, was believed to be enough to provide an unshakable foundation for their legitimacy. The concept of inalienable rights thus promised to protect humanity as a whole rather than particular individuals or groups.[47] The Rights of Man also presupposed that the individual did not need a place in the world in order for her fundamental human rights to be protected. Arendt says, "The Rights of Man, after all, had been defined as 'inalienable' because they were supposed to be independent of all governments," presumed to be guaranteed by nothing more than the bare fact of the human being's existence.[48]

Yet, Arendt explains that in their original formulation, these rights were not meant to protect individuals. Instead, they served to justify the sovereignty of the people who belonged to a particular nation-state. Hence, the rights of the abstract human being envisioned by the eighteenth-century framers of the Declaration of the Rights of Man collapsed into the rights of particular groups who justified their membership in their political communities on the basis of national or ethnic identity. She says:

> No paradox of contemporary politics is filled with a more poignant irony than the discrepancy between the efforts of well-meaning idealists who stubbornly insist on regarding as "inalienable" those human rights, which are enjoyed only by citizens of the most prosperous and civilized countries, and the situation of the rightless themselves.[49]

In providing justification for the sovereignty of peoples, the Rights of Man provided the ground for the rise of European nation-states along with juridical orders that were oriented by the national identity of certain collectives rather than the sacredness of man. Even those governments that derived their legitimacy directly from the Rights of Man discovered in the twentieth century that they had the grounds to justify denationalizing all those who were unfortunate enough "to be born into the wrong kind of race or the wrong kind of class or drafted by the wrong kind of government."[50] Upon being denationalized, stripped of the rights of citizenship and the protection of their own governments, stateless individuals found themselves living outside the pale of the law in a way that had not been seen before World War I. Neither their country of origin nor any other country would extend legal protection to them. Consequently, Arendt explains, stateless people became increasingly subject to the arbitrary force of the police. Masses of stateless people who were no longer citizens of any sovereign state thus emerged at the beginning of the twentieth century whose inalienable rights could not be enforced.[51]

The appearance of stateless people demonstrated that while one's fundamental freedoms were supposed to be guaranteed by the bare fact of being human alone, this promise proved meaningless for those who had lost the rights of citizenship and no longer belonged to a political community that was willing and able to protect them. Arendt says:

> The calamity of the rightless is not that they are deprived of life, liberty and the pursuit of happiness, or of equality before the law and freedom of opinion—formulas which were designed to solve problems *within* given communities—but that they no longer belong to any community whatsoever. . . . There is no question

that those who exist outside the pale of the law may have more freedom of movement than a lawfully imprisoned criminal or that they enjoy more freedom of opinion in the internment camps of democratic countries than they would in any ordinary despotism, not to mention in a totalitarian country. But neither physical safety . . . nor freedom of opinion changes in the least their fundamental situation of rightlessness.[52]

In making visible this space of rightlessness, the emergence of stateless people called into question the inalienability of the right to life, liberty, and happiness, or the notion that such rights exist without being guaranteed by a political community.[53] In other words, Arendt argues, the internal notion of freedom that has its origins in late-antiquity and becomes definitive of politics in the modern age proved inadequate for guaranteeing the rights of those who had been expelled from their political communities. What thus became apparent with the rise of stateless people, she says, is that "the world found nothing sacred in the bare fact of being human."[54] Upon losing their rights to belong to a political community, stateless people found themselves abandoned entirely by all laws and exposed to a space of rightlessness that opened up the unforeseen possibility of complete dehumanization. The appearance of stateless people in the period between the world wars thus clarified the inadequacy of the structure of the European nation-state for achieving the end of universal emancipation set forth by the Enlightenment presumption that human beings have inalienable rights and liberties.

THE LONELINESS OF LIBERAL SUBJECTIVITY

In view of this, we find that Arendt makes clear a paradox internal to the structure of the nation-state and the notion of the inalienable Rights of Man on which it is based. Yet, Arendt's concern for statelessness goes beyond this paradox. It also provides a critical commentary on the history of Western political thought, of which the decline of the nation-state is merely a chapter. By considering her analysis of statelessness in light of the development of the idea of freedom throughout the tradition of Western political thought, we find that statelessness is symptomatic of a broader crisis in Western notions of freedom. Understood as a property of the individual rather than as an event brought to bear on political life by speaking and acting with others, Arendt suggests that freedom has been left in the modern age with no way of appearing in the world. Statelessness offers a powerful illustration of the political danger involved in this, indicating that upon losing one's place in the world or the context of meaning that makes opinions significant and actions effective, one loses the ability to intervene in the necessity and meaninglessness of the automatic life processes. Rather than rising above these necessary processes by enacting one's freedom in the space of politics, human beings who have lost their place in their political communities are instead left entirely exposed to them. It is in consequence of this that human beings become susceptible to being reduced in their unrepeatable uniqueness to interchangeable and expendable parts of the cyclical movements of nature and history. That is to say, this displacement of the idea of freedom from the political sphere to a property of thought or the will has the effect of rendering human beings superfluous.

Through her analysis of statelessness, Arendt thus diagnoses a contradiction internal not only to the nation-state but also to the fundamental assumptions of the Western political tradition. As we have seen, this assumption, which has pre-modern origins, consists in the idea that freedom is an essential, internal, and inalienable property of the human being that is most fully realized through a retreat from the world into the inner domain of thought or the will. On Arendt's view, the emergence of stateless people revealed the fatal consequences of such a concept of freedom, making clear that freedom is meaningful only insofar as it can be actualized in a world with others. For this reason, she insists that freedom requires a space of appearance, calling for critical inquiry into the modern emphasis on securing liberty in the private sphere through a consideration of the political origins of the notion of freedom.

Arendt's analysis of statelessness brings her critical concerns regarding the epoch of the Enlightenment into focus, which helps to elucidate the centrality of the space of appearance for her positive political project. She believes that the internal notion of free will was brought to bear on the political realm in the modern age through the elevation of liberty and the protection of private rights to the highest political ideal. As a result, the infrastructure of the political underwent a fundamental shift in the modern age, no longer constituting a space in which individuals could come together for the sake of rising above the necessities of private life through speech and action in the public realm. Instead, government was transformed into a mechanism for securing the private rights of individuals, a mechanism that is fundamentally antithetical to the spontaneity and unrepeatability of human action. The rise of stateless people at the beginning of the twentieth century exposed a crisis in this understanding of freedom, demonstrating that freedom loses its meaning when individuals are expelled from their political communities and lose the space of appearance. We therefore find through Arendt's analysis of statelessness that the political structures of enlightened liberalism, in having their basis in the assumption that freedom begins where politics ends, leave no space for freedom to appear.

Arendt suggests that it is precisely in virtue of this that in the modern age, necessity, automation, and security have overtaken the space of politics, providing a platform for totalitarian governments to come into existence in the twentieth century. The model of the isolated modern subject on which Heidegger's critique of modernity is based thus takes on new significance in light of Arendt's efforts to account for the history of the Western political sphere. That such a notion of subjectivity could emerge, Arendt thinks, points to the loss of those spaces in which human plurality and natality can appear, which is to say, the loss of the political. As Arendt suggests in her 1951 letter to Jaspers, it is because of this that the history of Western philosophy is concerned above all with the individual, rendering it blind to its own complicity in the destruction of human plurality. For Arendt, Heidegger's own complicity in this path of thinking should therefore come as no surprise. Though he intended to undertake a destruction of the history of Western metaphysics, he fails to conceive of a space for the appearance of human plurality and, because of this, implicates himself in the very tradition that he seeks to overcome. Moreover, he remains blind to the ways in which this notion of subjectivity implicates him in a history of error in the Western political tradition, one that Arendt believes cannot but end in disaster. With this in view, we may read Arendt's critique of Heidegger in terms of her larger critique of the liberal political tradition and the forms of subjectivity that it produces. Moreover, we might consider this as the impetus for her to reformulate the idea of freedom and the task of politics more generally in terms of the space of appearance.[55]

As we have seen, being free for Arendt is a distinctly human capacity that is rooted not in certain inalienable properties but rather in our capacity to introduce new meaning into the world by acting in concert with others. In this, Arendt is clear that freedom is a political phenomenon to the extent that its appearance depends on the world and the plurality that constitutes it. She thus envisions the political as the space for the appearance of human plurality, or the space that enables human beings to act in concert with others while remaining individuated in order to disclose new meaning in the world. Arendt therefore believes that any event of authentic disclosedness will depend on a space existing in the world where individuals can appear together in their radical and irreducible singularity.

By elevating liberty in the private sphere to the highest political ideal, the public realm has been covered over in the modern age, making speech meaningless and action impossible, while leaving us without a means for contravening those automatic life processes that render human beings superfluous. The phenomenon of statelessness signaled a crisis in the epoch of the Enlightenment; it revealed that by divorcing freedom from the world and restructuring the sphere of politics accordingly, liberalism gives way to a political realm that is sustained by the automation of the masses. In response to this crisis, Arendt suggests that it is necessary to recover a more originary conception of political freedom, understood as a worldly phenomenon, in order to provide a means for overcoming the dangers and limits of the liberal political structures that organize contemporary political life.[56]

In what follows, I will turn to Arendt's political interpretation of the phenomenon of loneliness in modern life to clarify the importance of her critical relation to the liberal political tradition, one that brings into focus the possible risks for totalitarianism and populism in the forms of subjectivity that these structures produce. In so doing, we will find that her account of statelessness is not exhaustive of the dangers and limits of modern political life, but is instead symptomatic of the loneliness that she believes characterizes modern mass society. By turning to her diagnosis of the problem of loneliness as it unfolds in her account of the susceptibility of the structures of modern political life to totalitarian domination, I will argue that Arendt poses her notion of the space of appearance as an antidote to this problem. As such, I wish to show that she makes a novel contribution to discourses concerning the possibility for authentic communal life by developing a notion of political agency that forms the basis to critique the loneliness of liberal subjectivity.

NOTES

1. Hannah Arendt, *The Origins of Totalitarianism* (New York: Harcourt Inc., 1974), 145.
2. Hannah Arendt, "Concern for Politics in Recent European Thought," in *Essays in Understanding 1930–1954: Formation, Exile, and Totalitarianism*, ed. Jerome Kohn (New York: Schocken Books, 1994): 428–447, 433.
3. Hannah Arendt, *The Human Condition* (Chicago: University of Chicago Press, 1998), 7.
4. For more on Arendt's engagement with the Greek tradition see Roy T. Tsao, "Arendt against Athens: Rereading *The Human Condition*," *Political Theory* 30.1 (2002): 97–123. It is important to note, too, that Arendt is concerned to think beyond the Greek *polis* in ways that challenge the approach that Heidegger takes to the Greeks through her concern for Latin and the Roman *res publica*. This concern comes into view in her essay, "What Is Authority?" in *Between Past and Future* (New York: Penguin Books, 2006), 91–141. See also Jacques Taminiaux, "Athens and Rome," in *The Cambridge Companion to Hannah Arendt*, ed. Dana Villa (Cambridge: Cambridge University Press, 2000): 166 and Barbara Cassin, *Nostalgia: When Are We Ever at Home?* trans. Pascale-Anne Brault (New York: Fordham University Press, 2016), 75.
5. Seyla Benhabib offers an account of Arendt's conflicted relationship to the modern tradition in *The Reluctant Modernism of Hannah Arendt*, where Benhabib argues that the influence of Heidegger's anti-modernism coupled with Arendt's own experience as a persecuted Jew in the early twentieth century creates a tension that remains largely unresolved throughout her work. See Seyla Benhabib, *The Reluctant Modernism of Hannah Arendt* (New York: Rowman and Littlefield Publishers, Inc., 2000), xxxix.
6. Hannah Arendt, "What Is Freedom?" in *Between Past and Future: Eight Exercises in Political Thought*, ed. Jerome Kohn (New York: Penguin Books, 2006): 143–169, 161. See also Dana Villa, *Arendt and Heidegger: The Fate of the Political* (Princeton: Princeton University Press, 1995), 118.
7. Hannah Arendt, *On Revolution* (New York: Penguin Group, 2001), 29.
8. Ibid., 32.
9. Ibid., 29 and 32.
10. Ibid., 29.
11. Arendt, *The Human Condition*, 24.
12. Ibid., 30.
13. Ibid., 31.
14. Arendt, "What Is Freedom?" 155.
15. Arendt, *On Revolution*, 32. See also Arendt, "What is Freedom?", 155.
16. Arendt, "What Is Freedom?" 147.
17. Arendt, *On Revolution*, 32.
18. Arendt, "What Is Freedom?" 146–147.
19. Ibid., 146.
20. Ibid.
21. Ibid., 156.

22. Ibid., 160.
23. Ibid., 161.
24. Ibid., 143.
25. Ibid., 161.
26. Villa, *Arendt and Heidegger*, 121.
27. Arendt, "What Is Freedom?" 146.
28. Ibid., 155.
29. Ibid., 148.
30. Ibid.
31. Ibid.
32. Hannah Arendt, *The Origins of Totalitarianism* (New York: Harcourt, Inc., 1973), 139.
33. Arendt, "What Is Freedom?" 148–149.
34. She develops this, along with her discussion of Hobbes, in the section on "Imperialism" in *The Origins of Totalitarianism*. See Arendt, *The Origins of Totalitarianism*, 123–156.
35. Arendt, *The Origins of Totalitarianism*, 126.
36. Ibid., 126.
37. Ibid., 139.
38. Ibid.
39. Ibid., 138.
40. Ibid., 141.
41. Arendt, *The Human Condition*, 141.
42. Arendt, *The Origins of Totalitarianism*, 141.
43. Ibid., 143.
44. Ibid., 160.
45. Ibid., 123. There has been much debate about what has come to be known as Arendt's "boomerang thesis" or the idea that Europe's imperial experience in Africa had a direct impact on the rise of totalitarian bureaucracy, though it is beyond the scope of this project to develop that debate here. For an overview of this debate, see Richard King, "Introduction," in *Hannah Arendt and the Uses of History: Imperialism, Nation, Race and Genocide*, ed. Richard King and Dan Stone (New York: Berghahn Books, 2007): 1–20, 3. See also Kathryn T. Gines, *Hannah Arendt and the Negro Question* (Bloomington: Indiana University Press, 2014), 74, and Shiraz Dossa, "Human Status and Politics: Hannah Arendt on the Holocaust," *The Canadian Journal of Political Science*, 13.2 (1980): 309–323, 310.
46. Arendt, *The Origins of Totalitarianism*, 277.
47. Ibid., 297.
48. Ibid.
49. Ibid., 279.
50. Ibid., 295.
51. Ibid., 291–292.
52. Ibid., 295–296.
53. Ibid., 299.
54. Ibid.

55. In his discussion of Arendt's Heideggerian roots, Dana Villa uses the term "worldly phenomenon" to describe the kind of freedom that both figures prioritize in contrast to the more abstract notion of freedom conceived as an attribute of thought or the will that dominated the history of Western metaphysics. See Villa, *Arendt and Heidegger*, 119.

56. Arendt explains in *Between Past and Future* that it is necessary to return to the Greeks not for the sake of erudition but instead because we have lost the ability in the modern age to think of freedom in terms of action, and such a concept of freedom has not been so clearly articulated since antiquity. Given the depravity of the notion of freedom that has become pervasive in modern politics, she suggests that while it is important to leave behind the elitism of the ancient politics, the worldly concept of freedom that arises there should be revisited in the present age. See Arendt, *Between Past and Future*, 163–164.

5
The Politics of Loneliness: Another Origin of Totalitarianism

Arendt diagnoses a crisis in the epoch of the Enlightenment through her analysis of statelessness.[1] On the basis of this analysis, she offers a critical intervention in the tradition of classical liberalism, suggesting that the retreat of freedom from the realm of politics in the modern era, while taken by liberal thinkers to be the ground for universal emancipation, produced the conditions for totalitarianism to emerge in the twentieth century. We find through Arendt's analysis of statelessness that freedom is meaningless for individuals who remain isolated and invisible to one another in their private lives. In order for freedom to become meaningful, it must be brought to bear on the world or the context of meaningful relations in which individuals find themselves. Conceived as an event of appropriation rather than a fixed property of the human being, Arendt thus maintains that freedom requires a space of appearance, or a public realm in which individuals are able to appear to one another in the fullness of their humanity through speech and action. By reformulating the concept of freedom in terms of the space of appearance, Arendt is led to develop a lived and embodied conception of citizenship that is oriented above all by the active participation of individuals in the realm of politics.

The purpose of this chapter is to suggest that Arendt's concern for citizenship in her discourse on statelessness must be read in light of her critique of the concept of liberty and her insights into the dangers of the forms of subjectivity that the liberal political tradition has produced. Arendt's political philosophy has received renewed attention in recent years for the contribution it makes to current debate concerning the global possibilities for democratic citizenship. Yet, the emphasis scholars have placed on Arendt's notion of the right to have rights in order to advance these debates threatens to overshadow the scope and depth of her critical relation to the liberal tradition. My aim in what follows will be to show that Arendt's understanding of citizenship guides a prescient critique of the basic assumptions that underlie notions of citizenship inherited from the tradition of liberal political theory and the forms of subjectivity that they affirm. My argument thereby aims to shift the orientation of these debates in order to bring into renewed focus the decisive role that her concerns regarding liberalism play in her insights into the failures and dangers of modern political life.

To this end, I will turn in this chapter to a central but underappreciated dimension of Arendt's theoretical framework. Whereas Arendt's notion of citizenship and, with it, the right to have rights are often cast in terms of her critique of the failings of the European nation-state that became evident with the rise of stateless people in the period between the world wars, I maintain that her approach to citizenship answers not only to this, but also—and even more fundamentally—to her broader concern for the political stakes of the peculiar loneliness of the current age. Loneliness, she argues, epitomizes the experience of living together in the modern age. Symptomatic of the feeling of no longer belonging to a world, lonely individuals are unable to see themselves or others as who they are in their singularity. Loneliness thus leaves human beings dominated by a sense of worldlessness and superfluity, prepared to surrender their capacity for thinking to the compulsory force of logic that drives totalitarianism.[2]

By developing the problem of loneliness in a political register, we find that Arendt's discussion opens new paths to thinking the possibilities for authentic communal life today. As I will suggest, Arendt is led by her critique of liberal subjectivity to emphasize a rehabilitated notion of citizenship that is responsive to the peculiar loneliness of the current age and the vulnerability this loneliness creates to totalitarianism even among citizens in liberal and allegedly open societies. In this, Arendt's own notion of citizenship provides the basis to critique not only the problem of statelessness and the aporia of human rights, but also received ideas about citizenship that we have inherited from the liberal tradition. As I shall demonstrate, this dimension of Arendt's work puts into relief her view that the emphasis in the liberal tradition on the expansion of rights in the private sphere does not serve to remedy political exclusion, but, quite to the contrary, serves to reproduce the very loneliness that has made modern subjects susceptible to totalitarian domination. Arendt thus insists on a notion of citizenship that involves more than the protection of the right to pursue individual interests in the isolation of private life, aiming instead at drawing lonely liberal subjects out of their hiding and into the full illumination of the public realm. In turning to Arendt's discussion of loneliness, I wish to suggest that scholars who focus on Arendt's notion of rights at the price of her critical relation to the liberal tradition not only put a decisive feature of Arendt's concerns in jeopardy of being overlooked. Beyond this, they also risk misrepresenting an important critical perspective on assumptions of the liberal tradition that may remain operative in their work and, moreover, in the political structures that organize modern life.

FROM STATELESSNESS TO LONELINESS

Arendt's concern for citizenship grows out of her analysis of statelessness in *The Origins of Totalitarianism* and the danger she believes it reveals in denying individuals the right to belong to a political community. As we have seen, Arendt maintains that the space of rightlessness to which stateless people were subjected at the beginning of the twentieth century revealed a paradox internal to the notion of human rights born out of the eighteenth-century declarations of the Rights of Man. Whereas these rights, in their original eighteenth-century formulations, were purported to be inalienable properties of every human individual, the emergence of stateless people demonstrated that such rights could be lost without a political community willing and able to guarantee them.[3] Hence, on the basis of her analysis of the phenomenon of statelessness, Arendt says:

> Not the loss of specific rights, then, but the loss of a community willing and able to guarantee any rights whatsoever, has been the

calamity which has befallen ever-increasing numbers of people. Man, it turns out, can lose all so-called Rights of Man without losing his essential quality as a man, his human dignity. Only the loss of a polity itself expels him from humanity.[4]

In light of this, Arendt argues that rise of stateless people made the world aware of "the existence of the right to have rights (and that means to live in a framework where one is judged by one's actions and opinions) and a right to belong to some kind of organized community."[5] She thus offers what is perhaps her most emphatic statement concerning the importance of citizenship in this text, calling for a new conception of human rights rooted in the "the right to have rights" or the right to be a citizen of some sovereign state.[6]

In emphasizing the centrality of the right to have rights, scholars have focused on whether it is possible to provide rational or normative justification for her suggestion that the right to belong to a political community is a universal human right. Arendt, for her part, remains unresolved in her assessment of the viability of the global institution of human rights, leading scholars to disagree about the extent to which her own political categories are adequate for grounding the universal right to citizenship.[7] Even so, many continue to draw on her notion of the right to have rights as part of their efforts to advance debate concerning the global possibilities for democratic citizenship, interpreting Arendt in the service of expanding the structures of liberal democracy that guide political practice today. Those who approach Arendt this way thus assume that the forms of exclusion epitomized by statelessness are external to our liberal political structures and thereby risk overlooking the critique she develops in her discourse on citizenship regarding the basic assumptions that underlie the liberal tradition.

Seyla Benhabib, for instance, argues that Arendt's account of the right to have rights provides a vital starting point for critically engaging the conception of universal rights that is attached to liberal political practice. She insists, however, that in refusing to embrace a unified concept of human nature, Arendt leaves us without a normative foundation for transforming the right to citizenship into a universal human right.[8] Moreover, Arendt's concern regarding the decline of the public space in the modern era leads her to formulate a conception of politics based on the Greek notions of action and visibility, failing, in turn, to conceive of political life in ways that admit of a more enlightened theory of democratic legitimacy.[9] Benhabib thus argues that as significant as Arendt's critical insights are, they must be supplemented by the work of liberal theorists if we are to find an anchor for them in present day politics. To this end, she considers Arendt alongside figures such as Jürgen Habermas and John Rawls who develop methods for rehabilitating the political categories of the Enlightenment in order to morally and rationally justify the expansion of our liberal political structures.[10]

In contrast to Benhabib, both Peg Birmingham and Serena Parekh believe that it is possible to derive a universal ground for the right to have rights from Arendt's own theoretical framework. While these scholars thereby do important work to demonstrate the internal consistency of Arendt's political categories, their emphases on the question of rights keep Arendt's critical relation to the liberal tradition from coming into full view. Birmingham insists that while Arendt offers a profound indictment of the Rights of Man in drawing attention to their failure to protect stateless people from the death camps, Arendt nevertheless remains a humanist, searching throughout her career for a new principle of humanity to guarantee the right to have rights.[11] Rather than grounding this guarantee in a fixed and pre-political conception of human nature, however, Birmingham argues that Arendt locates it in the human condition of natality.[12] As Birmingham explains, Arendt conceives of natality as the fundamental condition of human existence, marking the singularity of each human being that is given by the fact that we are born into the world anew. In capturing the boundlessness of human action, Birmingham maintains that Arendt's notion of natality provides an ontological foundation for human rights that takes seriously the questions raised by the political disasters of the twentieth century.[13] In this, Birmingham clarifies the importance of Arendt's work for renewing a notion of human rights that is based not on the presumed sacredness of the human being, but rather on the global political responsibility we now have to come to terms with the human capacity for evil.[14]

Though Parekh differs from Birmingham in her angle of approach, she too argues that it is possible to derive a foundation for the right to have rights from Arendt's own political categories. Parekh explains, for instance, that when taken together with her understanding of political action as "love of the world," Arendt's conception of human rights offers a novel means of universally grounding our responsibility to address global injustices such as world poverty.[15] According to Parekh, Arendt achieves this by taking seriously the ethical demands of non-citizens without diminishing the importance of community as a human good, mediating between these seemingly contradictory ends through her account of judgment.[16] By drawing attention to the intervention Arendt makes in the debate between communitarian and cosmopolitan visions of international politics, Parekh, like Birmingham, demonstrates the importance of Arendt's work for rehabilitating a conception of rights that guarantees human solidarity on a global scale.[17]

Whereas these scholars stress the contribution Arendt makes to debates concerning the global expansion of the right to democratic citizenship, more may nevertheless be done to clarify the role that Arendt believes liberal theory and practice play in producing dangerous forms of subjectivity that perpetuate alienation and exclusion. To be sure, their interpretations of Arendt do recognize the ways in which her critique of the nation-state and her analysis of the aporia of human rights can serve to challenge and reshape liberal political practice. Less appreciated, however, is Arendt's discourse on loneliness, which brings into focus the full depth of her critique of the structures of modern liberalism and the forms of citizenship that accompany it. This critique is only tacitly expressed in her analysis of the plight of stateless people. Moreover, Arendt's notion of loneliness and her analysis of statelessness have only been developed in parallel in Arendt studies, and have yet to be considered as interconnected and interdependent concepts in Arendt's thought. In emphasizing the right to have rights and treating it as a stand-alone issue unrelated to the theme of loneliness, I maintain that scholars like Benhabib, Birmingham, and Parekh do not do enough to elucidate Arendt's novel critique of the liberal tradition, one that uncovers the possible risks for totalitarianism and populism in liberal notions of subjectivity. Hence, by shifting the focus of this discourse to loneliness, my aim is to put into relief a dimension of Arendt's political philosophy that has been overshadowed, but that is nevertheless central for capturing the prescience of her insights concerning the dangers and limits of the liberal political structures that organize modern life.

While loneliness is a persistent and orienting theme in Arendt's work, it rarely receives the kind of systematic treatment that is given to her discussion of the right to have rights, often taken instead to be an intriguing but incidental dimension of her broader theoretical framework.[18] I maintain, by contrast, that her account of loneliness is integral for clarifying the stakes involved in the concern for citizenship and political belonging that she expresses in her analysis of statelessness. Beyond this, it brings into focus the political stakes of the peculiar loneliness of the current age, demonstrating how this loneliness can become widespread even among those who have been endowed with the full rights of citizenship in liberal and allegedly open societies.

Arendt's concern for belonging to a political community turns on her view that it is only by working with others in the space of politics to enact our freedom that we renew the meaningfulness of the world, initiating something new in order to save it from the ruinous necessity that ordinarily governs human existence.[19] Political life thus engenders an authentic sense of human belonging; it opens a space in which human beings become visible to one another in their irreducible uniqueness and brings the meaningful reality of a common world into appearance.

Loneliness forms the other side of political belonging, arising when human beings discover that they no longer belong to a world with others who can bring the fullness of their humanity into relief. In this, loneliness can be understood as a symptom of what Arendt describes as worldlessness or world-alienation, which emerges when human beings have been deprived of their political existence and severed from the meaningful nexus of relations that constitute the common world. While much has been said about the existential, psychoanalytic and social dimensions of loneliness, Arendt's political interpretation of this problem puts into relief the dangers of this loneliness for our communal relations and responsibilities. As I shall demonstrate in what follows, Arendt believes that this displacement from the world is dangerous, as it prepares human beings to submit to totalitarian domination. In separating individuals from themselves and the truth of their experience, loneliness shields human beings from the reality of their deeds, enabling them, in turn, to step blindly into the mechanism of terror.

By turning to this aspect of Arendt's work, we find that statelessness is not exhaustive of Arendt's diagnosis of the problem of political exclusion as those who emphasize the right to have rights suggest; on the contrary, statelessness is symptomatic of a broader and more endemic form of exclusion expressed in the loneliness of modern individuals. Through her account of the political loneliness of modern mass society, Arendt demonstrates that totalitarianism cannot be thought apart from the liberal political structures that organize modern life, but must instead be understood as an effect of the worldlessness that these structures have produced. This worldlessness has its basis in the destruction of the public realm in the modern era, a consequence, she thinks, of the tendency to elevate the protection of liberty in the private sphere to the highest aim of politics.[20] To the extent that freedom has come to be understood within this tradition as an inner state of the human being rather than a worldly, political phenomenon, the structures of modern liberalism have kept the meaningfulness inherent in human action from coming into appearance and bringing a common world into view. For this reason, Arendt says, "World-alienation, and not self-alienation as Marx thought, has been the hallmark of the modern age."[21] Hence, rather than augmenting liberal political theory, I maintain that Arendt's concern for citizenship and political belonging in her discourse on statelessness serves as the basis to critique and, in turn, to remedy the loneliness that has been generated by some of the very principles that animate this tradition.

SOLITUDE, ISOLATION, AND LONELINESS

Arendt's understanding of loneliness echoes the work of Heidegger and Jaspers. Like Heidegger, Arendt intends to show through her account of loneliness that contemporary man is afflicted by a peculiar loneliness, having been set adrift by the technical automation of the world rather than brought together with the world and others by these advances. Yet, as we have seen, she is also critical of Heidegger's inability to recognize this peculiar loneliness as symptomatic of the loss of the political sphere in the modern age, which she believes leads him to develop a worldless notion of authenticity that can only be realized in isolation from others.[22] To be sure, Heidegger's existential analytic of Dasein as being-in-the-world seeks to de-center the isolated modern subject and, therefore, cannot be thought apart from Dasein's relation to others. Moreover, because authenticity is a mode of being-in-the-world, Dasein's authentic disclosedness is always bound up with the possibility of authentically being-with.[23] Yet, while Arendt, no less than the figures we have already considered, recognizes the importance of Heidegger's insights into Dasein's native vulnerability to being with others in inauthentic ways, she nevertheless believes that Heidegger leaves crucial possibilities for authentic being-with unfulfilled.[24] Arendt suggests that in failing to recognize the political significance of his own analysis of the they-self in *Being and Time*, Heidegger implicates himself in the philosophical prejudice against *praxis* central to the Western metaphysical tradition since Plato. Hence, she argues that while Heidegger undertakes the destruction of this tradition by developing a "this-worldly philosophy," he ultimately deprives Dasein of its native relationality in his account of authentic Dasein, while absorbing Dasein's radical singularity into a common destiny in his account of authentic historicity.[25]

In this divergence from Heidegger, Arendt's account of the political loneliness of modern life also has roots in Jaspers's concern for communication and his critical insights regarding the central position that solitude has come to occupy in Western metaphysics. As she says in *Men in Dark Times*, "Jaspers is, as far as I know, the first and the only philosopher who has ever protested against solitude, to whom solitude has appeared 'pernicious.'"[26] Like Jaspers, Arendt remains critical throughout her career of the tendency in the Western philosophical tradition to elevate contemplative life above practical life, suggesting that this tendency has kept thinking from thematizing human plurality and intervening in the mechanization of the modern world.[27] Even so, she believes that solitude has an important role to play in political life, enabling individuals who belong to a world to cultivate their capacity for thinking. Hence, in her discussion of loneliness, Arendt distinguishes herself from both of her mentors, deepening these aspects of their thought in ways that are responsive to the vulnerability that the loneliness of liberal subjectivity creates to totalitarian domination.

Arendt, for her part, maintains that the seeds of loneliness can be found in two different but interrelated concepts, namely, solitude and isolation.[28] For Arendt, the principle according to which solitude, isolation, and loneliness are related is the human condition of natality, which marks our inherent capacity for new beginnings and constitutes the source of our freedom.[29] As we have seen, Arendt wishes to show through her notion of natality that the distinguishing feature of our humanity resides not in our sameness but rather in the irreducible uniqueness that is bestowed upon us by the fact of our birth.[30] She says, "Each man is unique, so that with each birth something uniquely new comes into the world. With respect to this somebody who is unique it can be truly said that nobody was there before."[31] While Arendt has biological birth in mind, she interprets this in its existential significance as the appearance of the incalculable possibilities that are opened up by the uniqueness of each human being. This uniqueness can only be fully realized through action, or the native human capacity to bring something into the world that has never before been seen and could never have been predicted. While natality is a condition for the possibility of all human activity, it comes to appear most fully through speech and action in the realm of politics where human beings disclose who they are in their radical singularity to the world. We have already seen how Arendt conceptualizes action and speech, natality and plurality, in relation to the fundamental activities of human life. I return to these activities again to clarify their relation to her diagnosis of the political loneliness of modern life.

Arendt develops the relation between action and the realization of the human condition of natality through her discussion of the *vita activa*, or the fundamental activities of human life, which she designates as labor, work, and action.[32] Whereas labor and work are fundamental to human existence, only action, which is free, is definitive of it. Labor, Arendt explains, is the endless cycle of production and consumption that human beings undertake to satisfy their biological needs.[33] As *animal laborans*, she explains, we never rise above the necessity of the life processes.[34] For this reason, Arendt says, "When considered in their worldliness, [the products of labor] are the least worldly and at the same time the most natural of all things. Although they are man-made, they come and go, are produced and consumed, in accordance with the ever-recurrent cyclical movement of nature."[35] Labor, though necessary for human existence, is devoid of meaning, generating things that go in and out of existence according to the particular needs of human beings.[36] To the extent that labor is governed entirely by these natural processes, human beings in their capacity as *animal laborans* are indistinguishable from other living things. Hence, in being bound up with necessity, Arendt explains that labor corresponds to the human condition of life in general.[37]

In contrast to labor, which is driven entirely by the necessary movements of nature, work is that process by which we assert ourselves violently over nature in order to produce artifacts that can outlast it.[38] To the extent that fabrication brings things into the world that can endure the cyclical movement of nature, work, rather than labor, is world-building. In other words, Arendt says, "The work of our hands, as distinguished from the labor of our bodies—*homo faber* who makes and literally 'works upon,' as distinguished from the *animal laborans* which labors and 'mixes with'—constitutes the human artifice."[39] The artifacts we fabricate are relatively independent of those who produce and use them, giving them a permanence that distinguishes them from nature. Insofar as work produces artifacts that can endure these processes, the products of work, unlike labor, are able to stand between men and be shared in common.[40] In other words, human beings are able to create a home for themselves through work that can withstand the necessary movements of nature. For this reason, Arendt explains, work corresponds to the human condition of worldliness, insofar as it is the condition for the possibility of shared meaning and significance.

Work does distinguish human beings from other animals, giving the surrounding environment a permanence that she suggests exists nowhere in nature. Yet, work is not the definitive form of human action because it is driven by utility rather than spontaneity. Drawing on Aristotle's conception of *poïesis*, Arendt maintains that the process of fabrication is purposive, guided by a fixed end that is external to the activity itself. While man in his capacity as *homo faber* does exercise his will over nature, violently dominating it for the sake of producing a world, he does so only through means-end schematization. Hence, following both Plato and Aristotle, Arendt argues that the process of fabrication, in being "determined by the constant use of yardsticks, measurements, rules, and standards," is too predictable to be the activity that is most proper to human life.[41]

In contrast to labor and work, action, Arendt argues, is free and therefore definitive of human life. She says, "Action is not forced upon us by necessity, like labor, and it is not prompted by utility, like work."[42] Instead, action is the spontaneous enactment of one's inherent capacity for new beginnings. Whereas labor corresponds to the human condition of life, and work to the human condition of worldliness, action corresponds to the human condition of natality, or the fact that all human beings, simply in virtue of being born, come into the world as irreducibly unique and, as such, able to begin anew.

The experience of *solitude* does not diminish our irreducible uniqueness and, indeed, can even foster the complete realization of it by preparing us to engage thoughtfully in political life. When, by contrast, the political sphere of our lives has been destroyed and we find ourselves living in *isolation*, the condition of natality can no longer be fully realized but instead remains only partially developed in the context of work. Human natality is diminished even further in the context of *loneliness*, which develops when human beings have been reduced even in their productive capacities to laboring animals and are prevented entirely from realizing themselves in their radical uniqueness.

The extent to which our natality can be realized in these respective states of solitude, isolation, and loneliness depends on the relation we retain in each to the world and others. Arendt defines solitude as a temporary retreat from the world, but a retreat that is nevertheless indispensable for political life. As Roger Berkowitz explains, solitude nurtures our capacity for thoughtfulness, bringing us into relation with ourselves so that we are prepared to engage authentically with others.[43] Conceived as the cradle for thinking, solitude offers a sanctuary from what he describes as the "contagion of conformity" that threatens our capacity to realize our radical singularity in the context of political life.[44] In this, Berkowitz argues that solitude provides a vital safeguard against "the delusional fellowship promised by ideological and totalitarian fantasies."[45]

Yet, solitude, though a necessary aspect or moment of human existence, can only ever play a preparatory role in the full flourishing of human life and is never itself adequate for achieving this end. Because we are relational creatures, we find that while we may be together with ourselves in solitude, our wholeness and singularity as individuals remains unresolved when we are separated from others.[46] Solitude, Arendt explains, gives rise to the feeling of being "two-in-one," deflected from our individuality by the dual nature that arises when we have only our conscience to consult.[47] Hence, while solitude provides the foundation for the activity of thinking, enabling us to stand in an authentic relation to ourselves and those around us, one is always plagued by duality and doubt in the dialogue of thought. To be sure, this duality does not diminish the importance of solitude for cultivating our capacity for thought; on the contrary, Arendt insists that the fragmentation we find in ourselves forms the basis for the reflection we undertake in solitude, enabling us to ask timeless metaphysical questions about "God, freedom, and immortality (as in Kant), or about man and world, being and nothingness, life and death."[48] Even so, the feeling of being "two-in-one" that arises in solitude prevents us from authentically appropriating ourselves in our singular and irreducible uniqueness. For Arendt, it is only after our singularity has been illuminated by those around us that we can decide to be ourselves, a decision that is brought to completion when we announce who we are to the world. As she explains,

> We become one whole individual, in the richness as well as the limitations of definite characteristics, through and only through the company of others. For our individuality, insofar as it is one—unchangeable and unmistakable—we depend entirely on other people. . . . The great grace of companionship is that it redeems the two-in-one by making it individual.[49]

Solitude thus has the two-fold effect of bringing us into relation with ourselves, while at the same time revealing that we are always outside of ourselves when we are alone. It is therefore necessary for the full flourishing of human life because we are reminded in this confrontation with ourselves of our irrevocable interdependence, or the fact that we always remain incomplete in solitude and must therefore return to the world and the company of others in order to restore our individuality.

If we no longer belong to a world with others who can bring our singularity into relief, solitude becomes vulnerable to a dangerous extreme or limit experience of "complete solitude," which Arendt describes as loneliness.[50] Solitude is experienced at this limit, she says, "When man does not find companionship to save him from the dual nature of his solitude, or when man, as an individual, in constant need of others for his individuality, is deserted or separated from others."[51] Hence, while solitude may be necessary for the full flourishing of human life, it can also become dangerous when an individual is severed from a world, or community of others, who are able to bring that individual into relief in her singularity. As we shall see, individuals become susceptible to the dangers of solitude when they find themselves living in isolation and increasingly more so as they drift toward loneliness.

Human beings become isolated, Arendt explains, "When the political sphere of their lives, where they act together in the pursuit of a common concern, is destroyed."[52] Having lost the space that is most proper to human action, isolation keeps individuals from fully realizing themselves in their natality. She develops her account of isolation with reference to the distinction she finds in Montesquieu between the principles of action in republican and tyrannical governments.[53] On this view, Arendt argues, republican law springs from the joy of belonging to a group of individuals who, though radically different by birth, nevertheless recognize one another as equally valuable and powerful.[54] The experience of belonging to a group of distinct but equally powerful individuals gives rise to a love of equality and, with this, the principle of virtue that motivates individuals to act in concert with others in the public sphere. Thus, the principle of action in republican government rests on the twofold assumption that human beings are both irreducibly singular and interdependent, only capable of realizing their singularity, along with their power and freedom, with others in the full illumination of the public realm.[55]

The lawlessness of tyrannical government, as Arendt reads Montesquieu, depends by contrast on the impotence of radically isolated individuals.[56] Rather than virtue, the motivating principle of tyrannical government is fear, which springs from the feeling of despair one has over the impossibility of acting in concert with others. Because human beings are both singular and interdependent, their power and freedom as individuals can only be realized with others in the public realm, or that space in which human beings are able to appear in their singular uniqueness. Hence, the destruction of the public realm gives rise to isolation, preventing individuals from recognizing one another as equally powerful in their singularity.

Arendt thus defines isolation in reference to her interpretation of Montesquieu as the experience of living together "without sharing some visible, tangible realm of the world."[57] Through the destruction of the political sphere, isolation renders human beings incapable of fully realizing themselves through action, robbing them of the ability to be together in such a way that they are able to endow the world they have in common with meaning. Capable of seeing themselves and those around them only in their productive capacities, isolation thus makes human beings impotent, leading to a sense of despair over the feeling of powerlessness that develops when one is unable to act in concert with others.[58] No longer fully illuminated by the public realm, the human condition of natality is thus diminished in isolation, remaining only dimly lit in the human capacity for work.

Loneliness is a further and more radical iteration of the feeling of despair that sets in when human beings are no longer able to take collective action in the sphere of politics. Whereas isolated individuals may still be able to contribute something of their own to the world through their work, Arendt argues that loneliness arises once human beings have been reduced even in their productive capacities to "*animal laborans*, whose necessary 'metabolism with nature' is of concern to no one."[59] Loneliness thus develops when human natality has been altogether snuffed out, and human beings have been leveled in their intrinsic uniqueness to indistinct parts of the necessary movement of nature. This experience, Arendt explains, is unbearable; it involves not only the loss of companionship but also "the loss of one's own self which can be realized in solitude but confirmed in its identity only by the trusting and trustworthy company of my equals."[60] Because we are always outside of ourselves in solitude, we can easily lose ourselves in it if we no longer belong to a world with others who can bring our singularity into focus. Arendt thus describes loneliness as the anxiety we have over the loss of self that occurs upon being severed from a common world that can confirm the truth of our experience.[61] She explains that this anxiety causes individuals to lose trust in who they are and "the elementary confidence in the world which is necessary to make experiences at all. Self and world, the capacity for thought and experience are lost at the same time."[62] Upon falling into despair over this loss of self and the surrounding world, we become disoriented; loneliness overwhelms us with doubt and uncertainty regarding the truth of our experience in the world, leaving us without a tangible reality in which to ground ourselves. For this reason, Arendt says, the feeling of loneliness is "among the most radical and desperate experiences of man."[63]

As we have already seen, Arendt insists that the hallmarks of the modern epoch—namely, the political emancipation of the bourgeoisie, the rise of European imperialism, capital exploitation, industrialization, and the advance of modern science and technology—have created a breeding ground for loneliness. The increasing decay of our political institutions and traditions in the modern era have caused the world to collapse, leaving behind rootless individuals who are only capable of seeing themselves and others in terms of their utility and functionality. This, in turn, has generated a widespread feeling of loneliness, or the overwhelming sense of not belonging to any world at all.[64] Loneliness has thus come to epitomize the basic experience of living together in the modern world, such that individuals find themselves dominated not just by isolation and powerlessness but also by worldlessness and superfluity.[65] For this reason, Arendt describes loneliness as "the very disease of our time," a fact laid bare by the submission of the masses to totalitarian domination at the beginning of the twentieth century.[66]

LONELINESS AND TOTALITARIANISM

Arendt suggests through her discourse on loneliness that losing one's place in the world involves more than mere physical displacement; beyond this, it entails a deeper existential displacement, leaving individuals in exile from themselves and the radical singularity that is definitive of being human. The phenomenon of loneliness reveals, too, that such experiences of exile are not specific to the stateless, refugees, or otherwise marginalized individuals, but are instead widespread even among those who have secured a place within the borders of liberal and allegedly open societies. In this, Arendt's concern for loneliness indicates that the problem of exclusion epitomized in her discussion of statelessness is not external to the structures of modern political life, as those who emphasize the right to have rights suggest. On the contrary, she suggests that this problem is internal to the liberal political structures that organize modern life, which she believes can be seen above all in the vulnerability of liberal subjects to totalitarian domination.

Much has already been said of Arendt's approach to totalitarianism; my aim here will simply be to synthesize her principal concerns and elucidate her claim that we become increasingly susceptible to totalitarianism as the prevalence of loneliness within society increases.[67] While the sense of community promised by totalitarian movements such as National Socialism has been attributed to their ascendancy, Arendt's analysis offers an important critical perspective on this heightened sense of togetherness, clarifying that in order for such movements to become mainstream, the masses must have already been atomized and isolated to the point of loneliness. In this, we might interpret totalitarianism not as promising genuine belonging but rather as the most heightened and refined form of the peculiar loneliness of the current age.

Totalitarianism, Arendt maintains, is an unprecedented form of government, depending for its existence on widespread loneliness rather than fear and isolation alone. Unlike tyrannical rule, totalitarian government is not arbitrary and lawless but instead purports to be lawful in the purest sense, executing the law of nature or history without translating this law into the standards of right and wrong for individual behavior.[68] In this, it defies positive law, which derives its legitimacy from a natural or divine authority external to human beings, erecting boundaries between a plurality of individuals so that they are able to retain and enact their native capacity for spontaneous free action. Totalitarianism, by contrast, destroys human plurality, pressing men together in order to create "one man" in whom the law of history or nature can be realized.[69]

Totalitarianism accomplishes this through terror, which, Arendt says, "[provides] the forces of nature or history with an incomparable instrument to accelerate their movement."[70] By pressing isolated individuals together, terror ensures that the masses, no longer able to recognize themselves or others in their radical singularity, come to see that their particular existence is meaningful only insofar as it advances the species as a whole. In this, totalitarian terror draws its momentum from the loneliness of modern mass society "which, with its iron band, presses masses of isolated men together *and* supports them in a world that has become a wilderness for them."[71] By pressing men more tightly together in their loneliness, Arendt explains, this iron band of terror destroys the very source of human freedom, "which is given with the fact of the birth of man and resides in his capacity to make a new beginning."[72] By effectively outlawing human plurality, totalitarian terror ensures that the stream of necessity governed by natural or historical processes remains uninterrupted by any unforeseeable or spontaneous human act. In forcing individuals to see themselves and others as superfluous and interchangeable parts of a larger mechanism, terror guarantees that the subjects of totalitarian rule exist only to propel the death sentences that nature or history have supposedly pronounced for certain human beings. Hence, Arendt says, "The inhabitants of a totalitarian country are thrown into and caught in the process of nature or history for the sake of accelerating its movement; as such, they can only be executioners or victims of its inherent law."[73] This two-sided preparation, she explains, is the basis of totalitarian ideology.

Like its nineteenth-century predecessors, totalitarian ideology seeks total explanation, subordinating the reality of experience to some truer reality that is proclaimed to be concealed behind all perceptible things.[74] In striving to explain all historical happenings, the very structure of ideological thinking precludes the possibility of experiencing anything new, as the tangible reality of an event is never understood on its own terms but only with reference to a greater ideological truth. As Arendt says, "Once it has established its premise, its point of departure, experience no longer interferes with ideological thinking, nor can it be taught by reality."[75] Ideology thus emancipates thought from experience such that it is able to proceed with logical consistency that has no basis in reality.[76]

Yet, totalitarian ideology also distinguishes itself from other ideologies in that it is driven not by an idea, such as dialectical materialism or racism, but instead by the coercive force of the logical process itself.[77] That is, in addition to emancipating thought from experience by subordinating all perceptible reality to an ideological truth, totalitarian ideology transforms the stringent logicality inherent in all ideology into the principle of action that drives human behavior. As Arendt explains,

> The stringent logicality as an inspiration of action permeates the whole structure of totalitarian movements and totalitarian governments. The most pervasive argument, of which Hitler and Stalin were equally fond, is to insist that whoever says A must necessarily also say B and C and finally end with the last letter of the alphabet. Everything which stands in the way of this kind of reasoning—reality, experience, and the daily network of human relationships and interdependence—is overruled. . . . It is no longer race . . . that is the "ideal" which appeals, nor class or the establishment of a classless society, but the murderous network of pure logical operations in which one is caught up once one accepts either of them.[78]

Logical reasoning is the one capacity of the human mind that does not need the self, others, or the world to function properly. Hence, loneliness, as the experience of having been severed from all three, prepares men to submit to the coercive force of logic or, as Hitler put it, the "ice-cold reasoning," that accelerates totalitarian terror.[79] That is, she says, "Logicality is what appeals to isolated human beings, for man—in complete solitude, without any contact with his fellow men and therefore without any real possibility of experience—has nothing else he can fall back on but the most abstract rules of reasoning."[80] For this reason, totalitarianism can only rule over lonely individuals who, in the desperation of their loneliness, have lost trust in their experience as an originating source of truth, left to cling instead to the automated processes of logical deduction to supply their thoughts.

Mere logic, or reasoning without regard for facts or experience, is the inherent vice of solitude, a vice that "grows out of the despair of loneliness."[81] Upon being severed from the world and others, it is only possible to appease the despair of loneliness by remaining consistent in one's reasoning, which provides "the only reliable 'truth' human beings can fall back upon once they have lost the mutual guarantee, the common sense, men need in order to experience and live and know their way in a common world."[82] Totalitarianism rescues men from their loneliness, preying on the fear lonely individuals have of contradicting themselves.[83] Upon accepting the first premise of the movement's ideology, lonely individuals must follow through with the deduction it prescribes, or else risk rendering their lives meaningless.[84]

For this reason, Arendt argues, totalitarianism can perhaps best be understood as "organized loneliness."[85] In order to transform human beings into executioners and victims of the inherent law of history or nature, it is not enough to destroy the external reality of freedom in the political sphere through isolation and fear. Beyond this, individuals must also be willing to surrender their inner freedom, or their capacity for thinking, which Arendt describes as "the freest and purest of all human activities . . . the very opposite of the compulsory process of deduction."[86] Therefore, in addition to external coercion, totalitarianism depends on self-coercion, whereby lonely individuals who have become content to submit their capacity for thought to the ongoing process of deduction, compel themselves to step into the movement of terror.[87]

Arendt explains that the destruction of the public realm over the last two centuries has given rise to a society of atomized and isolated human beings who live together without sharing anything in common.[88] In this, she is clear that the liberal political structures that organize modern life are not antithetical to totalitarianism, but have instead laid the foundation for totalitarian rulers to organize European society as they did at the beginning of the twentieth century. By producing and affirming atomized and isolated subjects, these very structures have created a breeding ground for the peculiar loneliness of the current age. Hence, she says, "Hitler was able to build his organization on the firm ground of an already atomized society, which he then artificially atomized even further."[89] The all-consuming concern for instrumentality and individualism in Western liberal societies has not only isolated human beings but also left them desperately lonely, a fact that Arendt believes was made evident by the willing submission of so many to the logic of totalitarian terror.

Through her account of loneliness, we thus find that the danger involved in losing one's place in the world runs deeper than her analysis of statelessness initially suggests. In addition to characterizing the experience of being physically displaced, it also encompasses the broader experience of liberal subjects, who, despite living together in open, democratic societies, nevertheless find themselves homeless and uprooted in having lost a common world. Arendt's articulation of the dehumanizing effect of statelessness may therefore be generalized to include the lonely masses in the modern era. Loneliness strips individuals of the singularity and interrelatedness that is definitive of the human condition. Therefore, in much the same way as statelessness, loneliness expels human beings from humanity, reducing them in their unrepeatable uniqueness to interchangeable parts of a worldless society.

LONELINESS AND LIBERAL CITIZENSHIP

When considered in light of her account of loneliness, Arendt's concern for citizenship in her analysis of statelessness poses an important challenge to the forms of subjectivity and citizenship that grow out of the liberal tradition. Political membership, according to Arendt, is characteristically conceived within this tradition as an indefinitely expandable legal status that promises liberty in exchange for obedience to the law; in this, it purports to have found in the social contract a steadfast foundation for just society.[90] Yet, in guaranteeing the right to pursue one's private interests as far as possible so long as this does not preclude others from doing the same, the liberal tradition reproduces and affirms a notion of citizenship that lawfully promotes the separation of human beings. In other words, the terms of the contract itself presuppose a society of lonely liberal subjects, providing rational justification for the atomization and isolation that has made modern individuals susceptible to totalitarian domination.

Given this, we may wonder whether those discourses that emphasize the right to have rights do enough to capture the stakes involved in Arendt's concern for political belonging and citizenship. Those who focus on Arendt's discussion of rights for the sake of developing methods for expanding liberal citizenship on a global scale imply in their approach to her work that the forms of exclusion epitomized by statelessness stand outside the structures of liberal democracy. Yet, Arendt's account of loneliness suggests that the experience of no longer belonging to a world may be endemic for those who live within political structures of liberal provenance. If the problem of loneliness is understood as the loss of one's place in the world, and this loss is a consequence of the destruction of the political sphere in the modern age, then overcoming it involves more than simply extending the rights of liberal citizenship to those who exist outside our circles of inclusion; beyond this, what is called for is a critique of these structures and the very forms of subjectivity that they reproduce. In turning to Arendt's analysis of loneliness, we therefore find that her own concern for citizenship may be interpreted as forming a basis for a deeper critique of the liberal tradition that remains underdeveloped in her discussion of the right to have rights, but that is nevertheless integral to her broader insights concerning the failures and dangers of politics in the modern age. Arendt scholars who emphasize the right to have rights to the detriment of her critical relation to the liberal tradition not only risk missing this decisive feature of her political project but also, and more importantly, threaten to overshadow an important critical perspective on the assumptions of the liberal tradition that Arendt brings into view. These are assumptions that may remain at work not only in their efforts to develop new ways of justifying the expansion of democratic citizenship but, moreover, in the very structures of liberal democracy that organize political life today.

BEYOND THE LONELINESS OF LIBERAL SUBJECTIVITY

Arendt's insights into the political significance of the problem of loneliness not only put into relief her novel critical perspective on this liberal political tradition. Beyond this, they also give new orientation to her concern for political belonging and her call for the right to have rights, or the right to be a citizen of some sovereign state. Her concern for citizenship not only offers a response to the loss of rights that stateless people suffered but also constitutes a means of contravening the broader problem of loneliness, which she describes as "an everyday experience of the ever growing masses of our century."[91] Arendt's account of loneliness clarifies that her own call for the right to be a citizen cannot be reduced to a call for the expansion of our present political structures; on the contrary, it serves as the basis for an entirely new conception of citizenship that is able to return lonely individuals to themselves, the world, and others.

As Arendt explains, action in the modern era has been relegated to the realm of necessity, leading to a conception of politics that may promise liberty in the private sphere but that is entirely divorced from freedom and that renders us hidden and isolated from one another. It is Arendt's view that this loss of the space of appearance has led to widespread disorientation. This experience prepares men for totalitarian domination and, thus, Arendt suggests, what is called for in the wake of the political catastrophes of the twentieth century is a more robust sense of political belonging that can save us from the political loneliness of modern life. Drawing on a model of political life represented by the Greek *polis* and the Roman *res publica* Arendt thus envisions citizenship not in terms of the liberal pursuit of one's individual interests in the isolation of private life; instead, what it means to be a citizen for Arendt is to actualize one's inherent capacity for new beginnings with and through others in the space of politics.

While a trace of freedom is inherent in all human activity, Arendt explains that it can only develop fully when "action has created its own worldly space where it can come out of hiding, as it were, and make its appearance."[92] For this reason, her conception of citizenship consists in having the right to be seen by others in the space of appearance. Arendt argues that it is only through speech and action in the realm of politics that individuals reveal themselves to one another as human beings rather than mere physical objects.[93] Through action, we express our native capacity for new beginnings, which is given to us by the human condition of natality. Through speech, we announce that we are the authors of our action, confirming our radical singularity in the presence of others, realizing the human condition of plurality. Speech and action are only possible in a world with others; hence, rather than a collection of private rights and liberties, Arendt conceives of citizenship in terms of belonging to a space of appearance, which enables individuals to see themselves and those around them in the fullness of their humanity. Understood this way, Arendt's concern for political belonging culminates in a conception of citizenship that works against the isolation and atomization of liberal subjectivity insofar as it is oriented by the illuminative power of the public realm.[94]

This, alone, however is not enough for a conception of citizenship that can overcome the worldlessness of the modern era. Drawing on Heidegger's conception of thrownness, Arendt maintains that we find ourselves born into a world or set of relations that we have inherited but that are not our own.⁹⁵ Because of this, we can never fully liberate ourselves from the conditions of our existence, meaning that our freedom will always be a matter of appropriating these conditions anew. Arendt thus maintains that freedom must be understood as an event of appropriation, whereby citizens work in concert with one another for the sake of carrying the world they have in common from the past into the future. Arendt suggests as much in the following passage concerning the political virtue of courage. She says:

> For this world of ours, because it existed before us and is meant to outlast our lives in it, simply cannot afford to give primary concern to individual lives and the interests connected with them.... It requires courage to leave the protective security of our four walls and enter into the public realm, not because of the particular dangers which may lie in wait for us, but because we have arrived in a realm where the concern for life has lost its validity. Courage liberates men from their worry about life for the freedom of the world. Courage is indispensable because in politics, not life but the world is at stake.⁹⁶

In light of this, we find that what it means to be a citizen for Arendt is to have the courage to take responsibility for preserving and renewing the world in which one finds oneself. As such, Arendt's conception of citizenship does not simply grant individuals the right to the protection of the law; beyond this, it requires of them that they work to reclaim the significance of the world they share. That is, citizenship, for Arendt, promises political belonging only insofar as it demands of us that we act in concert for the sake of holding open the realm of politics, or that space in which freedom can appear. Citizenship, understood in terms of our responsibility to carry a common world from the past into the future, thus offers a powerful antidote to the political loneliness of modern life; in returning us to ourselves by bringing us into relation with others, it provides a means of reclaiming the significance of a world that has been overtaken by worldlessness and superfluity.

By drawing Arendt's analysis of statelessness together with her conception of loneliness, it is therefore possible to see that her conception of citizenship forms the basis to critique the loneliness of liberal subjectivity. With this, it provides a basis to develop an account of the forms of loneliness that may remain at work in our own society today. In what follows, I will suggest that Arendt's analysis of the political loneliness of modern life provides an important frame for interpreting the vulnerability of Western liberal democracies today to right-wing nationalism and populist politics. In this, I will argue that she puts before us the task of thinking the political sphere anew so that we might envision possibilities for authentic forms of communal life that are able to work against the loneliness of modern mass society and the vulnerability that it creates to dangerous and totalizing forms of communal life.

NOTES

1. This chapter is derived, in part, from an article I have published on this topic entitled "Another Origin of Totalitarianism: Arendt on the Loneliness of Liberal Citizens," *Journal of the British Society for Phenomenology*, 47.1 (2016): 1–17.

2. Hannah Arendt, "On the Nature of Totalitarianism: An Essay in Understanding," in *Essays in Understanding 1930–1954: Formation, Exile, and Totalitarianism*, ed. Jerome Kohn (New York: Schocken Books, 1994): 328–360, 360.

3. Hannah Arendt, "The Origins of Totalitarianism,* (New York: Harcourt Inc., 1974), 477.

4. Ibid., 297.

5. Ibid.

6. Ibid., 296–297.

7. In identifying a paradox at the heart of modern formulations of human rights Arendt seems at once to undermine the concept of human rights, while at the same time invoking this concept in her call for the universal right to citizenship. Her discourse on the right to have rights has thus left many to wonder whether this is merely a lacuna in her thought, or if she in fact views the very structure of the political institution of human rights to be aporetic. For more on Arendt's account of the paradox of human rights, see Jacques Rancière's critique of Arendt in "Who Is the Subject of the Rights of Man?" *South Atlantic Quarterly*, 103.2/3 (2004): 297–310; Ayten Gündogdu, "'The Perplexities of the Rights of Man': Arendt on the Aporias of Human Rights," *European Journal of Political Theory*, 11.1 (2011): 4–24; and Christoph Menke, "The 'Aporias of Human Rights' and the 'One Human Right': Regarding the Coherence of Arendt's Argument," *Social Research*, 74.3 (2007): 739–763.

8. Benhabib, *The Reluctant Modernism of Hannah Arendt*, 185.

9. Ibid., 200.

10. Ibid., 193–200. See also Seyla Benhabib, *Dignity in Adversity: Human Rights in Troubled Times* (Hoboken: Wiley Press, 2011), 57–76.

11. Peg Birmingham, *Hannah Arendt and Human Rights: The Predicament of Common Responsibility* (Bloomington: Indiana University Press, 2006), 5.

12. Peg Birmingham, "The An-Archic Event of Natality and the Right to Have Rights," *Social Research*, 74.3 (2007): 763–777, 766.

13. Ibid.
14. Birmingham, *Hannah Arendt and Human Rights*, 7.
15. Serena Parekh, "Arendt, Judgment, and Responsibility to the Global Poor," *Philosophical Topics*, 39.2 (2011): 145–163, 147.
16. Ibid.
17. Birmingham, *Hannah Arendt and Human Rights*, 57.
18. Several scholars including Dana Villa, Martin Shuster, and Roger Berkowitz have acknowledged the centrality of the theme of loneliness for Arendt's broader philosophical project. Villa develops this in relation to Arendt's concern for political action. Shuster considers the importance of loneliness for understanding Arendt's conception of language. Berkowitz turns to the concept of loneliness in Arendt's work in order to contrast it with solitude and to demonstrate its importance for thinking not just the loss of the public sphere but also the loss of the private sphere in the modern age. Arendt's conception of loneliness, however, has yet to be given systematic treatment in relation to her notion of citizenship. See Dana Villa, *Politics, Philosophy, Terror: Essays on the Thought of Hannah Arendt* (Princeton: Princeton University Press, 1999), 198–203; Martin Shuster, "Language and Loneliness: Arendt, Cavell, and Modernity," *International Journal of Philosophical Studies*, 20.4 (2012): 473–497; and Roger Berkowitz, "Solitude and the Activity of Thinking," in *Thinking in Dark Times: Hannah Arendt on Ethics and Politics*, edited by Richard Bernstein, 237–48. New York: Fordham University Press, 2009.
19. Arendt, *The Human Condition*, 246.
20. See Hannah Arendt, "What Is Freedom?" in *Between Past and Future* (New York: Penguin Books, 2006), 142–69. See also Arendt's discussion of world-alienation in *The Human Condition*, esp. 248–257.
21. Arendt, *The Human Condition*, 254.
22. See Villa, *Philosophy, Politics, Terror*, 67.
23. Heidegger's discussion of being-with (*mitsein*) as a mode of being-in-the-world, as well as his discussion of the inauthenticity of Dasein's publicly interpreted self appears in §25–27 of *Being and Time*. See Martin Heidegger, *Being and Time*, trans. Joan Stambaugh (Albany: SUNY Press), 111–26.
24. See Dana Villa, *Arendt and Heidegger: The Fate of the Political* (Princeton: Princeton University Press, 1995), 212–213.
25. Ibid., 232. For Arendt's criticism of Heidegger see Hannah Arendt, "What Is Existential Philosophy?" in *Essays in Understanding 1930–1954: Formation, Exile and Totalitarianism* (New York: Random House, Inc., 1994), 176–181.
26. Hannah Arendt, "Karl Jaspers: Citizen of the World?" in *Men in Dark Times* (New York: Harcourt, Brace, and World Inc., 1968), 81–94, 86.
27. Ibid., 87.
28. Arendt, "On the Nature of Totalitarianism," 358.
29. Arendt, *The Human Condition*, 9.
30. Ibid., 178.
31. Ibid.
32. Ibid., 7.
33. Ibid., 82.

34. Ibid., 96.
35. Ibid.
36. Villa, *Arendt and Heidegger*, 28.
37. Arendt, *The Human Condition*, 7.
38. Villa, *Arendt and Heidegger*, 28.
39. Arendt, *The Human Condition*, 136.
40. Ibid., 137.
41. Ibid., 166. See also Jacques Taminiaux, "Athens and Rome," in *The Cambridge Companion to Hannah Arendt*, ed. Dana Villa (Cambridge: Cambridge University Press, 2000), 166.
42. Arendt, *The Human Condition*, 177.
43. See Roger Berkowitz, "Solitude and the Activity of Thinking," in *Thinking in Dark Times: Hannah Arendt on Ethics and Politics*, ed. Richard Bernstein (New York: Fordham University Press, 2009), 239.
44. Ibid., 240.
45. Ibid., 237.
46. Arendt, "On the Nature of Totalitarianism," 358.
47. Ibid.
48. Ibid., 359.
49. Ibid., 358–359.
50. Ibid., 357.
51. Ibid., 359.
52. Arendt, *The Origins of Totalitarianism*, 474.
53. Arendt, "On the Nature of Totalitarianism," 335.
54. Ibid., 336.
55. Ibid.
56. Ibid., 337–338.
57. Ibid., 357.
58. Arendt, *The Origins of Totalitarianism*, 475.
59. Ibid.
60. Ibid., 477.
61. Arendt, "On the Nature of Totalitarianism," 336.
62. Arendt, *The Origins of Totalitarianism*, 477.
63. Ibid., 475.
64. Ibid.
65. Arendt, "On the Nature of Totalitarianism," 360.
66. Ibid., 358.
67. For a classic study of Arendt's analysis of totalitarianism, evil, and anti-Semitism, see Richard J. Bernstein, *Hannah Arendt and the Jewish Question* (Cambridge: MIT Press, 1996). For more recent accounts of the importance of Arendt's analysis of totalitarianism for advancing global political theory, see Patrick Hayden, *Political Evil in a Global Age: Hannah Arendt and International Theory* (New York: Routledge, 2009) and Lars Rensmann, "Grounding Cosmopolitics: Rethinking Crimes against Humanity and Global Political Theory with Arendt and Adorno," in *Arendt & Adorno: Political and Philosophical Investigations*, ed. Lars Rensmann and Samir Gandesha (Stanford: Stanford University Press, 2012).

68. Arendt, *The Origins of Totalitarianism*, 462.
69. Ibid.
70. Ibid., 466.
71. Ibid., 472.
72. Ibid., 466.
73. Ibid., 470.
74. Ibid.
75. Ibid., 471.
76. Ibid., 470–471.
77. Arendt, "On the Nature of Totalitarianism," 355.
78. Ibid., 355–356.
79. Arendt, *The Origins of Totalitarianism*, 471, 477.
80. Arendt, "On the Nature of Totalitarianism," 358.
81. Ibid.
82. Arendt, *On the Origins of Totalitarianism*, 477.
83. Ibid., 478.
84. Ibid., 473.
85. Ibid.
86. Ibid.
87. Ibid.
88. Arendt, "On the Nature of Totalitarianism," 356.
89. Ibid.
90. Arendt offers a critical interpretation of these assumptions of the liberal tradition in her discussion of European imperialism and the political emancipation of the bourgeoisie in *The Origins of Totalitarianism*, esp. pp. 124–141, as well as in her account of the difference between liberty and political freedom in her essay, "What Is Freedom?" in *Between Past and Future* (New York: Penguin Books, 2006), 146–149.
91. Arendt, "On the Nature of Totalitarianism," 356.
92. Arendt, "What is Freedom?", 167.
93. Arendt, *The Human Condition*, 176.
94. Arendt, "What is Freedom?", 152.
95. See Villa, *Arendt and Heidegger*, 120–123.
96. Arendt, "What Is Freedom?", 155.

6
Political Loneliness Today: America's Hidden Trump Supporter

By developing the peculiar loneliness of the current age in a political register, Arendt offers a novel critical perspective on the dangers of liberal subjectivity. She interprets the problem of our peculiar loneliness—or the fact that in an era of hyperbolic interconnectedness, we nevertheless find ourselves more extremely apart than ever before—as a symptom of the loss of the political sphere in the modern era. This loss, she suggests, is affirmed and reproduced by the forms of subjectivity inherited from the liberal political tradition, forms of subjectivity that have lost their political valence and have, in turn, left human beings isolated, atomized, and lonely.

In this chapter, I will suggest that Arendt's analysis of the political significance of the loneliness of modern mass society provides an important framework for interpreting several of the perplexities and presumptions of modern political life. First among these is the way in which totalitarian movements like National Socialism, which ordinarily appeal to the outer edges of the political spectrum, become mainstream. Though we may be inclined to attribute this appeal to the sense of community that such movements promise, this alone is not enough to account for the vast demographics across which they are able to cut. To be sure, such movements do promise a heightened sense of togetherness. Yet, Arendt's analysis offers an important critical perspective on this heightened togetherness, clarifying that in order for totalitarianism to have such wide and undifferentiated appeal, the masses must have already been atomized and isolated to the point of loneliness. Rather than promising genuine belonging through a collective cause or consciousness, totalitarian politics represents the most refined form of the peculiar loneliness of the current age, pressing individuals into an indistinguishable mass whose sole purpose is to accelerate the necessary movements of nature and history. Her analysis thus issues an urgent call, not to dismiss these movements as aberrations but to confront the breeding ground that loneliness creates for them to enter the mainstream.

Second, Arendt's political interpretation of the problem of loneliness provides a platform to critique our received ideas and assumptions about the liberal political tradition, highlighting the loneliness that these structures produce and the vulnerability that this loneliness creates to totalizing and dangerous forms of communal life. Whereas mainstream discourses in liberal political theory call for the expansion of these structures to address the exclusion and alienation of modern life, Arendt's analysis puts into relief the way in which they can affirm and reproduce the very loneliness that makes modern individuals susceptible to totalitarianism. Figures like Stauffer have already done important work to clarify the dangers of the problem of loneliness for those who have been cast out of their political communities. Equally important has been the work that scholars since Heidegger have done to make philosophically significant the peculiar character of the loneliness of modern mass society. Yet, Arendt provides a novel point of departure for interpreting the relation of this peculiar loneliness to the liberal political structures that organize Western democracies and the ways in which we implicate ourselves in the reproduction of this loneliness by uncritically calling for their expansion.

Third, and perhaps most importantly, Arendt provides a platform to interrogate the loneliness that remains at work in political life today. Her notion of political loneliness opens new paths to understanding our own "post-truth" era, a time in which "fake news" and "alternative facts" are referred to regularly to express suspicion over the reliability, not just of the words and deeds of others but also of the reality of the world itself. It provides a basis to consider why, in an era in which modern technology has made us more accessible to one another than ever before, we do not use this technology to cultivate spaces for genuine political discourse or to advance knowledge and creativity; instead, we turn to the echo chambers of Twitter and Facebook to reinforce our own views, to mine human data, and to develop metrics and algorithms to predict, coerce, and surveil one another. On Arendt's view, these tendencies are symptomatic of a widespread experience of loneliness, an experience that has been produced by the destruction of the political sphere of our lives. By considering the desperation that such loneliness creates, she also provides a basis to interpret the rise of far-right populism across Western liberal democracies today.

There are, to be sure, many contemporary phenomena one could point to in order to evaluate the loneliness that remains at work in contemporary political life. Yet, I will focus here on one phenomenon in particular that is especially illuminating in this regard: America's "hidden" Trump supporter. A contemporary political phenomenon that is easily passed over in favor of other perhaps more striking examples, I wish to suggest that the hidden Trump supporter is a crucial one for bringing into focus the political significance of the peculiar loneliness of the current age.

This term was introduced to the American political lexicon during the 2016 U.S. presidential election, referring to those who voted for Trump but who did not disclose this preference in public opinion surveys in the months and weeks leading up to the election for fear of being socially ostracized. While polling data in October 2016 suggested that Hillary Clinton's victory was all but inevitable, Donald Trump and his campaign team introduced this language to describe an undercurrent of support for his candidacy that they believed the polls were missing. Media outlets and pollsters cast doubt on the existence of these supporters in the days leading up to the election, arguing that Trump's underperformance at both the state and national level accurately reflected public opinion and suggested a clear path to victory for Hillary Clinton. Yet, when Donald Trump was declared the president-elect of the United States on November 9, 2016, the "hidden" Trump supporter became central to the political discourse, representing a vast, incongruent, and seemingly invisible part of the American electorate whose votes appeared to make possible one of the greatest political upsets in American history.

In the years since Trump was elected, political scientists have been working to understand why polling data failed to predict this outcome. There is much debate among political scientist about whether "hidden" or "shy" Trump supporters contributed to the surprising outcome of this election. Yet, whereas these debates have focused on the statistical significance of the hidden Trump supporter for understanding widespread polling errors at the state level, we have yet to consider the broader significance of the use of this language of hiddenness to describe so vast a swath of a democratic electorate. Arendt, for her part, provides a novel theoretical basis for understanding how the language of hiddenness could become so ubiquitous in a nation that prides itself on democratic participation. A phenomenon that is easily overlooked, I wish to suggest that this language of hiddenness is itself emblematic of the political loneliness to which Arendt draws our attention and the vulnerability it creates among liberal citizens to totalitarianism and populism.

It is, of course, crucial to recognize the complex nature of the circumstances that have led to the rise of right-wing populism today, no less than the specific conditions under which Arendt was developing her account of European totalitarianism in the early twentieth century. It would be not only overly simplistic to neglect these complexities but also inconsistent with recent scholarship in Arendt studies that cautions against reductive approaches to these complex political environments.[1] Yet, while it is crucial to acknowledge these complexities, Arendt's analysis nevertheless provides a useful framework for interpreting the loneliness that may remain at work in our own society today and the susceptibility this creates to totalizing forms of communal life. Whereas much work has been done to discuss other factors—for instance, growing economic inequality, globalization and technological change, structural racism, and global mass migration—this chapter emphasizes an element not typically explored, namely, the vulnerability of the liberal subject per se to right-wing populism in order to provide a broad framework for critically engaging more specific contexts like the contemporary political situation in the United States. Turning to scholars such as Wendy Brown and Bonnie Honig, both of whom point to the way in which neoliberal rationality has transformed political subjects, states, and public things in contemporary political life, I will suggest that we have good reason to extend Arendt's analysis of the loneliness of liberal subjectivity beyond her own historically specific context to neoliberal subjectivity today. Hence while we must acknowledge the contingent factors of the 2016 U.S. context, no less than the distinctive ways in which right-wing populism is taking shape in other regions, I nevertheless wish to suggest that we may turn to the loneliness of liberal subjectivity to consider how such contingent factors achieve their determining power.

AMERICA'S HIDDEN TRUMP SUPPORTER

10:30 PM: *Trump Showing Unexpected Strength in Battleground States*
11:40 PM: *Trump Takes Florida, closing in on a Stunning Upset*
2:30 AM: *TRUMP IS ON THE VERGE OF A STUNNING UPSET*
2:50 AM: *TRUMP TRIUMPHS: Shocking Upset as Outsider Harnesses Voters' Anger*[2]

These headlines appeared on *The New York Times* website over the course of November 8–9, 2016, pointing to what nearly every polling organization in the United States failed to predict: a Donald Trump victory on election day. This "stunning upset" suggested that something had been overlooked, some part of the American electorate left hidden, in the effort to forecast the outcome of this historic election. There is much debate among political scientists about whether "hidden" or "shy" Trump supporters had a decisive impact on the outcome of this election. Some have argued that "social desirability bias," or the refusal on the part of survey respondents to express openly their candidate preference for fear of being ostracized, did contribute in significant ways to these polling errors and had a decisive impact on the election. Others have suggested that the outcome was a consequence of late-deciding voters and overrepresentation of college-educated survey respondents in polling data.[3] Yet, I wish to suggest that the question itself—the question of whether there were large numbers of voters who remained hidden in the days and weeks leading up to this election—is worthy of our consideration regardless of the empirical results. The pervasiveness of the language of hiddenness to describe voters in a liberal and allegedly open democracy is itself significant, pointing to what might be interpreted as the loneliness of political life today.

The 2016 U.S. presidential election was characterized by division, not just between Republicans and Democrats but also between the so-called political elite and populist politicians who sought to galvanize the people against the status quo. The latter division appeared to be indifferent to party lines, dividing left liberals from their centrist counterparts, no less than the orthodox core of the Republican Party from fringe groups on the far-right.[4] Rather than viewing this election as a contest between political parties, it may therefore better be characterized as a contest between establishment and antiestablishment politics.

There is perhaps no greater establishment candidate in American politics today than the 2016 presidential nominee for the Democratic Party, Hillary Clinton. A registered Democrat since 1968, Clinton had spent thirty-one years in government life prior to her 2016 presidential run, serving as First Lady of Arkansas from 1983 to 1992, First Lady of the United States from 1993 to 2001, the United States Senator from New York from 2001 to 2009, and Secretary of State from 2009 to 2013. The second of two presidential campaigns, Clinton ran in 2016 on a center-left platform, proposing progressive social policies that emphasized inclusion, equality, and diversity, while distancing herself from both the far-left and the far-right, "both of whom," she said, "want to blow up the system and undermine it."[5] She advocated for the DREAM Act and a pathway to citizenship for undocumented immigrants, increased funding for Planned Parenthood, the expansion of Obamacare, increased taxes for high-income earners, a higher minimum wage, and stricter gun control. In contrast to her Democratic primary opponent, Senator Bernie Sanders, however, she did not call for a dramatic overhaul of the federal government, nor did she favor the kind of progressive populism that fueled his grassroots campaign. Instead, she proposed incremental change to the policies of her predecessor, Barack Obama, and a moderate economic approach to addressing such issues as healthcare reform, education, and income inequality.[6]

With the exception of Sanders, there is perhaps no greater antiestablishment figure in American politics today than Clinton's Republican opponent, Donald Trump. Whereas Clinton had spent thirty-one years in government life prior to her run for president in 2016, the multibillionaire real-estate mogul and reality television star entered the race without ever holding public office. In thirty-one years, Trump had switched political parties five times. Between 2009 and 2016 alone, he had been a Democrat, an Independent, and a Republican.[7] Trump treated his lack of political experience and lack of allegiance to a political party as an advantage, arguing that the nation was long overdue for a leader who, no longer beholden to Washington insiders, could disrupt the sluggish operations of federal bureaucracy and rid Washington of its corrupt political elite. As Trump said in a tweet on October 17, 2016, "I will Make Our

Government Honest Again—believe me. But first, I'm going to have to #draintheswamp."⁸

Trump leveraged his position as an outsider throughout the campaign, capitalizing on what the PRRI Research Center characterized as a sense of "anxiety, nostalgia, and mistrust" that has become increasingly pronounced among American voters in the last decade.⁹ Though Trump's platform combined center-right and, in some cases, center-left proposals with traditional conservative values, he framed his campaign promises in terms of right-wing populist rhetoric to challenge what he described as the political correctness of the Washington establishment. Trump promised to "make America great again" by building a wall along the U.S./Mexico border, deporting immigrants who he characterized as "drug dealers, criminals, and rapists," revoking the citizenship of children born in the United States to undocumented Mexican immigrants, temporarily "banning Muslims" from entering the United States, bringing manufacturing jobs back to the United States, rolling back environmental protection policies, and taking an "America first" approach to foreign trade policy.¹⁰ Unlike Clinton, Trump did not call for incremental change. Instead, he vowed to undo the corruption of the establishment and usher in a new era of American supremacy that would save the nation from what he portrayed as its descent into failure.

Trump's unfiltered rhetoric, his relentless attacks on dissenters both within and outside his own party, his dismissal of news media outlets that criticized him, and the support he found from figures associated with alt-right and white supremacist movements such as Steve Bannon and David Duke made him a challenging candidate even for the most loyal Republicans to endorse. To win the election, Trump would have to appeal to varied and seemingly incompatible pockets of the American electorate. Though he had found a base in the alt-right, it was unclear how Trump would appeal to the diverse interests of groups such as mainstream Republicans, evangelical Christians, and white working-class voters, many of whom tended to be politically neutral and some of whom had even voted for Barack Obama in the previous two elections. Polling data at both the national and the state level in the last month of the election reflected this, indicating to election forecasters that a Clinton victory was all but inevitable.

Trump had argued throughout his campaign that the polls were missing an undercurrent of his supporters who were not reporting their candidate preference in public opinion surveys but who nevertheless intended to cast their vote for him on election day. On

October 28, Trump's then campaign manager, Kellyanne Conway, told Fox News that "undercover" Trump supporters, or supporters who had kept their candidate preference private in public opinion surveys, would swing the election in Trump's favor.[11] Both *Politico*, on October 28, and *The New York Times*, on November 7, considered these claims and examined whether "social desirability bias," or a reluctance on the part of voters to express publicly a preference for Trump, had impacted polling data.[12] Both suggested that while there certainly might be "hidden Trump supporters," these voters would not have a significant impact on the outcome of the election.[13]

Election forecasters rely on public opinion surveys, mathematical modeling, and historical trends to predict voter shares for candidates at both the national and state level. It is important to note that because U.S. presidents are elected indirectly by the Electoral College rather than directly by the popular vote, state polling is crucial for forecasting election results. To be elected president, a candidate must win at least 270 of 538 electoral votes. Every state apart from Maine and Nebraska awards all of its electors to the candidate who wins the state. Hence, if a candidate wins a state even by a slim margin, he or she typically wins the entirety of that state's electoral votes. According to the Politico Battleground Project, there were at least 11 battleground states in 2016 that would deliver 147—nearly half—of the electoral votes required to win: Colorado, Florida, Iowa, Michigan, Nevada, New Hampshire, North Carolina, Ohio, Pennsylvania, Virginia, and Wisconsin.[14] In both 2008 and 2012, Obama had won the majority of these states, and the polls suggested that Clinton would have similar success.[15] This was especially true in "rust belt" states like Pennsylvania and Michigan, neither of which had elected a Republican president since 1988.[16]

Nearly every election forecast model suggested that a Trump victory was "virtually impossible or at least unlikely."[17] As early as October 18, Sam Wang of the Princeton Election Consortium tweeted his confidence in a Clinton victory, saying, "It's totally over. If Trump wins more than 240 votes, I will eat a bug."[18] Clinton's lead had narrowed in the final days of her campaign. According to Real Clear Politics, she led by 5.5 percent on October 16, 5.9 percent on October 23, 4.3 percent on October 30, and only 1.8 percent on November 8.[19] Yet, even as the race tightened, Clinton remained ahead in national polls and key battleground states, leading forecasters to put her chances of winning at 71 percent to 99 percent on election day (see figure 6.1 and table 6.1).[20]

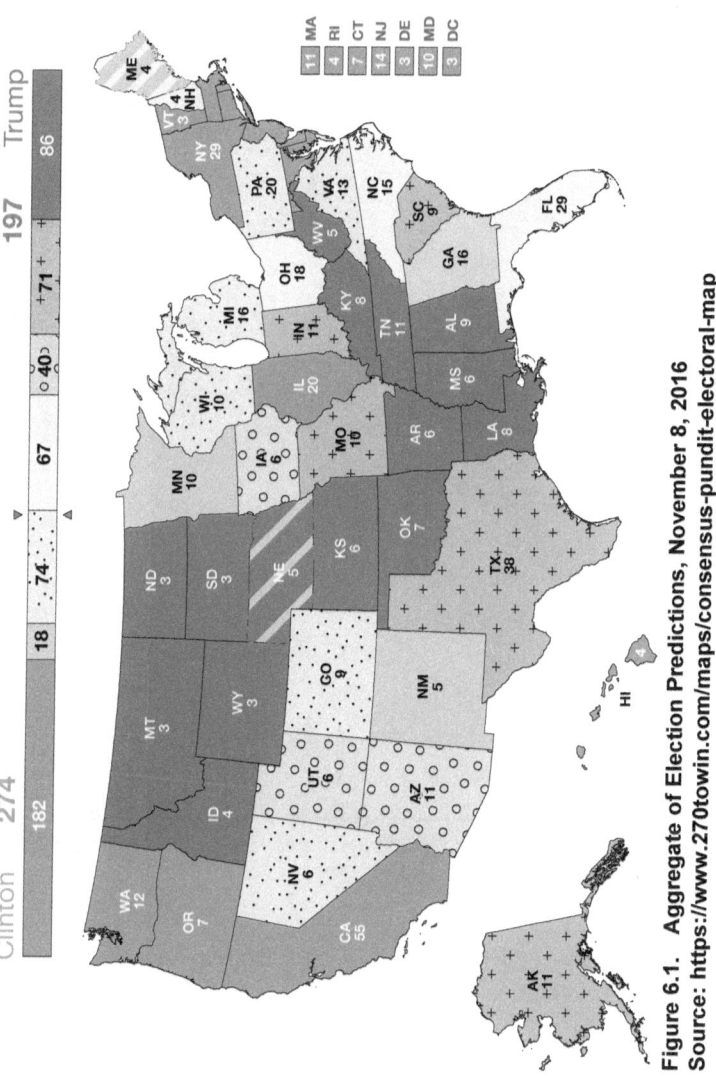

Figure 6.1. Aggregate of Election Predictions, November 8, 2016
Source: https://www.270towin.com/maps/consensus-pundit-electoral-map

Table 6.1. Individual Polling Organization Forecasts Used in Figure 6.1

	Polling Organization	Electoral Vote Forecasts for Clinton	Electoral Vote Forecasts for Trump
Statistical Modeling	Princeton Electoral Consortium	308	215
	PredictWise	322	215
	NYT Upshot	322	198
	FiveThirty-Eight Polls	272	214
Full-Time Analysts	Cook Political Forecast	278	214
	UVA Center for Politics	322	216
	Rothenberg and Gonzales	323	197
Media	CNN News	268	204
	Associated Press	274	190
	NBC News	274	170
	NPR News	274	114
	The Fix	275	215
	ABC News	274	188
	Fox News	274	215
	Louis Jacobson/ Governing	274	186

Source: https://www.270towin.com/content/forecasts-comprising-the-consensus-pundit-electoral-map

Casting doubt on the possibility of a Trump victory, the BBC reported on November 7:

> To prevail the Republican would have to either clear the table when it comes to [battleground] states or post a surprise win in a place like Pennsylvania, Michigan, or Virginia, where polling shows Mrs. Clinton ahead. Such a shoot-the-moon scenario is certainly possible . . . for this to become a reality, however,

Mr. Trump would essentially have to be perfect or polling would have to be off in a variety of disparate states that have decidedly different electorates.[21]

Yet, once the polls closed on the evening of November 8, this "shoot-the-moon" scenario began to materialize. At 10:39 PM EDT, Trump won Ohio, his first major battleground state. By 10:53 PM, he had taken Florida, making his path to victory begin to appear clearer than Clinton's. At 11:14 PM, he was declared the winner of North Carolina. He won Iowa at 12:06 AM, and then, at 1:35 AM, he had a stunning upset in Pennsylvania, putting him at 264 electoral votes. At this point, Trump only needed to win Wisconsin, Michigan, or Arizona to secure his victory. While he ultimately took all three, it was his win in Wisconsin at 2:30 AM on November 9, 2016, that enabled him to surpass the 270 electoral vote marker, making him the next president-elect of the United States (see figure 6.2 and table 6.2).[22]

Clinton conceded the race at 2:35 AM on November 9, 2016, and while it eventually became clear that polling data had accurately predicted her victory at the national level, an unanticipated surge of support for Trump at the state level left election forecasters in disbelief. This support not only decided the election but also raised the question of who these voters were, why they had gone unnoticed by pollsters in the days and weeks leading up to the election, and how such an incongruent mass could have cast their votes for a candidate whose right-wing populist rhetoric seemed out of accord with many of their interests and values.

In the days following the election, media outlets across the United States returned to the notion of the "hidden," "reluctant," or "shy" Trump supporter who Trump's campaign team had insisted would decide the election and who, in the end, seemed to have made possible one of the greatest political upsets in American history. As *The Washington Post* reported on November 12, "One possibility is that polls were off because people were uncomfortable openly sharing that they planned to vote for Trump. . . . In short, identifying as a Trump supporter may have seemed—at least to some people—as socially undesirable."[23] *The Guardian* reported on November 10 that the phenomenon of the shy or hidden Trump supporter was perhaps most pronounced in white women who concealed their preference for Trump because of his hostile and predatory remarks toward women throughout the campaign, but who ultimately cast

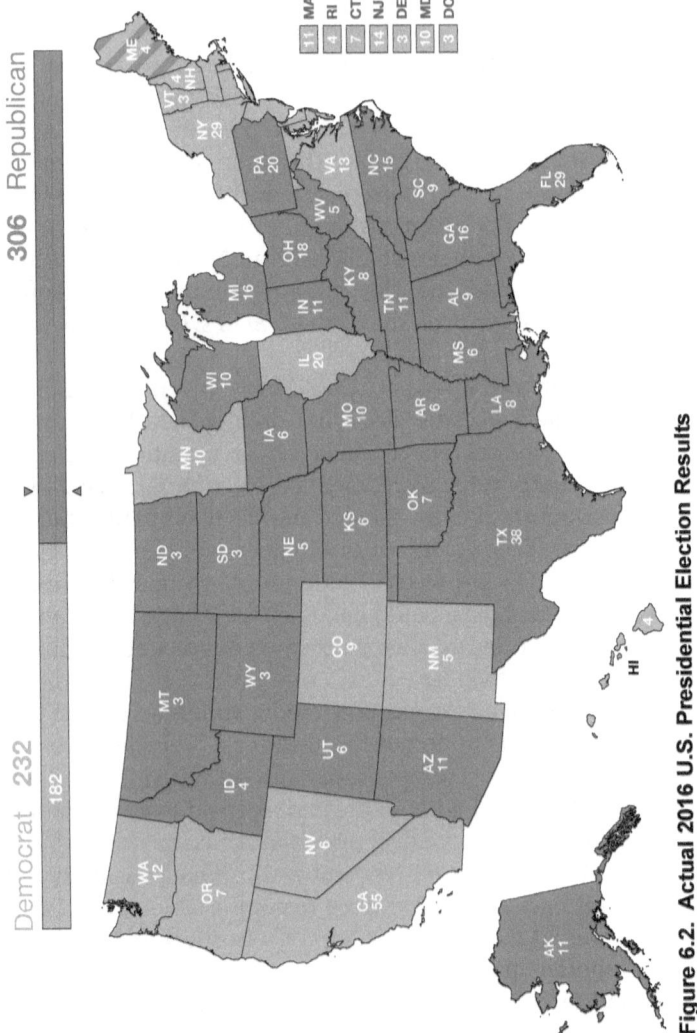

Figure 6.2. Actual 2016 U.S. Presidential Election Results
Source: https://www.270towin.com/2016_Election

Table 6.2. Actual 2016 U.S. Presidential Election Results

Candidate and Party	Electoral Vote	Popular Vote
Donald Trump (Republican)	306 (304)	62,980,169
Hilary Clinton (Democrat)	232	65,845,063
Gary Johnson (Libertarian)	0	4,488,931
Jill Stein (Green Party)	0	1,457,050
Evan McMullin (Independent)	0	728,830

Source: https://www.270towin.com/2016_Election

their vote for him in spite of this.[24] *USA Today* suggested on November 9 that hidden Trump supporters could have been a likely culprit in 2016 presidential election polling errors.[25] So, too, did *The Boston Globe* on November 9, *The New York Times* on November 16, and National Public Radio on November 9.[26] Though some media outlets disagreed with this assessment of the election results, the language of hiddenness, reluctance, and shyness nevertheless became ubiquitous, giving articulation to a seemingly incongruent mass of voters who, for no reason apart from what seemed to be anger and discontent, galvanized behind a right-wing populist outsider, transforming Trump's seemingly impossible odds of winning into a historic victory.

Political scientists have since approached this phenomenon by focusing on the quality of the samples that pollsters took throughout the election, the disparity between the accuracy of national and state forecasts, and the extent to which the statistical models used to forecast the election might have been flawed. Peter Enns, Julius Lagodny, and Johnathan Schludt have argued that there is evidence in public opinion surveys taken in mid-October to suggest that hidden Trump supporters were an important factor in explaining why the polling errors in the 2016 U.S. presidential election were so widespread. They say, "We define hidden Trump supporters as survey respondents who did not directly express their preference for Trump in the survey, but who nevertheless appeared as if they would support Trump on the basis of their responses to other survey questions."[27] By using the answers that survey respondents provided to these other questions, rather than focusing on candidate preference alone, the study shows that it would have been possible to accurately predict the outcomes of five of seven swing states in the 2016 U.S. presidential election. Enns, Lagodny, and Schludt suggest on the basis of these findings that there were likely a statistically significant number of voters, both because of social desirability bias and what they call "top of the head" considerations, who decided as early as mid-October to vote for Trump, but who did not reveal this preference in polling surveys.[28] Others such as Alexander Coppock have argued that while so-called hidden Trump supporters might have existed, they were not widespread enough to decide the 2016 U.S. presidential election. Coppock thus casts doubt on the statistical significance of the "hidden Trump supporter," opting instead to explain the surprising outcome of this election in terms of late-deciding voters, or voters who reported their candidate preference honestly in surveys in October, but who changed their vote in the final week of the election.[29] The American Association for Public Opinion Research released a report in 2017 evaluating the reason for such widespread polling errors in the 2016 election. This study indicates that while national polls were correct, state polls in the Upper-Midwest underestimated Trump support for three reasons. The first was real change in voter preference during the final week of the election. The second was a failure on the part of pollsters to adjust for over-representation of college graduates, which proved to be a critical consideration for this election. Third, the report indicates that some Trump supporters who participated in pre-election polls did not reveal themselves as Trump supporters until after the election, out-numbering late revealing Clinton supporters, and pointing to a "shy Trump supporter effect" as well as evidence of late reporting voter preference.[30]

Given how difficult it is to verify empirically a concealed preference for one candidate or another, it is unclear whether political scientists will come to a consensus about the impact that hidden Trump supports had on the outcome of the 2016 U.S. presidential election. Yet, it is clear that regardless of the impact, these voters existed. In view of this, I wish to suggest that the fact that the language of hiddenness itself has become so ubiquitous to describe a vast swath of the American electorate warrants our attention. It is significant that Trump's campaign team used this language in the weeks leading up to the election to suggest that the polls were wrong. It is equally notable that the surprising outcome of this election left media outlets and political scientists alike wondering whether this phenomenon was real. As I will suggest in what follows, Arendt's novel critical perspective on the loneliness of liberal subjectivity provides an important theoretical frame for interpreting contemporary political phenomena like this one. Though such a framework by no means proves empirically the statistical significance of these voters, it does provide a platform to consider the significance and potential dangers of this new part of our political lexicon. With this, it opens up possibilities for considering how this phenomenon and others like it might help us to understand the vulnerability of Western liberal democracies today to right-wing nationalism and populist politics.

LONELINESS AND NEOLIBERAL SUBJECTIVITY TODAY

As we saw in the previous chapter, Arendt takes loneliness to be a symptom of the loss of a common world, a loss that cannot be thought apart from the destruction of the political sphere in the modern era. She attributes this loss to the atomized and isolated forms of subjectivity that are affirmed and reproduced by the liberal political structures that organize modern life. She insists, too, that totalitarianism can only begin to take shape after the masses have been rendered lonely. In what follows, I will attempt to demonstrate that this language of hiddenness is one among a number of contemporary political phenomena that may be interpreted as a symptom of the loneliness that remains at work in political life today. Given that Arendt's account unfolds in the context of the rise of European totalitarianism at the beginning of the twentieth century, one might argue that it would be reductive of our own complex political environment to apply her concept of loneliness to a contemporary phenomenon like the hidden Trump supporter. Yet, recent scholarship has similarly problematized the decline of the political sphere, attributing this decline to the global ascendance of neoliberalism over the last half-century.

We see this, for instance, in Wendy Brown's 2015 analysis of the ways in which neoliberalism has accelerated the decline of Western liberal democracies in *Undoing the Demos: Neoliberalism's Stealth Revolution*. Though neoliberalism itself is a contentious term, widely acknowledged by scholars to have no fixed or easily definable coordinates, Brown argues that we can, at the very least, understand neoliberalism as economic rather than political in nature.[31] Her task, in light of this, is to consider the ways in which the economic underpinnings of neoliberal rationality have transformed political subjectivity and statehood today.

Broadly understood, Brown says, neoliberalism may be defined as "an ensemble of economic policies in accord with the root principle of affirming free markets."[32] What distinguishes neoliberalism is not that it marketizes and monetizes all spaces from without but rather that it attacks from within, transforming subjects into economic actors whose value is measured by nothing more than the metrics of utility, efficiency, and accumulation. In this, she says:

> Neoliberalism is best understood not simply as economic policy, but as a governing rationality that disseminates market values and metrics to every sphere of life and construes the human itself exclusively as *homo oeconomicus*. Neoliberalism thus does not merely privatize—turn over to the market for individual production and consumption—what was formally publically supported and valued. Rather, it formulates everything, everywhere, in terms of capital investment and appreciation, including and especially humans themselves.[33]

By remaking citizen and state alike into projects of capital management and investment, Brown explains that neoliberal rationality has reconfigured the way that we conceptualize cornerstones of political life such as justice, individual and popular sovereignty, law, and democratic citizenship. Neoliberal rationality compels us to conceive of these concerns not as shared public matters but rather as issues that must be subsumed under the project of capital enhancement, recede altogether, or be radically transformed as they are economized.[34]

Moreover, Brown argues, neoliberal rationality does not just transpose these broader ideals from a political to an economic register. Beyond this, it refashions noneconomic domains of life into spaces that are governed by the metrics of utility, efficiency, and accumulation. The reach of this rationality is so expansive, she argues, that it informs where we choose to send our children to school, how we are evaluated at work, the methods we use to conduct and evaluate research in the academy, how food production and consumption is undertaken, how we pursue health and fitness, and even how we date.[35] Though there is certainly continuity between liberalism and neoliberalism, Brown argues that this feature of neoliberal rationality—its expansion of the metrics of utility and accumulation to all domains of life—distinguishes it from classical liberalism, whose theorists, she argues, were careful to preserve the space between public, private, and economic life. By contrast, Brown says, "Neoliberal rationality disseminates the *model of the market* to all domains and activities—even where money is not at issue—and configures human beings exhaustively as market actors, always, only, and everywhere as *homo oeconomicus.*"[36]

At stake in this, Brown argues, is the transposition of concepts such as freedom and citizenship from a political register into an economic one. She says, "One important effect of neoliberalization is the vanquishing of liberal democracy's already anemic *homo politicus*, a vanquishing with enormous consequences for democratic institutions, cultures, and imaginaries."[37] In Brown's view, this not only fundamentally changes the ways in which society is ordered, but, even more than this, undermines the very conditions under which concepts like citizenship can remain meaningful. When we are no more than *homo oeconomicus*, when every domain has been refashioned according to economic metrics, Brown says:

> The foundation vanishes for citizenship concerned with public things and the common good. Here, the problem is not just that public goods are defunded and common ends are devalued by neoliberal reason, although this is so, but that citizenship itself loses its *political* valence and venue. Valence: *Homo oeconomicus* approaches everything as a market and knows only market conduct; it cannot think public purposes or common problems in a distinctly political way.[38]

She explains that this has devastating consequences for political life. First, it makes the existence of anything we might consider a public good increasingly difficult to speak of or secure. The government comes to be associated not with the public but "only as an alternate market actor," while transforming citizens into "investors or consumers, not as members of a democratic polity who share power and certain common goods, spaces, and experiences."[39] Second, it transforms democracy itself, giving economic valence to the distinctly political value of such ideals as equality, autonomy, and freedom.[40] In consequence of this, democracies come to be understood as requiring "technically skilled human capital, not educated participants in public life and common rule."[41] Third, it reconfigures subjects and, especially citizen subjects according to today's market metrics of self-investing human capital, which, she says, "is distinctly not concerned with acquiring the knowledge and experience needed for intelligent democratic citizenship."[42] Finally, she says, it transforms knowledge, thought, and training into things that are valued and desired exclusively for their contribution to capital enhancement. As such, she says, "Knowledge is not sought . . . for developing the capacities of citizens, sustaining culture, knowing the world, or envisioning and crafting different ways of life in common. Rather, it is sought for 'positive ROI'—return on investment."[43] In view of this, Brown explains that the very conditions of democracy—which include limits on wealth and poverty as well as educated citizens oriented toward the problems of public life—are severely challenged by neoliberal rationality and policy.[44]

Significantly, Brown argues that in reducing all domains of life to *homo oeconomicus*, this rationality produces a "limited form of human existence," one that she, following Arendt and Aristotle, describes as mere life or, as Marx puts it, a life "confined by necessity."[45] Neoliberal rationality, she explains, hollows out the distinctiveness of human life, leaving behind subjects who are only able to see themselves and others in terms of the struggle for existence and wealth accumulation.[46] An ordering that strips life of its distinctively human quality, she says, "Neoliberalism is the rationality through which capitalism finally swallows humanity—not only with its machinery of compulsory commodification and profit-driven expansion, but by its form of valuation."[47] Brown, in 2015, thus identifies conditions very similar to those that Arendt identifies in her own critique of the loneliness of liberal subjectivity. In particular, both identify the ways in which liberal and neoliberal rationality not only alter and diminish the public sphere of human existence but also render human beings superfluous, interchangeable, and expendable.

We find a similar critique of the dangers and limits of neoliberalism in Bonnie Honig's 2017 work *Public Things: Democracy in Disrepair*. Honig sets out in this work to articulate the importance of public things—emphasizing the importance of the word "things" in the Latin, *"res publica"*—for binding communities together. In focusing on public objects rather than public subjects, Honig attempts to demonstrate the danger of the unrelenting privatization of much of American life while deepening Brown's analysis of the all-consuming power of neoliberal rationality. Honig explains that there is today "the contemporary impulse to privatize everything (though in the United States, 'privatization' is often supported by public state power)."[48] Though this impulse is often guided by the concern to improve efficiency and to reduce waste and sloth among civil servants, Honig maintains that the value of public things far exceeds these metrics. It is Honig's view that democracy requires public things that are irreducible to their instrumental value, things that citizens of a democracy have a shared concern for and that provide a basis for common, public engagement. Democracy, she argues, is rooted in the love for and contestation of public things. Without these things, citizenship risks being reduced to repetitive private work and democratic participation to something concerned only with extraordinary crisis as opposed to a more sustained engagement in debate over the public good.[49] Brown and Honig are not alone in expressing these concerns for the way in which neoliberal rationality has diminished the possibility for public life. They are also apparent in the recent work of such figures as William Davies, who treats the rise of Donald Trump in the United States and Brexit in the United Kingdom as the revenge of the political on the economic order produced by neoliberal policies and practices, as well as in Lars Cornelissen's work on the possibilities for resistance and alternative rationalities that are responsive to neoliberal rationality.[50]

While Arendt's critique of the atomization and isolation that she believes liberalism produces is specific to her own historical and political context of European society in the period leading up to the Second World War, we nevertheless find resonant concerns in recent scholarship for the alienated forms of subjectivity that are produced by the neoliberal structures that organize contemporary political life. As atomizing as Arendt suggests the liberal political structures that organize modern life are and as destructive as she suggests they have been to the political sphere, we see in these more recent discourses how the further refinement of these structures by neoliberal rationality only makes Arendt's concerns more relevant. In view of this, I maintain that while Arendt develops her analysis in a specific, complex historical context, this does not diminish the importance of her theoretical framework for our own world today. Instead, by turning to these recent discourses, we find that her analysis is as prescient as ever before and is therefore useful for examining the loneliness that may remain at work in such contemporary political phenomena as the hidden Trump supporter.

POLITICAL LONELINESS AND THE HIDDEN TRUMP SUPPORTER

If we take seriously the analysis that figures like Brown and others offer of the neoliberal rationality of contemporary life, we can justifiably bring Arendt's discourse on loneliness to bear on contemporary political phenomena. With this, we might interpret the language of hiddenness that became pervasive during the 2016 U.S. presidential election, no less than its relation to the ascendance of far-right populism in the United States, as symptomatic of the kind of political loneliness that Arendt identifies. Without a space to appear, to announce oneself to the world and to present one's views in the presence of others, the possibility for seeing oneself as a member of a common world fades away. The other of appearance is hiddenness, and with this hiddenness comes the widespread sense of loneliness and desperation. The decay of the political, or that space in which we appear to one another in the fullness of our humanity, is the very condition under which something like a hidden Trump supporter becomes possible. Unable to see oneself as belonging to a common world, this hiddenness is dangerous; under such conditions, Arendt suggests, we lose the ability to see one another in the fullness of our humanity and become willing, in turn, to surrender to totalizing forms of communal life.

We can see the danger of this hiddenness in several especially resonant passages from *The Origins of Totalitarianism*. In her own analysis of the conditions that gave way to totalitarian movements in Europe at the beginning of the twentieth century, Arendt begins by considering the effect that the collapse of class-based societies into mass societies had on political life. This collapse, she argues, revealed that the subjects of the nation-state had lost the political sphere of their lives, and, because of this, had become atomized and isolated in unprecedented ways. That is, Arendt says, "The apolitical character of the nation-state's population came to light only when the class system broke down and carried with it the whole fabric of visible and invisible threads which bound the people to the body politic."[51] Whereas the party system had held in check these apolitical masses by representing their class interests in government, the collapse of the class system meant also the collapse of this party system, setting in motion the rise of mass movements. No longer willing to believe that party politicians actually represented their interests in government, Arendt argues that these hidden masses suddenly became politically efficacious in ways that had never before been seen. She says:

> The fall of the protecting class walls transformed the slumbering majorities behind all parties into one great unorganized, structureless mass of furious individuals who had nothing in common except their vague apprehension that the hopes of party members were doomed, that, consequently, the most respected, articulate and representative members of the community were fools, and that all the powers that be were not so much evil as they were equally stupid and fraudulent.[52]

Characterized by this discontent with the status quo, Arendt argues that mass movements began to form in response to widespread disenchantment with the political elite. While party politicians had taken these masses to be politically indifferent and unimportant for securing their own political power, Arendt is clear that it was precisely this neglect that enabled these silent majorities to become politically relevant. She explains:

> The . . . democratic illusion exploded by totalitarian movements was that the politically indifferent masses did not matter. . . . They made apparent what no other organ of public opinion had ever been able to show, namely, that democratic government had rested as much on the silent approbation and tolerance of the indifferent and inarticulate sections of the people as on the articulate and visible institutions and organizations of the country. Thus, when totalitarian movements invaded parliament with their contempt for parliamentary government . . . they succeeded in convincing the people at large that parliamentary majorities were spurious and did not necessarily correspond to the realities of the country.[53]

While these masses had remained hidden, covered over, forgotten by mainstream party politicians, Arendt argues that this sudden awakening to their atomization and isolation gave rise to a "new terrifying negative solidarity."[54] This solidarity formed among individuals with interests so divergent that, under different circumstances, they would have had no reason to align with one another. Arendt explains that what drew this undifferentiated mass together was no real common bond, but rather a pervasive sense of having been rendered expendable and a willingness, in light of this, to surrender themselves to whatever alternative presented itself. This, in turn, not only drew the small property owner and the unemployed laborer together but also attracted members of the elite, who, she says, were the most illustrative example and articulate spokesmen for this more general phenomenon. That so strange a coalition was able to form was indicative of a distinctive form of loneliness, one that had only become increasingly pronounced as these masses were pressed more closely together by the instruments of modern economic and techno-scientific rationality. As Arendt explains,

> The truth is that the masses grew out of the fragments of a highly atomized society whose competitive structure and concomitant loneliness of the individual had been held in check only through membership in a class. The chief characteristic of the mass man is not brutality and backwardness, but his isolation and lack of normal social relationships.[55]

This insight that "the mass man" is not characterized by brutality or backwardness, but rather by isolation and a lack of normal social relationships is a crucial one. While one may instinctively presume this backwardness in characterizing those who join such movements, Arendt is clear that they arise not from this but rather from the loneliness that is produced and affirmed by the political structures that organize modern life. If only the most backward and brutish people found themselves compelled by totalitarian ideology, then these movements would never have been able to appeal across such disparate demographics, nor would they have had any chance of becoming mainstream political institutions. It was rather the loneliness of modern mass society that made it possible for so many seemingly ordinary citizens, citizens who might have otherwise been politically indifferent, to be compelled to give themselves over to the delusional fellowship promised by totalitarianism.

Further evidence of this widespread loneliness, Arendt argues, can be found in the susceptibility of these ordinary citizens to totalitarian propaganda. As we have seen, it is Arendt's view that the possibility for a shared reality and a sense of common belonging depends on being able to appear to others in the full illumination of the public sphere. She therefore argues that it was in virtue of the loss of this space that made totalitarian rhetoric compelling to so many, a rhetoric, she argues, that made visible what had otherwise remained hidden and socially unacceptable. She says:

> The spokesmen for totalitarian movements possessed an instinct for anything that ordinary party propaganda or public opinion

did not care to touch. Everything hidden, everything passed over in silence, became of major significance, regardless of its own intrinsic importance.... Truth was whatever respectable society had hypocritically passed over, or covered up with corruption.[56]

Upon being severed from the world and the relations that constitute it, left only to see themselves as superfluous and expendable, Arendt argues that individuals lose their orientation toward the reality of the world. She suggests that the loneliness this produces is easily appeased by totalitarian propaganda. By making visible these masses who had been presumed by party politicians to be of no consequence, totalitarian leaders were able to compel them toward their own murderous ends. While such propaganda has no basis in reality, Arendt argues that it is among the most striking features of totalitarian movements that it can have such broad appeal. She says:

> The effectiveness of this kind of propaganda demonstrates one of the chief characteristics of the modern masses. They do not believe in the reality of their own experience; they do not trust their eyes and ears but only their imaginations, which may be caught by anything that is at once universal and consistent with itself. What convinces the masses are not facts, and not even invented facts, but only the consistency of the system of which they are presumably a part.[57]

While loneliness on its own cannot give rise to totalitarianism, it is the condition, Arendt argues, that gives the contingent factors that make possible totalitarianism their determining power. Arendt is clear that there will always be far-right movements on the fringes of the political spectrum. What enables the normalization and expansion of these movements is the experience loneliness, which she says is the one thing that "prepares men for totalitarianism in a non-totalitarian world."[58]

In view of this, we might consider the echoes of these passages in such recent phenomena as the hidden Trump supporter and the 2016 U.S. presidential election more generally. A similar negative solidarity appears to have formed among seemingly divergent groups such as evangelical Christians, white-supremacists, center-right fiscal Republicans, and the white working class. They have aligned behind a member of the economic elite, whose political incorrectness and personal lifestyle, no less than his economic interests, have little in common with these groups, groups which themselves have very little in common with each other. The effectiveness of Donald

Trump's rhetoric both during and after his 2016 campaign seems to turn not on his ability to appeal to these interests but rather on his ability to make significant "everything hidden, everything passed over in silence . . . regardless of its own intrinsic importance" and to insist that the "truth is whatever respectable society had hypocritically passed over, or covered up with corruption."[59] We see, too, the neglect on the part of establishment politicians like Clinton of these seemingly apolitical masses. Whereas Trump held rallies in rust belt states like Michigan eight times and Wisconsin five times during his campaign, Clinton campaigned in Michigan three times and did not set foot in Wisconsin.[60] To be sure, polling data suggested that Clinton had no need to campaign in these states; yet, what this polling data seems to have overlooked were those slumbering majorities to which Arendt points.

The outcome of the 2016 U.S. presidential election seems to point to the very democratic illusion that Arendt identifies, namely, "That democratic government had rested as much on the silent approbation and tolerance of the indifferent and inarticulate sections of the people as on the articulate and visible institutions and organizations of the country."[61] Trump's right-wing populist rhetoric effectively galvanized this negative solidarity, challenging the "political correctness" of the status quo. If we follow Arendt, we might, in turn, recognize that this rhetoric compels, not because it has any hook in reality or fact, or because it speaks to the interests of these groups, but because it is consistent. That the language of fake news and alternative facts has become pervasive, and the current president of the United States able to appeal to this mistrust of reality in his own rhetoric, should remind us of Arendt's remarks on the ways in which loneliness leaves human beings unable to trust the reality of their own experience, using not their eyes and ears to orient them but rather their imagination. Such rhetoric, Arendt argues, can only be effective in a world in which loneliness has already set in and individuals no longer see themselves as belonging to a common world.

These echoes should give us pause. While it is crucial to remain attentive to the differences between the conditions that gave rise to totalitarianism in Arendt's era and our own political situation today, we nevertheless find that her insights provide an important platform to consider the loneliness of neoliberal subjectivity today and the extent to which it has created a vulnerability among citizens in Western liberal democracies to right-wing nationalism and populist politics. We usually associate totalitarianism with a form of government, often fascism and sometimes communism; we then treat liberalism as the other of totalitarianism. Arendt, for her part, thinks differently about this, treating totalitarianism as the closure of the political sphere, a closure that is possible in any society, including our own liberal democratic society. That the language of hiddenness could become so pervasive during a democratic election today points to this closure. That it could be perceived as a vehicle for the ascendance of a far-right, antiestablishment populist politician makes clear the dangers of this closure. To be sure, our era is decidedly different from the one that Arendt is describing. We do not live in a totalitarian society, nor has a new Hitler come to power. Even so, Arendt's insights should prompt us to reflect on the loneliness that may remain at work in our own society today. After all, Arendt says, "Loneliness, once a borderline experience . . . has become an everyday experience of the evergrowing masses of our century. The merciless process into which totalitarianism drives and organizes the masses looks like a suicidal escape from this reality."[62] Hence, while our own political environment is irreducible to Arendt's, and while we may be far from the totalitarian society that she is describing, the problem of political loneliness today has nevertheless prepared us for this possibility.

What, then, might we learn from the phenomenon of the hidden Trump supporter? First, the very language of hiddenness points to a broader failure within our own society to create robust political spaces for the appearance of speech and action. In the absence of such spaces, we tend to retreat into the lamplight of the private, creating echo chambers for ourselves that leave us hidden from one another. Second, and in consequence of this, this phenomenon indicates that those with whom we share the world have become lonely, isolated, and atomized, no longer able to see themselves or others as belonging to a common world. Third, and perhaps most importantly, we might anticipate the dangers that this experience of loneliness creates for engendering a new form of totalitarianism today. Far-right movements are becoming increasingly mainstream, galvanizing support across classes and political interest groups who have nothing in common except for a shared frustration with the powers that be. These movements are finding their greatest appeal in nations that purport to be the most liberal, democratic, and progressive on earth, pointing to the need for critical engagement with the ways in which these political structures might produce and perpetuate the very loneliness that is making liberal citizens vulnerable to the populist politics of the day.

By developing the peculiar loneliness of the current age in a political register, we thus find that Arendt opens new paths for thinking the possibilities for communal life today. Not simply a question of thinking the "we" anew, Arendt indicates that the task before us is to think of the conditions under which we come to see ourselves as a "we" in terms of a rehabilitation of the political sphere. With this, it requires that we think of citizenship, not as an indefinitely expandable legal status, but rather as a responsibility to make one another visible in the realm of politics. While this would no doubt work against the loneliness of modern life, Arendt reminds us that such a rehabilitation requires that we have the courage to appear before our political opponents, to speak and act with them in order to take shared responsibility for the world we have inherited.[63] As I will suggest by way of conclusion, it demands what might be described as a politics of appearance, or a politics that is able to contravene the loneliness of neoliberal subjectivity by drawing us out of our hiding and into the full illumination of the public realm.

NOTES

1. See, for instance, Ian Storey, "The Politics of Defining Today: Towards a Critical Historicism of Judgment," *Arendt Studies*, 1 (2017): 61–86, DOI: 10.5840/arendtstudies2017957.

2. Mark Bulik and Stephen Hiltner, "In 13 Headlines: The Drama of Election Night," *The New York Times*, November 16, 2016, https://www.nytimes.com/2016/11/17/insider/in-13-headlines-the-drama-of-election-night.html. See also Peter Enns, "Understanding the 2016 US Presidential Election Polls: The Importance of Hidden Trump Supporters," *Statistics, Politics and Policy*, 8.1 (2017): 41–63.

3. There is extensive literature on social desirability bias and whether it can help to explain polling errors in election forecasting. This theory suggests that polling errors in races in which women and people of color appear to be outperforming their opponents but ultimately lose the race can be attributed to survey respondents' unwillingness to report their true preference for fear of being perceived as a racist or sexist. For more on this, see Samara Klar, Christopher R. Weber, and Yanna Krupnikov, "Social Desirability Bias in the 2016 Presidential Election," *The Forum*, 14.4 (December 2016): 433–443. Andy Brownback and Aaron Novotny, "Social Desirability Bias and Polling Errors in

the 2016 Presidential Election," *Journal of Behavioral and Experimental Economics*, 74 (June 2018): 38–56; Pei-Shan Liao, "Social Desirability Bias and Mode Effects in the Case of Voting Behavior," *Bulletin de Méthodologie Sociologique*, 132.1 (October 2016): 73–83; and Gregory J. Payne, "The Bradley Effect: Mediated Reality of Race and Politics in the 2008 U.S. Presidential Election," *American Behavioral Scientist*, 54.4 (December 2010): 417–435.

4. Akeel Bilgrami, "Reflections on Three Populisms," *Philosophy and Social Criticism*, 44.4 (2018): 453–62.

5. Ezra Klein, "What Hillary Clinton Really Thinks," *Vox*, Sept. 13, 2017, https://www.vox.com/policy-and-politics/2017/9/13/16298120/hillary-clinton-what-happened-interview.

6. See "Clinton, Hillary Rodham," History, Art and Archives: United States House of Representatives, https://history.house.gov/People/detail/11751, and "About Hillary," The Office of Hillary Rodham Clinton, hillaryclinton.com/about/.

7. See "Donald Trump: About," https://www.donaldjtrump.com/about/; Zachary Crocket, "Donald Trump Is the Only President Ever with No Political or Military Experience," January 23, 2017, https://www.vox.com/policy-and-politics/2016/11/11/13587532/donald-trump-no-experience.

8. Donald J. Trump Twitter Post, October 18, 2016, https://twitter.com/realdonaldtrump/status/788402585816276992?lang=en.

9. Betsy Cooper, Daniel Cox, Rachel Lienesch, and Robert P. Jones, "Anxiety, Nostalgia, Mistrust: Findings from the 2015 American Values Survey," November 17, 2015, https://www.prri.org/research/survey-anxiety-nostalgia-and-mistrust-findings-from-the-2015-american-values-survey/#.Vktmid-rRTZ.

10. Ibid.

11. "Trump Campaign: Undercover Trump Supporters Helped Deliver Upset Victory," *Fox News*, November 9, 2018, https://www.foxnews.com/politics/trump-campaign-undercover-supporters-helped-deliver-upset-victory.

12. See Stephan Shepard, "Poll: Shy Trump Supporters Are a Mirage," *Politico*, November 3, 2016, https://www.politico.com/story/2016/11/poll-shy-voters-trump-230667 and Peter Enns and Jonathan P. Schuldt, "Are There Really Hidden Trump Voters," *New York Times*, November 7, 2016, https://www.nytimes.com/2016/11/07/opinion/are-there-really-hidden-trump-voters.html.

13. David Byler, "Poll Position: Where Clinton, Trump Stand on Election Eve," *Real Clear Politics*, November 7, 2016, https://www.realclearpolitics.com/articles/2016/11/07/poll_position_where_clinton_trump_stand_on_election_eve_132270.html.

14. Charlie Mahtesian, "Where Are the Swing States in 2016?" *Politico*, June 15, 2016, https://www.politico.com/blogs/swing-states-2016-election/2016/06/what-are-the-swing-states-in-2016-list-224427.

15. In 2008 Obama won WI, PA, OH, IA, IL, VA, NC, FL, CO, and NV, putting him at 365 electoral votes over McCain's 173. In 2012, Obama won all of these states again with the exception of NC, putting him at 332 electoral votes

over Romney's 206 electoral votes. See "2008 Presidential Election," *270 to Win*, https://www.270towin.com/2008_Election/.

16. Ibid.

17. Elizabeth Connors, Samara Klar, and Yanna Krupnikov, "There May Have Been Shy Trump Supporters After All," *Washington Post*, November 12, 2016, https://www.washingtonpost.com/news/monkey-cage/wp/2016/11/12/there-may-have-been-shy-trump-supporters-after-all/.

18. Ibid.

19. David Byler, "Poll Position: Where Clinton, Trump Stand on Election Eve," *Real Clear Politics*, November 7, 2016, https://www.realclearpolitics.com/articles/2016/11/07/poll_position_where_clinton_trump_stand_on_election_eve_132270.html.

20. Ibid.

21. Anthony Zurcher, "US Election: Is Trump or Clinton Going to Win," *The BBC*, November 7, 2016, https://www.bbc.com/news/election-us-2016-37884603.

22. "Election Result Timeline," https://www.theguardian.com/us-news/2016/nov/08/presidential-election-updates-trump-clinton-news.

23. Connors, et al., "There may have been Shy Trump Supporters Afterall."

24. Lois Beckett, "The Real 'Shy Trump Vote'—How 53% of Women Pushed Him to Victory," November 10, 2016, https://www.theguardian.com/us-news/2016/nov/10/white-women-donald-trump-victory. This article cites, in particular, how women survey respondents might have concealed their preference in early October, when the infamous 2005 Access Hollywood tape was released, capturing Trump's lewd and predatory remarks about women he had tried or wanted to seduce. See David Fahrenthold, "Trump Recorded Having Extremely Lewd Conversation about Women in 2005 (Posted 2016–10–07 20:01:27): On Soap Opera Set, the GOP Nominee Bragged about Groping and Trying to Have Sex with Women," *The Washington Post*, October 7, 2016. http://ezpro.cc.gettysburg.edu:2048/login?url=https://ezpro.cc.gettysburg.edu:2609/docview/1827430259?accountid=2694.

25. Nathan Bomey, "How Did Pollsters Get Trump, Clinton Election So Wrong?" *USA Today*, November 9, 2016, https://www.usatoday.com/story/news/politics/elections/2016/2016/11/09/pollsters-donald-trump-hillary-clinton-2016-presidential-election/93523012/.

26. Michele McPhee, "The Hidden Trump Voter: The Police," *The Boston Globe*, November 9, 2016, https://www.bostonglobe.com/opinion/2016/11/09/the-hidden-trump-voter-police/71MUxHoqBzNCKZZcpH42nO/story.html; Peter Enns and Jonathan P. Schuldt, "Did Moderates Help Elect Trump," November 16, 2016, https://www.nytimes.com/2016/11/16/opinion/did-moderates-help-elect-trump.html; and Ron Elving "Trump Confounds the Pros, Connects with Just the Right Voters," *National Public Radio*, November 9, 2016, https://www.npr.org/2016/11/09/501387988/trump-confounds-the-pros-connects-with-just-the-right-voters.

27. Peter Enns, Julius Lagodny, and Johnathan Schludt, "Understanding the 2016 US Presidential Election Polls: The Importance of Hidden Trump Supporters," *Statistics, Politics and Policy*, 8.1 (2017): 41–63, 43.

28. Enns et al., 44.
29. See Alexander Coppock, "Did Shy Trump Supporters Bias the 2016 Polls? Evidence from a Nationally Representative List Experiment," *Statistics, Politics, and Policy*, 8.1 (2017): 29–40. DOI: 10.1515/spp-2016-0005.
30. "An Evaluation of 2016 Election Polls in the US" *American Association for Public Opinion Research*, https://www.aapor.org/Education-Resources/Reports/An-Evaluation-of-2016-Election-Polls-in-the-U-S.aspx.
31. Wendy Brown, *Undoing the Demos: Neoliberalism's Stealth Revolution* (New York: Zone Books, 2015), 22.
32. Brown, 28.
33. Ibid., 178.
34. Ibid., 22.
35. Ibid., 33–34.
36. Ibid., 31.
37. Ibid., 35.
38. Ibid., 39.
39. Ibid., 176.
40. Ibid., 177.
41. Ibid.
42. Ibid.
43. Ibid., 177–178.
44. Ibid., 178–179.
45. Ibid., 43.
46. Ibid.
47. Ibid., 44.
48. See Bonnie Honig, *Public Things: Democracy in Disrepair* (New York: Fordham University Press, 2017), 15.
49. See Honig, 7. For more on the notion of "extraordinary crisis" see Lauren Berlant, *Cruel Optimism* (Durham: Duke University Press, 2011), 5.
50. See William Davies, *The Limits of Neoliberalism: Authority, Sovereignty, and the Logic of Competition* (Washington D.C.: Sage Press, 2017), and Lars Cornelissen, "On the Subject of Neoliberalism: Rethinking Resistance in the Critique of Neoliberal Rationality," *Constellations*, 25 (2018): 133–146.
51. Hannah Arendt, *The Origins of Totalitarianism* (New York: Harcourt Inc., 1974), 314.
52. Ibid., 315.
53. Ibid., 312.
54. Ibid., 315.
55. Ibid., 317.
56. Ibid., 351.
57. Ibid.
58. Ibid., 478.
59. Ibid., 351.
60. Linda Poon and George Joseph, "Mapping How Clinton's Blue Wall Came Down," *City Lab*, November 10, 2016, https://www.citylab

.com/equity/2016/11/the-shattering-of-clintons-blue-wall-in-two-maps/507149/.

61. Ibid., 317.
62. Arendt, *The Origins of Totalitarianism*, 478.
63. Hannah Arendt, "What is Freedom?" in *Between Past and Future*, ed. Jerome Kohn (New York: Penguin Books, 2006): 142–169, 155.

Conclusion

I draw this book to its conclusion on the eve of the 2020 U.S. presidential election cycle. Rather than engaging in genuine debate about the best path forward, Americans have only dug their heels deeper into their respective political camps, becoming less recognizable to one another as citizens who share and are responsible for the world in which they find themselves. While Democratic leaders are investing their energies and political capital into what will likely be fruitless impeachment hearings, Republican leaders continue to participate in what Jaspers might call "anonymous responsibility," reluctantly endorsing divisive and reckless leadership for the sake of remaining loyal to their party. Meanwhile, ordinary citizens are becoming less and less able to talk with one another about their views, to argue and think collectively about how to act into the future. Anecdotally, I have found this to be no more apparent than among my students, many of whom will vote in a presidential election for the first time in November 2020, and who, while fully integrated into networks of technology that make them entirely accessible to each other, nevertheless continue to express that no spaces exist where they can speak publically with their peers about their political views. Instead, students across the political spectrum have said that they tend only to talk with those who agree with them because they fear being labeled, judged, and ostracized by those with whom they disagree.

There is, I think, much evidence to suggest that we find ourselves living in an age in which the closure of the political has become commonplace, and the possibilities for speech and action in an Arendtian sense are few and far between. While we may be hyperbolically interconnected, able to access, evaluate, and monitor each other more easily than ever before, this has not made us more visible in our natality and plurality. On the contrary, it seems to have left us hidden from one another, unable to appear in our irreducible singularity and irrevocable interdependence as members of a common world. Arendt, for her part, would suggest that this hiddenness cannot be thought apart from the closure of the political. While we might be reluctant to acknowledge this closure in our own liberal and allegedly open societies, Arendt is clear that it is among the most important conditions under which totalitarianism becomes possible. Putting into relief the loneliness of liberal subjectivity, Arendt thus brings into focus the political significance of the peculiar loneliness of the current age—or the fact that we find ourselves more extremely together and more extremely apart than ever before. With this, she makes clear how this peculiar loneliness, when considered in a political register, can become dangerous, rendering liberal citizens vulnerable to totalizing forms of fellowship.

The dangers of this loneliness are apparent, not only in the political trends of the United States but also across Europe, which has seen surges of voter support for right-wing nationalism and populism that are matched only by surges seen in the period between the world wars. In July 2019, conservative leader Boris Johnson became prime minister of the United Kingdom after spearheading the Brexit campaign and finding majority support from voters for his "one-nation" agenda. Alternative for Germany (AfD), a right-wing, anti-Euro German nationalist party that favors strict anti-immigration policies and employs a rhetoric that breaks longstanding anti-Nazi taboos, is now the strongest opposition party in Germany. AfD has secured seats in every state parliament and, in October 2019, defeated Angela Merkel's Christian Democratic Party (CDU) in the eastern state of Thuringia, a defeat that came as "a shock to the political establishment."[1] Though France's far-right National Front Party (FN) leader Marie Le Pen and Italy's Matteo Salvini, leader of the far-right League Party, have both faced political defeats in their home countries, both nevertheless remain key figures in Europe's rising nationalist scene. Other far-right nationalist parties, including the Vox party in Spain, Austria's Freedom Party (FPÖ), the Law and Justice Party (PiS) in Poland, and Viktor Orban's far-right nationalist party in Hungary, have continued to gain political ground over the last five years and remain strongholds as we move into 2020. Though there are numerous contingent historical, political, and economic factors that have contributed to the rise of such movements in these specific regions, this widespread trend suggests that European voters appear at least in part to be frustrated with the political establishment and anxious about increasing globalization, immigration, and the dilution of a sense of national identity.[2]

A primary focus of this book has been to diagnose the problem of political loneliness and to suggest the ways in which we might use this framework as a point of departure for interpreting these trends today. Because of this, it would be beyond the scope of the present work to develop a comprehensive political framework that is able to provide an alternative to these lonely forms of subjectivity. Yet, I would nevertheless like to suggest that Arendt's novel critical perspective on the loneliness of liberal subjectivity does give way to a potential response to the peculiar loneliness of modern mass society, one that not only deepens discourses in continental philosophy concerned with envisioning possibilities for authentic communal life but also sets the stage for further inquiry into the implications of this loneliness for political life today.

If we take seriously Arendt's analysis of the political loneliness of modern mass society, I maintain that we are called upon to develop a politics of appearance or a politics that draws lonely liberal subjects out of their hiding and into the full illumination of the public realm. Much has been said about how we might improve the structures of liberal democracy in order to accomplish this end. We see this even in the decisive critiques of scholars like Brown and Honig, both of whom emphasize the ways in which neoliberalism destroys democracy, but who also offer methods for improving our liberal democratic structures. Arendt's analysis of loneliness, by contrast, reminds us that these very practices can have as much of a role in perpetuating political loneliness as the neoliberal structures of which they are born. A politics of appearance thus offers an alternative to this approach, one that does not simply call for an improved version of liberal democracy but that instead involves a sustained effort to critically engage the ways in which our democratic practices and liberal institutions keep citizens from appearing in their singularity as members of a common world.

Arendt's notion of appearance is keyed not to making visible the isolated modern subject per se, but to a conception of political action that fundamentally reshapes this notion of subjectivity. For Arendt, holding open a space of appearance depends on thinking the singular individual anew, not as a self-contained, self-interested subject that is endowed with pre-given, inalienable rights and liberties, but instead as always already constituted in and through the others with whom she shares the world. That is to say, Arendt's notion of appearance presumes human plurality, or the fact that we find ourselves always already in a world with others on whom we depend in order to become visible as who we are in our singularity. On the basis of this, we might turn to a politics of appearance, for instance, to think the concept of citizenship anew, not as an indefinitely expandable legal status that promises rights and liberties in the private sphere, but rather as a shared responsibility to make one another visible in the public realm. This in turn, might require that we think anew the idea of freedom, conceiving of it not as an inalienable right to pursue one's own self-interest as far as possible, but rather as a lived and embodied activity that comes to appear in the world by speaking and acting with others in the space of politics. A politics of appearance would depend, too, on reformulating the task of politics, treating it not simply as the space for democratic practice and policy formation but also, and more importantly, as a space of appearance in which we find ourselves beholden to the words and deeds of others and responsible for creating a space in the world in which these words and deeds can appear.

In requiring a new conception of the citizen subject, a politics of appearance opens the possibility for thinking beyond the lonely forms of subjectivity that have been produced and affirmed by the liberal structures that organize political life. Yet, in so doing, it not only demands a reformulation of singular individual but also provides a platform to rehabilitate the notion of a common world. Whereas we live in an age in which "alternative facts" and "fake news" are referred on a regular basis to express suspicion over the reality the world we share in common, a politics of appearance is predicated on a notion of politics that seeks to recover this shared reality. As Arendt explains, it is distinctive of speech and action in the political sphere that they do not only disclose the singular individual but also make visible what lies between human beings. She says:

> Action and speech go on between men . . . and retain their agent-revealing capacity even if their content is exclusively "objective," concerned with the matters of the world of things in which men move, which physically lies between them and out of which arise their specific, objective, worldly interests. These interests constitute, in the word's most literal significance, something which *inter-ests*, which lies between people and therefore can relate and

bind them together. Most action and speech is concerned with this in-between, which varies with each group of people, so that most words and deeds are *about* some worldly objective reality in addition to being a disclosure of the acting and speaking agent.[3]

In requiring a fundamentally different conception of the subject, Arendt thus insists that the very notion of interest shifts from self-interest in the private realm to shared *"inter-est,"* or interest that goes between people insofar as it concerns the world they have in common. She goes on to say:

> Since this disclosure of the subject is an integral part of all, even the most "objective" intercourse, the physical worldly in-between along with its interests is overlaid and, as it were, overgrown with an altogether different in-between which consists of deeds and words and owes its origin exclusively to men's acting and speaking directly *to* one another.[4]

In reformulating the citizen subject in terms of her irrevocable interrelatedness and irreducible singularity, a politics of appearance requires the rehabilitation of the shared reality of a common world. Yet, Arendt is careful to insist that this world is not common or shared because it is grounded in the sameness of a people or a totalizing collective. Rather, for Arendt, the common world that comes into appearance is always being negotiated, contested, augmented, and reconfigured precisely because it originates from the speech and action of a plurality of actors. Indeed, for Arendt, it is only insofar as this world in common is constituted by plurality that it is able to appear. In this, we see that a politics of appearance not only offers a way to think about the "we" in a way that does not absorb the singular into a collective but, in so doing, also contravenes the loss of a common reality that arises from the widespread experience of loneliness.

Though Arendt offers few modern examples to clarify what she means by the space of appearance, she does point to two concrete models that she suggests offer alternatives to modern forms of government. The first is the model of the town hall meeting integral to the ward system of the early American Republic, and the second is the council system that grew out of the European labor movements from 1848 to the 1956 Hungarian Revolution.[5] Though much has already been said about Arendt's interest in citizen councils throughout her work, most significant for our purposes is the fact that she treats these councils as the only opportunity in the modern world for an experience of "the political" as she envisions it—namely, as a space of appearance.[6] What is distinctive about these councils and town hall meetings is that they consist in direct, face-to-face political engagement, standing in contrast to the anonymity of representative models of democracy that have become the standard model of Western liberal democracies. As Shmuel Lederman has argued, it is precisely this direct and embodied form of political engagement that Arendt believes enables human beings to become visible to one another, offering the opportunity to contravene the loneliness of modern mass society. He says, "Against the dominant tendencies of the modern age—mass society, the decline of politics, the rise of the 'social,' the prevalence of ideology—an alternative vision emerged [from the citizen council]. It carried with it the hope of breaking mass society into individuals who act and speak together in numerous 'spaces of appearance.'"[7] Of course, Arendt acknowledges that these councils have historically failed to sustain themselves as institutionalized governments. Yet, she nevertheless takes them to be the very alternative that emerges throughout history for the sake to contravening the closure of the political.[8]

One might wonder whether this is too traditional and outdated a model for politics to contravene the loneliness of neoliberal subjectivity today. Yet, if these models are thought in light of Arendt's broader concern for thinking appearance as an antidote to the peculiar loneliness of the current age, then I would argue that they in fact promise a radical alternative to our own forms of political engagement today. It is true that we must intervene in the reductive metrics of utility and instrumentality that may organize communal life but that are productive of the peculiar loneliness of the current age. Arendt, however, reminds us in the prologue of *The Human Condition* that in order to undertake such an intervention, we must first "think what we are doing."[9] Not a scientific task, but a political one to the greatest extent, Arendt would suggest that such an intervention thus depends first on developing a politics of appearance, or a politics in which we come face-to-face with one another, engaging directly in the matters that go between us. Such a model of politics, she thinks, enables us to become visible to one another, not as entities that are reducible to metrics and algorithms but rather as irreducibly unique and capable of acting against the overwhelming odds of statistical law and probability. How, then, might we think of this in the context of contemporary political life?

Movements such as Occupy Wall Street, Black Lives Matter, and the Women's March have been crucial for raising awareness of marginalized, oppressed, and excluded groups, for bringing issues of income inequality to the fore and for resisting the normalization of bigotry, racism, and sexism in the United States. Yet, they have not prevented such events as the Unite the Right Rally in Charlottesville, Virginia, which culminated in deadly violence in 2017. They have neither contravened the emergence of such groups as Blue Lives Matter and White Lives Matter nor dissuaded far-right groups like the Proud Boys, who, amid fears of violence, went head-to-head with far-left anti-fascist group Antifa in Portland in August 2019. While protest and assembly may be necessary at times, it is not obvious that this approach on either side of the political spectrum is working. Even more importantly, it is not clear how such movements serve to contravene the loneliness and isolation that Arendt suggests makes liberal citizens vulnerable to nationalism, populism, and fascism. A politics of appearance, or a politics that demands of us that we take responsibility for making one another visible in the public realm, requires a different angle of approach. Though it would not render protest and assembly irrelevant, it would require a different starting point, one that began with an effort to open spaces for speech and action. While social media has been an important tool for galvanizing these movements and rallies, we have yet to think what we are doing as we engage in such forms of communication. By opening political spaces for speech and action, we might come to recognize that social media has also had the effect of siloing political discourse, cordoning us off in our respective political camps before spaces for speech and action can be secured. Hence, rather than turning to the echo chambers of Facebook, Twitter, and Instagram, a politics of appearance would depend on embodied engagement and, with this, mutual courage and trust in those others on whom we depend in order to appear in our singularity. While this courage and trust are not required in the anonymous digital spaces of social media, they are crucial for enabling human beings to become visible to one another as members of a shared world. As effective as social media might be for galvanizing mass movements, a politics of appearance seeks to attend to the loneliness that such forms of technology can reproduce, demanding that citizens come to see one another as belonging to and responsible for a common world.

One could object to this notion of appearance by turning to the criticism that figures like Derrida and Butler have leveled against

Heidegger for perpetuating the very metaphysics of presence that Heidegger himself seeks to overturn. The notion of appearance might raise the question of whether Arendt has not also fallen prey to a metaphysics of presence that presumes that individuals are objective and self-contained entities that can appear in their entirety without remainder. Whereas Derrida makes clear the limits of such a notion of appearance through such concepts as the trace, the phantom, and the specter, Butler's early analysis of performativity indicates that we are never reducible to any fixed identity that appears in the world as such, but are instead always negotiating, contesting, choosing between identities that we then perform in the space of politics.[10] Yet, while both Derrida and Butler might read Arendt as implicating herself in a metaphysics of presence by insisting on a notion of appearance, I would argue that in conceiving of this notion *politically*, she in fact offers a viable response to this objection. To be sure, Arendt believes that the political provides the context for the announcement of who one is, constituting that sphere of human existence where we speak and act with others in order to bring something into the world that has never before been seen and that could never have been predicted. "In acting and speaking," Arendt explains, "men show who they are, reveal actively their unique personal identities and thus make their appearance in the human world . . . this disclosure of the 'who' in contradistinction to 'what' somebody is . . . is implicit in everything somebody says or does."[11] Yet, in conceiving of the political as arising directly out of this, Arendt wishes to suggest that the "who," as opposed to the "what" that appears, is never reducible to a fixed presence or identity that can be defined in advance. Rather, she would insist that this, too, is something that is always in flux, requiring contestation, negotiation, and augmentation.

While there are a number of ways to bring this into focus, Arendt's account of the stranger in her 1954 essay "Understanding and Politics" is especially helpful for putting into relief how Arendt envisions the meaning of political appearance in her efforts to think the possibilities for authentic communal life. As she says here, "Every single person needs to be reconciled to a world into which he is born a stranger and in which, to the extent of his distinct uniqueness, he always remains a stranger."[12] The stakes of our finitude thus consist for Arendt in determining how we might bear the world together from out of this condition of strangerhood.[13] As Phillip Hansen has argued, Arendt's notion of the stranger provides a decisive point of departure for capturing her contribution to a notion of communal life that is responsive to the loneliness of modern mass society. For Arendt, this "bearing with strangers" is not a contingent feature of human existence from which we can choose to abstain. Rather, Hansen says, "It is an essential element of our existence as plural beings—a refusal to bear with strangers is a refusal of plurality."[14] Hence, rather than asserting similarities in advance, he explains that for Arendt, "We must start with the reality of being strangers, and move to the creation of conditions under which understanding, 'the understanding heart,' is possible."[15] This gift of an understanding heart is neither a matter of sentiment nor a mental calculation that can be reduced to logical processes.[16] Rather, Arendt says, "Understanding, as distinguished from correct information and scientific knowledge ... is an unending activity by which, in constant change and variation, we come to terms with and reconcile ourselves to reality, that is, try to be at home in the world."[17] In this, understanding—the kind required for reconciling ourselves to a world in which we are forever strangers—never produces final results, but is instead characterized by an "interminable dialogue," or openness to that which escapes our ordinary sentiments, vocabularies, and methods of categorization. Significantly, Arendt argues that only an understanding heart is able to bear the burden of human action, remaining open to the incalculable possibilities of each newcomer who enters the world. In view of this, we may interpret Arendt's concern for making one another visible in the public sphere as a matter of learning how to bear the world with strangers, which depends not on intimate personal ties or shared sentimentality but on "being generous enough to bridge abysses of remoteness until we can see."[18] Hence, rather than transforming the stranger into something familiar, Arendt believes that it is a requirement of authentic communal life that the stranger appear in her singularity, as it is only with and through her that we are able to disclose new, previously unrecognized binds that make it possible to bear the world together.

Notions of communal life grounded in pre-given affinities and obvious similarities are, in Arendt's view, fundamentally antipolitical precisely because they fall prey to the presumptions of a metaphysics of presence. A politics of appearance, by contrast, is rooted in respect for the demands of human plurality. As Amy Allen has argued in the context of feminist theory, this provides an important framework for theorizing collectives without appealing to reductive identity categories.[19] According to Allen, Arendt's notion of political community is distinctive because it requires a notion of solidarity that is neither established beforehand nor grounded in obvious similarities; instead, it is the consequence of acting in concert. Allen says, "Action both individuates and establishes relationships; it sets us apart and binds us together."[20] The significance of Arendt's account thus lies in the interplay between commonality and distinctness that is always at stake in human plurality. The ground of this commonality arises not from what can be decided in advance about those with whom we share the world but rather from a shared commitment to a common goal or principle—"a promise to act in concert"—that is always open to reinterpretation and revision in order to sustain the bond between actors.[21]

Allen is clear that for Arendt, identities, including Arendt's own Jewish identity, no less than the identity of womanhood, are significant political facts; to deny them is delusional and dangerous. Yet, because Arendt conceives of these identities as *political* facts, Allen says, "they are not fixed, natural, or historically determined, but knit out of a fabric of difference and distinction."[22] Allen develops this with reference to Arendt's account in *Eichmann in Jerusalem* of the success of the Danish resistance to the Nazis. This example is significant, first, because, Arendt says, "it is the only case we know of in which the Nazis were met with *open* native resistance and the result seemed to have been that those exposed to it changed their minds."[23] Denmark's public denouncement of the Final Solution and its vow to protect its stateless people was "resistance based on principle," rather than national identity, ethnic similarity, or class consciousness.[24] In this, it constituted a political act that gave collective power to a multitude of actors who intervened in all manner of ways to resist the assumption that mass extermination was simply a matter of course.[25] Second, it is significant because although Jewish identity was important to this resistance movement, the binds of solidarity that emerged were based not on a shared essence, history, or experience of oppression but rather on a reciprocal commitment. Arendt cites, in particular, the moment when, upon being approached by the Nazis to distribute the yellow star, the Danish King vowed to be the first to wear it even though he was not a Jew.[26] This, Allen argues, epitomizes what Arendt means by political action.[27] It consists not in asserting a fixed identity, but instead, Allen says, "in the commitment of distinct individuals to work together for the attainment of a common goal."[28] Such reciprocal commitments create binds of solidarity that are powerful precisely because they exist between individuals who are able to appear to one another in their irreducible singularity and who share a commitment to preserving a world in which this singularity can appear. In this, Arendt's notion of appearance offers an important alternative to exclusionary and reductive collectives, while illustrating the urgency of a notion of communal life that is responsive to the loneliness of modern mass society.[29]

In view of this, I would argue in contrast to those who might suggest that Arendt implicates herself in a metaphysics of presence through her notion of appearance that such a conception of politics does not reinscribe a notion of the isolated modern subject into the realm of politics; rather, it assumes that we depend on others to confirm our own singularity no less than the reality of the world to which we belong. While both are undoubtedly in flux, there is no sense in which one is isolated and atomized on this view of politics. Moreover, such a conception of politics makes possible the appearance of the spontaneity of human action, thereby reminding us of our responsibility to hold open a space in the world for the incalculable possibilities of each newcomer and the plurality that this entails. At stake in Arendt's notion of appearance, then, is not a metaphysics of presence but rather an attempt to develop a notion of politics that contravenes the loneliness and hiddenness of modern life, and the vulnerability that this creates to dangerous and totalizing forms of fellowship.

It would be beyond the scope of this project to offer a single, definitive model of politics that can address this problem. Rather, in turning to the notion of a politics of appearance, I aim only to provide one potential response, while setting the stage for a broader discourse on how we might respond to this problem in contemporary political life. Even so, I do wish to suggest that we find in Arendt's novel critical perspective on the liberal tradition new ways of thinking the possibilities for more authentic forms of communal life that are able to work against the peculiar loneliness of the current age. The problem of this loneliness—or the fact that our ability to conquer all distances through technological and scientific advancement has nevertheless brought us no nearer to ourselves, others, or the world—has only become increasingly urgent today. What Arendt makes clear, and what perhaps distinguishes her from others who have attempted to address this problem, is her suggestion that attending to this problem depends first on thinking what we are doing. A task, she suggests, that cannot be thought apart from a rehabilitation the political sphere of our lives, Arendt not only brings into focus the political significance of this peculiar loneliness but, in so doing, clarifies the opportunity that the political provides for contravening the loneliness that may remain at work in our own liberal societies today.

NOTES

1. "Europe and Right Wing Nationalism: A Country By Country Guide," *The BBC*, November, 13, 2019, https://www.bbc.com/news/world-europe-36130006.

2. Ibid. For more on the rise of right-wing movements in Europe see Jude Hayes, Junghyun Lim, and Jae-Jae Spoon, "The Path from Trade to Right Wing Populism in Europe," *Electoral Studies*, 60 (August 2019): 1–13; Albana Shehaj, Adrian J. Shin, and Ronald Inglehart, "Immigration and Right Wing Populism: An Origin Story," *Party Politics*, Online First: May 17, 2019, https://doi.org/10.1177/1354068819849888; and Daniele Caramani and Luca Manucci, "National Past and Populism: The Re-elaboration of Fascism and Its Impact on Right-Wing Populism in Western Europe," *West European Politics*, 42.6, (2019): 1159–1187, DOI: 10.1080/01402382.2019.1596690.

3. Hannah Arendt, *The Human Condition* (Chicago: University of Chicago Press, 1998), 183.

4. Arendt, *The Human Condition*, 183–184.

5. Arendt's most notable accounts of the American town halls and the French popular societies appear in *On Revolution*. Her analysis of the councils that emerged from European labor movements from 1848 to 1956 appear quite notably in the "Action" section of *The Human Condition*. See Hannah Arendt, *On Revolution* (New York: Penguin Books, 2006), 231–247, and *The Human Condition*, 216.

6. For recent scholarship on Arendt's concern for the council system, see Shmuel Lederman, "Hannah Arendt, the Council Tradition and Contemporary Political Theory," in *Council Democracy: Towards a Democratic Socialist Politics*, ed. James Muldoon (New York and London: Routledge, 2018); Mike McConkey, "On Arendt's Vision of the European Council Phenomenon: Critique from an Historical Perspective," *Dialectical Anthropology*, 16 (1991): 15–31; Jeffrey C. Isaac, "Oases in the Desert: Hannah Arendt on Democratic Politics," *American Political Science Review*, 88.1 (1994): 156–168; John F. Sitton, "Hannah Arendt's Argument for Council Democracy," in *Hannah Arendt: Critical Essays*, ed. Lewis Hinchman and Sandra K. Hinchman (New York: SUNY Press, 1994); James Muldoon, "The Lost Treasure of Arendt's Council System," *Critical Horizons*, 12.3 (2011): 396–417; and James Muldoon, "The Origins of Hannah Arendt's Council System," *History of Political Thought*, 37.4 (2016): 761–789.

7. Shmuel Lederman, "The Centrality of the Council System in Arendt's Politics," in *Arendt on Freedom, Liberation, and Revolution*, ed. Kei Hiruta (New York: Palgrave Macmillan, 2019): 253–276, 264.

8. See Hannah Arendt, "Thoughts on Politics and Revolution," in *Crisis of the Republic* (New York: Harcourt Brace, Inc., 1972), 230. See also Lederman, 258.

9. Arendt, *The Human Condition*, 5.

10. See Judith Butler, *Gender Trouble: Feminism and the Subversion of Identity* (New York: Routledge, 1990). See also Amy Allen, "Solidarity after Identity Politics: Hannah Arendt and the Power of Feminist Theory," *Philosophy and Social Criticism*, 25.1 (1999): 97–118.

11. Arendt, *The Human Condition*, 178.

12. Hannah Arendt, "Understanding and Politics," in *Essays in Understanding 1930–1954: Formation, Exile, and Totalitarianism*, ed. Jerome Kohn (New York: Schocken Books, 1994): 307–327, 308.

13. See "Understanding and Politics," 322. See also Phillip Hansen, "Hannah Arendt and Bearing with Strangers," *Contemporary Political Theory*, 3 (2004): 3–22, 5.

14. Hansen, 10.

15. Ibid., 6.

16. Arendt, "Understanding and Politics," 322.

17. Ibid., 308.

18. Ibid., 323.

19. Amy Allen, "Solidarity after Identity Politics: Hannah Arendt and the Power of Feminist Theory," *Philosophy and Social Criticism*, 25.1 (1999): 97–118, 107.

20. Ibid., 109.

21. Ibid., 113.

22. Ibid., 109.

23. Hannah Arendt, *Eichmann in Jerusalem: A Report on the Banality of Evil* (New York: Penguin, 2006), 175.

24. Ibid.

25. Ibid., Allen, 112.

26. Arendt, *Eichmann in Jerusalem*, 171. Allen, 113.

27. Allen, 114.

28. Ibid.

29. Allen's discussion of this grows out of a larger discourse on Arendt's notion of solidarity. I have drawn portions of what I have said here from an article I have published on this topic entitled "Solidarity in Dark Times: Arendt and Gadamer on the Politics of Appearance," *Philosophy Compass*, 13.12 (2018), https://doi.org/10.1111/phc3.12554. For more on Arendt's discourse on solidarity, see Ken Reshaur, "Concepts of Solidarity in the Political Theory of Hannah Arendt," *Canadian Journal of Political Science*, 25.4 (1992): 723–736; Samuel Butler, "Arendt and Aristotle on Equality, Leisure, and Solidarity," *Journal of Social Philosophy*, 41.4 (2010): 470–490; and Phillip Hansen, "Hannah Arendt and Bearing with Strangers," *Contemporary Political Theory*, 3 (2004): 3–32.

Bibliography

Allen, Amy. "Solidarity after Identity Politics: Hannah Arendt and the Power of Feminist Theory." *Philosophy and Social Criticism* 25, no. 1 (1999): 97–118.
Arendt, Hannah. *Between Past and Future*. Edited by Jerome Kohn. New York: Penguin Books, 2006.
———. *Crises of the Republic*. New York: Harcourt Brace Jovanovich, Inc., 1972.
———. *Eichmann in Jerusalem: A Report on the Banality of Evil*. New York: Penguin Books, 2006.
———. *Essays in Understanding 1930–1954: Formation, Exile, and Totalitarianism*. Edited by Jerome Kohn. New York: Schocken Books, 1994.
———. *The Human Condition*. Chicago: University of Chicago Press, 1998.
———. *Men in Dark Times*. New York: Harcourt, Brace, and World Inc., 1968.
———. *On Revolution*. New York: Penguin Group, 2001.
———. *The Origins of Totalitarianism*. New York: Harcourt Inc., 1974.
Arendt, Hannah, and Karl Jaspers. *Hannah Arendt, Karl Jaspers: Correspondence, 1926–1969*. Edited by Lotte Kohler and Hans Saner. Translated by Robert and Rita Kimber. New York: Harcourt Brace & Company, 1992.
Arendt, Hannah, and Martin Heidegger. *Letters 1925–1975*. Edited by Ursula Ludz. Orlando: Harcourt, 2004.
Barash, Jeffrey Andrew. "Martin Heidegger, Hannah Arendt, and the Politics of Remembrance." *International Journal of Philosophical Studies* 10, no. 2 (2002): 171–182.
Bax, Chantal. "Otherwise than Being-With: Levinas on Heidegger and Community." *Human Studies* 3 (2017): 381–400.
Beiner, Ronald. "The Presence of Art and the Absence of Heidegger." *Arendt Studies* 2 (2018): 9–15.
Benhabib, Seyla. *Dignity in Adversity: Human Rights in Troubled Times*. Hoboken: Wiley Press, 2011.

———. *The Reluctant Modernism of Hannah Arendt*. New York: Rowman and Littlefield Publishers, Inc., 2000.

Benjamin, Andrew. *Towards a Relational Ontology: Philosophy's Other Possibility*. Albany: SUNY Press, 2016.

Berkowitz, Roger. "Solitude and the Activity of Thinking." In *Thinking in Dark Times: Hannah Arendt on Ethics and Politics*. Edited by Richard Bernstein, 237–48. New York: Fordham University Press, 2009.

Berlant, Lauren. *Cruel Optimism*. Durham: Duke University Press, 2011.

Bernstein, Richard J. *Hannah Arendt and the Jewish Question*. Cambridge: MIT Press, 1996.

Bilgrami, Akeel. "Reflections on Three Populisms." *Philosophy and Social Criticism* 44, no. 4 (2018): 453–462.

Bird, Greg. *Containing Community: From Political Economy to Ontology in Agamben, Esposito, and Nancy*. Albany: SUNY Press, 2016.

Birmingham, Peg. "The An-Archic Event of Natality and the Right to Have Rights." *Social Research* 74, no. 3 (2007): 763–777.

———. *Hannah Arendt and Human Rights: The Predicament of Common Responsibility*. Bloomington: Indiana University Press, 2006.

Blumenberg, Hans. *Care Crosses the River*. Translated by Paul Fleming. Stanford: Stanford University Press, 2010.

Brogan, Walter. "The Parting of Being: On Creation and Sharing in Nancy's Political Ontology." *Research in Phenomenology* 40 (2010): 295–308.

Brown, Wendy. *Undoing the Demos: Neoliberalism's Stealth Revolution*. New York: Zone Books, 2015.

Brownback, Andy, and Aaron Novotny. "Social Desirability Bias and Polling Errors in the 2016 Presidential Election." *Journal of Behavioural and Experimental Economics* 74 (June 2018): 38–56.

Butler, Judith. *Gender Trouble: Feminism and the Subversion of Identity*. New York: Routledge, 1990.

———. "Precarious Life, Vulnerability, and the Ethics of Cohabitation." *Journal of Speculative Philosophy* 26, no. 2 (2012): 134–151.

Butler, Samuel. "Arendt and Aristotle on Equality, Leisure, and Solidarity." *Journal of Social Philosophy* 41, no. 4 (2010): 470–490.

Calcagno, Antonio. "The Role of Forgetting in Our Experience of Time: Augustine of Hippo and Hannah Arendt." *Parrhesia* 13 (2011): 14–27.

Caramani, Daniele, and Luca Manucci. "National Past and Populism: The Re-elaboration of Fascism and Its Impact on Right-Wing

Populism in Western Europe." *West European Politics* 42, no. 6 (2019): 1159–1187, DOI: 10.1080/01402382.2019.1596690.

Cassin, Barbara. *Nostalgia: When Are We Ever at Home?*, translated by Pascale-Anne Brault. New York: Fordham University Press, 2016.

Chandler, David, and Julian Reid. *The Neoliberal Subject: Resilience, Adaptation, and Vulnerability.* New York: Rowman and Littlefield, 2016.

Clark, Barry, and Lawrence Quill. "Augustine, Arendt, and Anthropy." *Sophia* 48, no. 3 (2010): 253–265.

Claviez, Thomas, editor. *The Common Growl: Towards a Poetics of Precarious Community.* New York: Fordham University Press, 2016.

Coppock, Alexander. "Did Shy Trump Supporters Bias the 2016 Polls? Evidence from a Nationally Representative List Experiment." *Statistics, Politics, and Policy* 8, no. 1 (2017): 29–40. DOI: 10.1515/spp-2016-0005.

Cornelissen, Lars. "On the Subject of Neoliberalism: Rethinking Resistance in the Critique of Neoliberal Rationality." *Constellations* 25 (2018): 133–146.

Costache, Adrian. "On Solitude and Loneliness in Hermeneutical Philosophy." *Meta: Research in Hermeneutics, Phenomenology and Practical Philosophy* 5, no. 1 (2013): 130–149.

Dallmayr, Fred. *Twilight of Subjectivity: Contributions to a Post-Individualist Theory of Politics.* Amherst: University of Massachusetts Press, 1981.

Davies, William. *The Limits of Neoliberalism: Authority, Sovereignty, and the Logic of Competition.* Washington D.C.: Sage Press, 2017.

Derrida, Jacques. "Force of Law: The 'Mystical Foundations of Authority.'" In *Deconstruction and the Possibility of Justice.* Edited by Drucilla Cornell, Michael Rosenfeld, and David Gray Carlson, 3–67. New York: Routledge, 1992.

Di Cesare, Donatella. *Utopia of Understanding: Between Babel and Auschwitz.* Albany: SUNY Press, 2012.

Dossa, Shiraz. "Human Status and Politics: Hannah Arendt on the Holocaust." *The Canadian Journal of Political Science* 13, no. 2 (1980): 310.

Dungey, Nicholas. "(Re)turning Derrida to Heidegger: Being-with-Others as Primordial Politics." *Polity* 33, no. 3 (Spring 2001): 455–477.

Enns, Peter, Julius Lagodny, and Johnathan Schludt. "Understanding the 2016 US Presidential Election Polls: The Importance of Hidden Trump Supporters." *Statistics, Politics and Policy* 8, no. 1 (2017): 41–63.

Figal, Gunter. *Objectivity: The Hermeneutical and Philosophy*. Translated by Theodore George. Albany: SUNY Press, 2011.
Gadamer, Hans-Georg. "Friendship and Solidarity." *Research in Phenomenology* 39 (2009): 3–12.
———. "Isolation as a Symptom of Self-Alienation." In *Praise of Theory: Speeches and Essays*. Translated by Chris Dawson. New Haven: Yale University Press, 1988, 101–113.
———. *A Century of Philosophy: A Conversation with Ricardo Dottori*. Translated by Rod Coltman and Sigrid Koepke. New York: Continuum, 2003.
Gaffney, Jennifer. "Another Origin of Totalitarianism: Arendt on the Loneliness of Liberal Citizens." *Journal of the British Society for Phenomenology* 47, no. 1 (2016): 1–17.
———. "At Home with the Foreign: Arendt on Heidegger and the Politics of Care." *Epoché, A Journal for the History of Philosophy* 23, no. 1 (2018): 146–163.
———. "Solidarity in Dark Times: Arendt and Gadamer on the Politics of Appearance." *Philosophy Compass* 13, no. 12 (2018). https://doi.org/10.1111/phc3.12554.
George, Theodore. "Are We a Conversation? Hermeneutics, Exteriority, and Transmittability." *Research in Phenomenology* 47 (2017): 331–350.
Gines, Kathryn T. *Hannah Arendt and the Negro Question*. Bloomington: Indiana University Press, 2014.
Grunenberg, Antonia, and Adrian Daub. "Arendt, Jaspers, and Heidegger: Thinking through the Breach in Tradition." *Social Research: Hannah Arendt Centenary: Political and Philosophical Perspectives* 74, no. 4.2 (Winter 2017): 1003–1028.
Gündogdu, Ayten "'The Perplexities of the Rights of Man': Arendt on the Aporias of Human Rights." *European Journal of Political Theory* 11, no. 1 (2011): 4–24.
Hansen, Phillip. "Hannah Arendt and Bearing with Strangers." *Contemporary Political Theory* 3 (2004): 3–22.
Hayden, Patrick. *Political Evil in a Global Age: Hannah Arendt and International Theory*. New York: Routledge, 2009.
Hayes, Jude, Junghyun Lim, and Jae-Jae Spoon. "The Path from Trade to Right Wing Populism in Europe." *Electoral Studies* 60 (August 2019): 1–13.
Heidegger, Martin. *Being and Time*. Translated by Joan Stambaugh, revised by Dennis J. Schmidt. Albany: SUNY Press, 2010.

———. *Plato's Sophist*. Translated by Richard Rojcewicz and Andre Schuwer. Bloomington: Indiana University Press, 1997.

———. "The Thing." In *Poetry, Language, Thought*. Translated by Albert Hofstadter. New York: Harper Collins Books, 1971.

———. "Transcendence." In *The Heidegger Reader*. Translated by Jerome Veith, 68–78. Bloomington: Indiana University Press, 2009.

Honig, Bonnie. *Public Things: Democracy in Disrepair*. New York: Fordham University Press, 2017.

Isaac, Jeffrey C. "Oases in the Desert: Hannah Arendt on Democratic Politics." *American Political Science Review* 88, no. 1 (1994): 156–168.

Jaspers, Karl. *Man in the Modern Age*. Translated by Eden and Cedar Paul. New York: Routledge, 2010.

Kattago, Siobhan. "Why the World Matters: Hannah Arendt's Philosophy of New Beginnings." *The European Paradigm: Toward New Paradigms* 18, no. 2 (2013): 170–184.

King, Richard, and Dan Stone, editors. *Hannah Arendt and the Uses of History: Imperialism, Nation, Race, and Genocide*. New York: Berghahn Books, 2007.

Klar, Samara, Christopher R. Weber, and Yanna Krupnikov. "Social Desirability Bias in the 2016 Presidential Election." *The Forum* 14, no. 4 (December 2016): 433–443.

Lederman, Shmuel. "Hannah Arendt, the Council Tradition and Contemporary Political Theory." In *Council Democracy: Towards a Democratic Socialist Politics*. Edited by James Muldoon. New York and London: Routledge, 2018.

———. "The Centrality of the Council System in Arendt's Politics." In *Arendt on Freedom, Liberation, and Revolution*. Edited by Kei Hiruta, 253–276. New York: Palgrave Macmillan, 2019.

Leshem, Dotan. *The Origins of Neoliberalism: Modeling the Economy from Jesus to Foucault*. New York: Columbia University Press, 2017.

Liao, Pei-Shan. "Social Desirability Bias and Mode Effects in the Case of Voting Behavior." *Bulletin de Méthodologie Sociologique* 132, no. 1 (October 2016): 73–83.

McConkey, Mike. "On Arendt's Vision of the European Council Phenomenon: Critique from an Historical Perspective." *Dialectical Anthropology* 16 (1991): 15–31.

Menke, Christoph. "The 'Aporias of Human Rights' and the 'One Human Right': Regarding the Coherence of Arendt's Argument." *Social Research* 74, no. 3 (2007): 739–763.

Muldoon, James. "The Lost Treasure of Arendt's Council System." *Critical Horizons* 12, no. 3 (2011): 396–417.

———. "The Origins of Hannah Arendt's Council System." *History of Political Thought* 37, no. 4 (2016): 761–789.

Nancy, Jean-Luc. "The Being-with of Being-there." *Continental Philosophy Review* 41 (2008): 1–15.

———. *Being Singular Plural*. Stanford: Stanford University Press, 2000.

Ortega, Mariana. *In-Between: Latina Feminist Phenomenology, Multiplicity, and the Self*. Albany: SUNY Press, 2016.

Overgaard, Soren. "Heidegger's Early Critique of Husserl." *International Journal of Philosophical Studies* 11, no. 2 (2003): 157–175.

Parekh, Serena. "Arendt, Judgment, and Responsibility to the Global Poor." *Philosophical Topics* 39, no. 2 (2011): 145–163, 147.

———. *Hannah Arendt and the Challenge of Modernity: A Phenomenology of Human Rights*. New York: Routledge, 2008.

Payne, Gregory J. "The Bradley Effect: Mediated Reality of Race and Politics in the 2008 U.S. Presidential Election." *American Behavioral Scientist* 54, no. 4 (December 2010): 417–435.

Polt, Richard. *Heidegger: An Introduction*. New York: Routledge, 1999.

Rancière, Jacques. "Who Is the Subject of the Rights of Man?" *South Atlantic Quarterly* 103, no. 2/3 (2004): 297–310.

Rensmann, Lars. "Grounding Cosmopolitics: Rethinking Crimes against Humanity and Global Political Theory with Arendt and Adorno." In *Arendt & Adorno: Political and Philosophical Investigations*. Edited by Lars Rensmann and Samir Gandesha. Stanford: Stanford University Press, 2012.

Reshaur, Ken. "Concepts of Solidarity in the Political Theory of Hannah Arendt." *Canadian Journal of Political Science* 25, no. 4 (1992): 723–736.

Risser, Jim. *The Life of Understanding*. Bloomington: Indiana University Press, 2012.

Sallis, John. *The Logic of Imagination: The Expanse of the Elemental*. Bloomington: Indiana University Press, 2012.

Scott, Charles. "Care and Authenticity." *Martin Heidegger: Key Concepts*, edited by Bret Davis, 57–68. Durham: Acumen Publishing, 2010.

Shehaj, Albana, Adrian J. Shin, and Ronald Inglehart. "Immigration and Right Wing Populism: An Origin Story." *Party Politics*, Online First: May 17, 2019. https://doi.org/10.1177/1354068819849888.

Shuster, Martin. "Language and Loneliness: Arendt, Cavell, and Modernity." *International Journal of Philosophical Studies* 20, no. 4 (2012): 473–497.

Sitton, John F. "Hannah Arendt's Argument for Council Democracy." In *Hannah Arendt: Critical Essays*. Edited by Lewis Hinchman and Sandra K. Hinchman, 307–334. New York: SUNY Press, 1994.

Sloterdijk, Peter. "Nearness and Dasein: The Spatiality of Being and Time." *Theory, Culture, and Society* 29, no. 4/5 (2012): 36–42.

Stauffer, Jill. *Ethical Loneliness: The Injustice of Not Being Heard*. New York: Columbia University Press, 2015.

Stawarska, Beata. "Reversability and Intersubjectivity in Merleau-Ponty's Ontology." *Journal of the British Society for Phenomenology* 33, no. 2 (2002): 155–166.

Storey, Ian. "The Politics of Defining Today: Towards a Critical Historicism of Judgment." *Arendt Studies* 1 (2017): 61–86. DOI: 10.5840/arendtstudies2017957.

Taminiaux, Jacques. *The Thracian Maid and the Professional Thinker: Arendt and Heidegger*. Translated by Michael Gendre. Albany: SUNY Press, 1997.

———. "Athens and Rome." In *The Cambridge Companion to Hannah Arendt*. Edited by Dana Villa, 165–177. Cambridge: Cambridge University Press, 2000.

Tatmen, Lucy. "Arendt and Augustine: One More Kind of Love." *Sophia* 52, no. 4 (2013): 625–635.

Topolski, Anya. *Arendt, Levinas, and a Politics of Relationality*. New York: Rowman and Littlefield, 2015.

Tsao, Roy. "Arendt's Augustine." In *Politics in Dark Times: Encounters with Hannah Arendt*, edited by Seyla Benhabib, 39–57. New York: Cambridge University Press, 2008.

Tsao, Roy T. "Arendt against Athens: Rereading *The Human Condition*." *Political Theory* 30, no. 1 (2002): 97–123.

Villa, Dana. *Arendt and Heidegger: The Fate of the Political*. Princeton: Princeton University Press, 1995.

———. *Politics, Philosophy, Terror: Essays on the Thought of Hannah Arendt*. Princeton: Princeton University Press, 1999.

Von Hermann, Friedrich-Wilhelm. *Hermeneutics and Reflection: Heidegger and Husserl on the Concept of Phenomenology*. Translated by Kenneth Maly. Toronto: University of Toronto Press, 2013.

Walhof, Darren. "Friendship, Otherness, and Gadamer's Politics of Solidarity." *Political Theory* 34, no. 5 (2006): 569–593.

Wolin, Richard. *The Politics of Being: The Political Thought of Martin Heidegger*. New York: Columbia University Press, 1990.

Young-Bruehl, Elizabeth. *Hannah Arendt: For Love of the World*, 2nd edition. New Haven: Yale University Press, 2004.

Index

action, political, 6, 14, 93–94, 96–99, 101, 136, 138, 150, 190, 195–96; and freedom, 95–96, 100, 139; versus labor and work, 94, 138–39; as a new beginning, 95–96. *See also* birth; natality

alienation, 3, 4, 31; as self-alienation, 136; as world-alienation, 6, 135–36

Allen, Amy, 195–97

alterity, 2, 11–12, 52–53, 59, 65–66, 68–70, 81

animal laborans, 138–39, 140; and totalitarianism, 143. *See also* labor

anonymity, 10; of the they-self, 16, 22, 43

anonymous responsibility, 2, 56–57, 76

anticipatory resoluteness, 44, 87–88, 99. *See also* authenticity

anxiety (*Angst*), 31, 41, 43, 66, 89

appearance, 5, 17, 27, 97; as co-appearance, 68; and the political, 97–98, 193, 197. *See also* phenomenology; politics of appearance; space of appearance

appropriation, 66, 79, 129. *See also* freedom, as existential

Arendt, Hannah, 4–6, 15, 53, 77, 86, 91; *Eichmann in Jerusalem: A Report on the Banality of Evil*, 196; on Heidegger, 13, 84–91, 93–94, 98–100, 102n7, 107–8, 111–12, 120, 124, 126nn4–5, 136–37; *The Human Condition*, 13, 90–91; on the liberal tradition, 6, 13, 82, 107, 129–30, 133–34, 136, 148–49; *Der Liebesbegriff bei Augustin*, 85, 102n12, 103n13; on loneliness, 130–31, 134–35, 153n18, 171, 176, 188; *The Origins of Totalitarianism*, 120; on techno-scientific rationality, 91–93, 136. *See also* action, political; natality; plurality; political loneliness; right to have rights; space of appearance; speech, political; statelessness

Aristotle, 23, 24, 47n10, 85, 139

Augustine, 87, 111, 115–16. *See also* freedom, as a property of thought or the will

authentic alliance, 42, 44. *See also* being-with, as authentic; leaping ahead

authentic communal life, 2–5, 9, 11–13, 23, 51–52, 56, 58, 81, 100, 107, 189; and the political, 107, 125, 152, 194, 197. *See also* authenticity; being-with, as authentic; political community

authenticity, 41–45, 72, 84–85, 88, 90, 99. *See also* anticipatory

resoluteness; being-toward-death; being-with, as authentic
automation, 93, 125, 119
averageness, 38, 39. *See also* the they; they-self

Beiner, Ronald, 91
being, 23–31, 60, 66–68; forgetfulness of, 24, 28, 101, 108, 110; question of, 24–25, 29. *See also* Heidegger, Martin, *Being and Time*
being-in, 32, 34, 85
being-in-common, 66–68, 75. *See also* the common/commonality
being-in-the-world (*in-der-Welt-sein*), 10, 21, 29–34, 31–32, 35, 37, 39, 40, 60, 85, 89; as being-with, 37; Dasein as being-in-the-world, 31–32
being-toward-death, 43, 45, 60, 63, 86, 88
being-with (*Mitsein*), 4, 10, 12, 36–38, 40, 45, 52, 57, 60–64, 66, 68–69, 71–72, 136, 153n23; as authentic, 17, 42, 44–46, 52, 56, 60, 62–63, 65, 76–77; as inauthentic, 22, 38–40, 66; and the political, 13, 97, 108. *See also* authentic communal life; inauthentic communal life
being-with-others, 38, 45
belonging, 2, 8, 70; and Dasein, 22, 31, 37, 42; political belonging, 149–150, 178
Benhabib, Seyla, 132–33
Benjamin, Andrew, 4, 12, 52, 59, 72–76
Berkowitz, Roger, 140
Birmingham, Peg, 133–34
birth, 95, 97; as a new beginning, 95. *See also* natality
Blumenberg, Hans, 42–43

bourgeoisie, political emancipation of, 14, 116–18, 155n90. *See also* Hobbes, Thomas
Brexit, in the United Kingdom, 175
Brogan, Walter, 66–67
Brown, Wendy, 160, 171–74, 176, 189. *See also* neoliberalism, and neoliberal rationality
bureaucracy, state, 55, 119
Butler, Judith, 9, 11, 51, 57, 193–94

call of conscience, 43–44. *See also* authenticity
capitalism, 117; and neoliberalism, 172, 174
care (*Sorge*), 10, 11, 21, 22, 30, 33, 36, 41–44, 63, 85; versus *caritas*, 87; and others, 36, 37, 41–42, 63; and things, 33; and truth, 30. *See also* Dasein; leaping ahead; leaping in
certainty, epistemological, 27, 28, 30, 43. *See also* epistemology; knowledge, scientific
Christianity, 111, 115. *See also* Augustine
citizenship, 4, 15, 74, 129–30, 134–36, 149; liberal, 4, 15, 83, 130–131, 148; neoliberal, 172; as a political activity, 112, 135, 149, 151, 190. *See also* right to have rights; statelessness
Clinton, Hillary, 159, 162–64, 166–70, 180; campaign platform of, 162; presidential election defeat of, 167. *See also* 2016 U.S. presidential election
collective identity, 70, 195–96
the common/commonality, 61–62, 68, 71, 73–75, 196; three modes of, 61–62
the common world, 6, 7, 14, 83, 180, 190–91

communication, 67, 68, 79n39, 68; and modern technology, 1, 45, 54
community, 2, 7, 8, 64–65, 66, 75, 158, 197; totalizing forms of, 2, 8, 61, 160. *See also* authentic communal life; inauthentic communal life; political community
consciousness, 10, 29; versus care, 33. *See also* intentionality; subject, modern
continental philosophy, 2, 4, 10, 11, 46, 59, 65; and the problem of loneliness, 23, 56
Coppock, Alexander, 170
council system, 191–192, 198n6
courage: as the highest political virtue, 151, 193
critical theory, 5

Dasein, 10–12, 21, 25, 26, 29, 31, 60, 70; as being-in-the-world, 31–33; existential analytic of, 26–27, 31; as a thrown project, 31, 33. *See also* authenticity; being-in-the-world; care; inauthenticity
de-distancing, 34, 35; as a tendency toward nearness, 34–35, 37, 40. *See also* spatiality
democratic illusion, 177, 180
democracy, Western liberal, 4, 8, 9, 10, 16, 82, 189, 192; representative versus deliberative model of, 4, 83, 192; vulnerability to populism and nationalism, 82, 152, 171. *See also* liberal political tradition; liberal subjectivity; neoliberalism; neoliberal subjectivity
Derrida, Jacques, 9, 57–58, 193–194; on Heidegger, 57–58

Descartes, Rene, 28, 30, 71, 115. *See also* epistemology; subject, modern
destiny (*Geschick*), 45, 52, 60, 63, 67; of a people (*Volk*), 45, 52, 63–67, 68. *See also* being-with, as authentic; historicity
difference, 12, 52, 75. *See also* alterity; exteriority
directionality, 34–35. *See also* de-distancing; spatiality, of Dasein
disclosedness, 30, 33
discourse. *See* communication
Dungey, Nicholas, 57
dwelling (*wohnen*), 32–33, 35, 85. *See also* being-in

election forecasting, 164, 167, 169; national versus state polling, 159, 163–64, 169. *See also* hidden Trump supporter; 2016 U.S. presidential election
Electoral College, in the United States, 164
enlightenment, 133; crisis of, 129; ideal of universal emancipation, 120, 122
Ens, Peter, 170
Epictetus, 111, 115–16. *See also* freedom: as a property of thought or the will; stoicism
epistemology, 28–30
essence, 25, 66; as co-essence, 66, 68; versus existence, 26. *See also* being
everydayness, 27, 29, 33, 43; and others, 38, 43. *See also* inauthenticity
existence, 21, 25, 26, 29, 44, 60–61, 66, 69; as co-existence, 65–66, 68; versus essence, 25–26. *See also* Dasein
experience, 7, 28–29; and the political, 92–93, 96–97; and

totalitarianism, 135, 143, 145–148. *See also* phenomenology; reality
exteriority, 12, 53, 61, 62. *See also* alterity; difference

facticity, 35, 37; hermeneutics of, 49n90
facts, 179–80; alternative facts, 9, 15, 180, 190; political facts, 196
fake news, 9, 15, 180, 190. *See also* reality
fate (*Schicksals*), 45. *See also* historicity
Fichte, Johann Gottlieb, 72, 74
finitude, 26, 33, 43, 63; and the political, 97, 194. *See also* temporality
freedom, 6, 100, 151; in antiquity, 108, 112–13, 128n56; as communal, 113; as existential, 42, 44, 99, 107; history of the idea of, 109, 122; in the liberal tradition, 109, 112, 136; as a metaphysical problem, 111; as a political activity, 14, 95–97, 111–13, 119, 125, 129, 150–151, 190; as a property of thought or the will, 14, 109, 111, 115–17, 122–23. *See also* action, political; liberty; natality

Gadamer, Hans-Georg, 2, 56, 77; on friendship and solidarity, 2, 57, 77; on Heidegger, 56; hermeneutics of facticity, 57, 78n19; on the loneliness of modern life, 2, 56

Habermas, Jürgen, 133
handiness (*Zuhandenheit*), 34, 36
Hansen, Phillip, 194–95
Hegel, 72, 75–76
Heidegger, Martin, 1–2, 4, 8, 10–12, 21–22, 52, 55, 72, 75–76, 81, 85; *Being and Time*, 10–11, 21, 23–24, 40–41, 51, 60–64, 81, 85; loneliness as a philosophical problem, 2, 11–12, 21–23, 31, 37–38, 41, 46, 51–53, 58–59, 81, 84; on the method of phenomenology, 27, 29–30; on the modern subject, 21, 52–53, 136; and National Socialism, 45, 60, 65, 88, 100. *See also* Arendt, Hannah, on Heidegger; Derrida, Jacques, on Heidegger; Gadamer, Hans-Georg, on Heidegger; Nancy, Jean-Luc, on Heidegger
hiddenness, 9, 15, 176–77, 188; and the hidden Trump supporter, 160–61, 170–71, 180; and loneliness, 171
hidden Trump supporter, 9, 15, 159, 164, 170, 175, 184n24; debates regarding, 159, 167, 170; versus late-deciding voters, 161, 170; and loneliness, 171, 179–81; and social desirability bias, 161, 164, 170, 182n3; theoretical significance of, 170–71, 175, 179. *See also* election forecasting; 2016 US presidential election
historicity (*Geschichtlichkeit*), 44–45, 52, 60, 67; and communal life, 60, 62
Hitler, Adolf, 85, 146–47, 181; rise to power, 87
Hobbes, Thomas, 116–17. *See also* bourgeoisie, political emancipation of
homo economicus, 172–74. *See also* neoliberalism

homo faber, 138–39. *See also* work
Honig, Bonnie, 160, 174–75, 189
human being, 24, 33, 67, 71, 92; existential interpretation of, 84, 99. *See also* Dasein
human condition, 93–96, 138; escape from, 91–92; and the political, 5–6, 98. *See also* natality; plurality; *vita activa*
Husserl, Edmund, 27–30, 40, 115; and the *epoché* 28, 30; Heidegger's critique of, 28–30, 47n23; and the transcendental ego, 27, 28. *See also* phenomenology

ideology, 145; totalitarian ideology, 7, 145–47, 178. *See also* totalitarianism
imperialism, 118–119, 127n45, 155n90. *See also* bourgeoisie, political emancipation of; capitalism
inauthentic communal life, 2, 55, 76; and nationalism, 66, 77; as totalizing, 8, 15, 58, 61, 65, 82, 152, 158, 197. *See also* being-with, as inauthentic; inauthenticity; they-self
inauthenticity, 10, 38–41, 43, 45–36, 62–63, 86. *See also* the they; they-self
instrumental rationality, 2, 147, 192. *See also* techno-scientific rationality
intentionality, 11, 28–30. *See also* consciousness; subject, modern
interdependence, 5, 10, 41, 141
isolation, 7, 137–139; and the loss of the political, 139–142

Jaspers, Karl, 2, 11, 51, 55, 56, 76, 100; and Arendt, 85, 136–37;
critique of techno-scientific rationality, 54, 55; and Heidegger, 77n3; *Man in the Modern Age*, 53
judgment, political, 133

Kant, Immanuel, 72, 89, 115, 140
knowledge/knowing, 28, 32–33; as discovery, 33; and neoliberal rationality, 174; scientific, 27–28, 92

labor, 5, 93–94, 96–97, 117, 138. *See also animal laborans*; necessity; *vita activa*
leaping ahead, 41–42, 44, 46, 63–64. *See also* authentic alliance; being-with, as authentic
leaping in, 41–42, 46, 62. *See also* being-with, as inauthentic
Lederman, Shmuel, 192
Levinas, Emmanuel, 3, 58
liberal political theory, 5, 8, 116–17, 132–33, 158
liberal political tradition, 5, 6, 8, 10, 81, 98–99, 118, 125, 129, 136, 158; classical liberalism versus neoliberalism, 172; emphasis on rights and liberties in the private sphere, 98, 107–109, 123; and loneliness, 134, 148–149; structures of, 4, 9, 13, 83
liberal subjectivity, 4, 9, 10, 17, 84, 120, 124, 130, 157; as atomized and isolated, 119, 124, 189; loneliness of, 13, 14, 16, 85, 125, 130, 134, 137, 144, 161, 170–171, 188–189, 192; vulnerability to totalitarianism, 16, 125, 134, 144, 147–48, 182. *See also* liberal political tradition; neoliberal subjectivity

liberty, 6, 14, 107, 116–117, 122, 129, 136; in antiquity, 112; versus freedom, 112, 117; and the private sphere, 6, 10, 107, 125, 150; and statelessness, 124
Locke, John, 117
logic: and totalitarianism, 7, 146
logocentrism, 57–58
logos. See communication
loneliness, 1, 5, 7–8, 10–11, 12, 15; ethical loneliness, 3; and modern mass society, 55, 90, 135; peculiar, 1, 2, 4, 8–11, 21–23, 31, 38, 40–42, 46, 52, 55–56, 59, 72, 76–77, 82, 107, 111, 125, 158, 188, 192; as a philosophical problem, 2, 10–11, 12, 21, 23, 31, 37, 41, 46; and totalitarianism, 6, 14. *See also* political loneliness

Marx, Karl, 6, 136, 174
mass society, modern, 6, 8, 54–55, 94, 143, 179; as apolitical, 176, 180; automation of, 125, 147; and the liberal tradition, 125; loneliness of, 15, 55, 135, 145, 149, 177–78, 192; and the rise of mass movements, 177; and the rise of totalitarianism, 145
meaning, 60, 66–69, 71; as co-constituted, 66, 68
Merleau-Ponty, Maurice, 58
metaphysics of presence, 9, 26, 31, 194–95, 197. *See also* objective presence
mineness, 52, 63. *See also* being-toward-death
mob rule, 118–19
modernity, 2, 6, 93, 101, 108, 124. *See also* mass society, modern
Montesquieu, 141–42

Nancy, Jean-Luc, 2, 4, 12, 52, 59–72, 77, 86; *Being Singular Plural*, 65–66; on Heidegger, 52, 60–72, 108; on modern subjectivity, 66
natality, 94–97, 137–38, 187; destruction of, 145; and the political, 124; relation to action, 94, 97; in relation to loneliness, 137, 141–42, 145. *See also* action, political; birth
National Socialism, 7, 8, 45, 60, 65, 144, 157, 196
nation-state, European, 130, 134, 176; paradox of, 120, 122–23
nationalism, 58, 65–66, 77
necessity, 93, 119, 124–25; of nature and history, 8, 94, 123, 138–39, 145; and totalitarianism, 145. *See also* private sphere
negative solidarity, 177–80. *See also* mass society, modern; 2016 U.S. presidential election
neoliberalism, 5, 18n8, 171, 189; and democracy, 173–75; and neoliberal rationality, 171–76; and statehood, 171. *See also* citizenship, neoliberal
neoliberal subjectivity, 3, 9, 160, 172–73, 175; loneliness of, 174, 180

Obama, Barack, 162–64, 184n15. *See also* 2016 U.S. presidential election
objective presence, 26, 29, 32–33, 35–37, 57. *See also* metaphysics of presence
ontology, 4, 24, 29; as fundamental ontology, 52, 55, 60, 67, 100; as ontology of existence, 21, 23; as ontology of relation, 2, 10, 11, 51, 59, 67, 73–76; as political ontology, 83

origin, 68–69, 71–72, 75–76; co-origin, 69; as myth, 75
Ortega, Mariana, 59
the other/others, 6, 12, 36, 38, 70, 96; being-other, 68; as a condition for being an individual, 141; Dasein and, 36, 37, 38, 39, 42; Dasein's subservience to, 38, 39. *See also* being-with; they-self

Parekh, Serena, 133–34
party system, European, 176; and the collapse of the class system, 177–78. *See also* mass society, modern, and the rise of mass movements
phenomenology, 27–30; existential phenomenology, 5, 27–28; as the method of ontology, 27, 29; political, 5, 87–88. *See also* appearance; Heidegger, Martin, on the method of phenomenology; Husserl, Edmund
phenomenon, 31–32. *See also* appearance
phronesis, 86
place, 75–76. *See also* origin
Plato, 23, 24, 27, 137, 139
plural event, 4, 72–74, 76
plurality/the plural, 2, 6, 12, 66–72, 74, 87, 91, 93–94, 97–98, 108, 187, 190–191, 196; as anoriginal plurality, 73–74; in the history of western metaphysics, 101, 108; and the political, 124, 195; and speech, 96
polis, 110, 113, 126n4, 150
political community, 121–22, 134–35; universal right to belong to, 131–32. *See also* right to have rights

political elite, 161–162, 177
political loneliness, 3–5, 9, 13–15, 53, 77, 82, 83, 91, 100, 110, 118, 130, 135, 137–38, 148–49, 151, 157, 159, 176–77, 188–89, 195, 198; and the destruction of the political sphere, 135, 140–42, 159; and the hidden Trump supporter, 16, 160, 175, 181; and the liberal tradition, 134, 149, 190; and natality, 140, 143; present day, 16, 159, 160, 171, 176, 180; relation to solitude and isolation, 142–43; and totalitarianism, 134–35, 142–43, 144, 146, 176, 182. *See also* alienation, as world-alienation; loneliness
political sphere, 5, 13, 66, 76–77, 82–84, 90–91, 94, 96–99, 107, 150, 159, 198; in antiquity, 112, 113; and the *bios politkos*, 112; in contemporary political life, 66, 135; as the in-between, 91, 191; forgetfulness of, 100–101, 108, 110; loss of, 5, 8–9, 13, 83–84, 101, 107, 111, 119, 125, 149, 159, 174–75, 181, 187–88; in the modern age, 107, 111. *See also polis*; public realm
politics of appearance, 9, 16, 182, 189–95, 197; and citizenship, 190–91; as embodied political activity, 193; and freedom, 190
populism, 161, 182; progressive, 162, 193; right-wing, 9, 16, 163, 167, 176, 188
possibility, 10, 11, 25–26, 31, 41, 46, 57, 75; as leveled down, 38, 39. *See also* being-toward-death; Dasein; existence; they-self
potentiality, 73, 76; potentiality-of-being, 42

power, 116, 118, 142–43, 196
praxis, 66, 100, 137. *See also* action, political
principles, political, 141, 146
private sphere, 6, 13, 14, 107, 117–19; as the household realm (*oikia*), 112–13; and necessity, 112–13, 119, 123–24, 150
privatization, 174–75
projection, 26, 31, 33. *See also* Dasein, as a thrown project
propaganda: of political parties, 177; totalitarian, 177–79
public goods, 173–75
publicness (*Öffentlichkeit*), 39, 57, 84, 90, 100. *See also* inauthenticity; they-self
public realm, 9, 100, 113; transformation in the modern age, 118. *See also* political sphere

racism, 7, 57, 75, 77
Rawls, John, 133
reality, 54; and appearance, 27; and loneliness, 143, 145, 178–80, 190
relationality, 10, 12, 21, 22, 30, 35, 37, 59, 67–68, 72–74, 76–77, 84; as anoriginal relation, 72–76; of Dasein, 30, 37, 46, 65, 85. *See also* being-in-the-world; being-with
republican government; law of, 141; principle of equality, 142. *See also* principles, political
res publica, 110, 126n4, 150, 174
rights, 14, 75–76, 131–34; and citizenship, 121, 132; and the private sphere, 124
Rights of Man, 109, 120–21, 133; aporia of universal human rights, 130–131, 152n7; as inalienable, 120–22
right to have rights, 15, 130, 134–135, 149; normative justification for, 132–33; as the right to belong to political community, 131–32
right-wing movements: in Europe, 188, 198n2; in the United States, 163, 176, 181, 193
Risser, James, 56

Sanders, Bernie, 162. *See also* 2016 U.S. presidential election
science, modern, 29, 34, 54, 56, 91–92, 109; and phenomenology, 27–28. *See also* human condition, escape from; knowledge, scientific; technology, modern; techno-scientific rationality
Scott, Charles, 33
security, 6, 13; as the aim of politics and government, 117–18, 134; and liberalism, 116–17
self-interest, private, 4, 6, 13, 82, 98, 107; and the modern political sphere, 117. *See also* liberal political tradition
the self/selfhood, 40, 54, 57, 84, 88–89; and loneliness, 140–41, 143
the shared, 68, 73–74. *See also* the common/commonality
singularity, 5–6, 11, 12, 44, 52, 57, 61–62, 67–71, 73, 75–76, 96, 98, 138, 140, 197; loss of, 38, 76, 144; and the political, 98, 191
singular-plural, 68. *See also* Nancy, Jean-Luc
social contract, 116, 148
social media, 1, 9, 159, 193

solidarity, 2, 56, 196–97, 199n29
solitude, 7, 115, 137, 139, 140–41. *See also* isolation; loneliness; political loneliness
space of appearance, 5–6, 97–98, 150, 189–90, 194; loss of, 108, 123, 125, 181; and freedom, 6, 111, 123, 129. *See also* polis; political sphere
spatiality, 37; as an ontological concept, 34–35, 48n53, 70; as a mathematical concept, 34, 35. *See also* de-distancing; directionality
speech, political, 92, 93, 96–99, 138, 150, 190; and plurality, 96–97. *See also* action, political; plurality
Stalin, Joseph, 146
statelessness, 14, 109–110, 119–124, 129–131, 133, 135–36, 148–49; as the loss of citizenship and political community, 121, 123, 135; and rightlessness, 120–21, 131
Stauffer, Jill, 3, 4, 8, 83, 158
Stawarska, Beata, 58
stoicism, 111, 117. *See also* Epictetus; freedom, as a property of thought or the will
subject, modern, 5, 13, 28, 31, 32, 52, 54, 56, 57, 61, 66, 70, 72, 83, 190; versus Dasein, 25, 30, 32, 36, 61; epistemological, 2, 4, 27, 28, 31, 72; as isolated, 2, 5, 10, 21, 30, 53, 65, 85, 93, 108, 119, 197; subject-object relation, 27, 28, 29, 32. *See also* liberal subjectivity; neoliberal subjectivity
superfluity, 7, 15, 101, 123, 125, 130, 143, 145, 174. *See also* modern mass society; political loneliness; totalitarianism

Taminiaux, Jacques, 85
technology, modern, 1, 11, 54, 56, 91–92, 109, 187, 193. *See also* science, modern
techno-scientific rationality, 2, 10, 51, 53–55, 91–93, 178
temporality, 26–27, 29, 31, 33, 35; as Dasein's horizon, 26, 29, 31, 33
the they (*das Man*), 30, 38–40, 63, 66, 70, 99
they-self, 10, 11, 22, 37, 38–42, 45–46, 51, 62, 71, 84–85, 90, 99; loneliness of, 31, 38–39, 108
thinking, 67, 92, 140, 147
thrownness, 31, 33. *See also* Dasein, as a thrown project
touch, 58, 70–71
totalitarianism, 4–5, 8, 10, 15, 16, 82, 110, 124–25, 129, 134–35, 143–44, 154n67, 158, 178, 180–181, 188; relation to contemporary right-wing movements, 16, 160, 171, 181; government and law of, 144–45; mass movements, 7, 177–79; as organized loneliness, 15, 83, 147; terror, 135, 145–47. *See also* ideology; propaganda
town hall meeting, 191–92, 198n5. *See also* council system
Trump, Donald, 15, 159, 162–64, 166–70, 175, 180; campaign platform, 163; presidential election victory, 167. *See also* 2016 U.S. presidential election
truth, 7, 30; as *aletheia*, 30, 85; and loneliness, 143, 147; post-truth era, 9, 158
Tsao, Roy, 86
2016 U.S. presidential election, 15, 159, 161–64, 166–70, 176,

179; battleground states of, 164; and the Democratic Party, 161–62, 187; and electorate interests, 160, 163, 170, 179; as establishment versus anti-establishment politics, 162–163; polling errors during, 16, 160, 167, 169–70; and the Republican Party, 161–62, 187; rustbelt states, 164, 180. *See also* election forecasting; hidden Trump supporter

tyrannical government, 14, 147; fear as the political principle of, 142; lawlessness of, 141. *See also* principles, political

universal and particular, relation of, 73–74, 76

utility, metrics of, 6, 11, 36, 81, 97, 143, 172, 192; and work, 96, 139

Villa, Dana, 99

vita activa, 94, 138. *See also* human condition

the we, 4, 13, 52, 59–61, 65, 77; and the political, 182, 191

Western metaphysical tradition, 23–25, 27, 30, 31, 47n10, 64, 73–74, 99; and being-with, 64, 66–67, 70; destruction of, 13–14, 30, 84; history of, 10, 14, 27, 30, 73, 101; and totalitarianism, 64–65, 100. *See also* plurality, in the history of western metaphysics

Western political tradition, 71, 110, 111, 120, 123; destruction of, 14, 84–85; history of, 101, 110, 119, 122, 124. *See also* freedom; liberal political tradition; political sphere

the with, 65–67, 70; as the structure of existence, 2, 56, 60, 71–72

Wollin, Richard, 40

work, 5, 94, 96–97, 138–39. *See also vita activa*

world, 5–6, 10–11, 29, 31, 69–70, 93, 99; love of, 87, 133

worldlessness, 6, 15, 118, 120, 130, 135–36, 143, 147, 150. *See also* alienation; political loneliness

worldliness, 94, 99, 138. *See also* work

www.ingramcontent.com/pod-product-compliance
Lightning Source LLC
Chambersburg PA
CBHW022012300426
44117CB00005B/141

Praise for *A Nurse's Step-By-Step Guide to Transitioning to an Academic Role*

"*In* A Nurse's Step-by-Step Guide to Transitioning to an Academic Role, Dr. Mercy Ngosa Mumba provides critically insightful perspectives on becoming an academic in the US. Although written from the perspective of the US academy, especially the field of medical nursing, the book has wider implications. It offers invaluable lessons to academics in other jurisdictions and disciplines. Written with impeccable clarity, Dr. Mumba's book raises practical issues that can either make or break one's dreams as an aspiring academic. This is a timely book that also challenges some conventional wisdom and biases in higher education."

–Kenneth K. Mwenda, PhD, LLD, DSc(Econ)
Rhodes Scholar
Program Manager, The World Bank, Washington, DC, USA
Extraordinary Professor of Law, University of Lusaka, Zambia

"The academic environment can be daunting to new graduates or practicing nurses. Dr. Mumba has authored a must-read primer for nurses and other healthcare professionals pursuing a career in academia. A Nurse's Step-by-Step Guide to Transitioning to an Academic Role *provides a window into academia and is bursting with pragmatic information and real-world examples of what to expect and how to navigate a successful and balanced academic career.*"

–Richard Ricciardi, PhD, CRNP
Professor, George Washington University
Past President, Sigma

"In her outstanding book, Mercy Mumba does an exceptional job of providing an essential 'tool box' that will help ensure the success of individuals transitioning to an academic role. This masterful publication prepares individuals for what to expect, provides critical information to answer commonly asked questions, and outlines key tactics to thrive in academia."

–Bernadette Mazurek Melnyk, PhD, APRN-CNP, FAANP, FNAP, FAAN
Vice President for Health Promotion
University Chief Wellness Officer
Dean and Helene Fuld Health Trust Professor of Evidence-Based Practice, College of Nursing
Professor of Pediatrics & Psychiatry, College of Medicine
Executive Director, the Helene Fuld Health Trust National Institute for EBP
The Ohio State University